Praise for *Hatchet Job*

'A passiona᠁ ᠁fence of criticism in the time of Twitter᠁ ᠁᠁ ᠁᠁ ᠁᠁ engaging and, frequently, spot᠁ ᠁ *Su᠁ ᠁᠁᠁es*

'A wry, robust and developed defence of accountable critical voices' – *Total Film*

'Entertainingly incendiary stuff' – *Empire*

'Very accessible, entertaining and relevant . . . Warmly recommended.' – Den of Geek

'Engaging, informative and funny . . . a thoroughly enjoyable and accessible book . . . buy it now' – Vada Magazine

'Populist, entertaining . . . A very personal examination of the usefulness and value of film criticism . . . will delight fans of Kermode's previous books, and offers a fascinating glimpse behind the curtain into the life of a professional film critic' – Vérité

'A passionate history of his craft [from] Britain's premier film critic' – Sp!ked

'Entertaining . . . lively . . . valiant . . . he still reacts to cinema with the open-minded enthusiasm of someone who sees going to the pictures as a treat' – *New Statesman*

HATCHET JOB

Mark Kermode is resident film critic for BBC Radio 5 live and the BBC News Channel. He is the author of several books on cinema, including *The Good, the Bad and the Multiplex* and a BFI Modern Classics monograph on *The Exorcist*. He has written and presented a number of film documentaries for the BBC and Channel 4. He is a contributing editor to *Sight & Sound* magazine, and recently became chief film critic for the *Observer*. He plays bass and harmonica in the skiffle-and-blues band The Dodge Brothers.

Follow Mark on Twitter @KermodeMovie

MARK KERMODE

HATCHET JOB

LOVE MOVIES, HATE CRITICS

PICADOR

First published 2013 by Picador

First published in paperback 2013 by Picador

This edition first published 2014 by Picador
an imprint of Pan Macmillan, a division of Macmillan Publishers Limited
Pan Macmillan, 20 New Wharf Road, London N1 9RR
Basingstoke and Oxford
Associated companies throughout the world
www.panmacmillan.com

ISBN 978-1-4472-3053-3

9 8 7 6 5 4 3 2 1

A CIP catalogue record for this book is available from the British Library.

Printed and bound by CPI Group (UK) Ltd, Croydon, CR0 4YY

Visit **www.picador.com** to read more about all our books
and to buy them. You will also find features, author interviews and
news of any author events, and you can sign up for e-newsletters
so that you're always first to hear about our new releases.

'So tell me, how did you love the picture?'

Samuel Goldwyn

Acknowledgements

As always, during the writing of this book I called regularly upon the expertise and assistance of others whose detailed knowledge of films and film criticism is far greater than mine. Each of them contributed immeasurably to the finished book, and I would like to thank:

Linda Ruth Williams, my partner, friend, and ongoing source of love and inspiration, who made me see the light on the subject of *A.I.* – and indeed everything else.

Hedda Archbold at HLA, my trusted friend and colleague, without whose guidance and advice my career would doubtless be in the doghouse.

Paul Baggaley and Kris Doyle at Picador, for proving (once again) that the heart of publishing lies not in good writing, but in excellent editing (something which *cannot* be done by robots!).

Tim Clifford, for the thoroughness and beauty of his index, and his extraordinary attention to detail.

Kim Newman, for running his encyclopaedic eye over the manuscript, and for generally raising the bar of film criticism.

Andrew Collins, Boyd Hilton, Nick James, and Tim Robey, all of whom generously gave their time and energy to read various drafts and make essential suggestions and corrections (along with helpfully encouraging noises) for which I am eternally grateful.

Nigel Floyd and Alan Jones, for being there from the start.

Dave Norris, for making sure the technical stuff was in the correct aspect ratio.

Finally, I'd like to thank all the film critics with whom I have been proud to share screening rooms – and sandwiches – for the last twenty-five years.

Contents

PROLOGUE

SHARK SANDWICH

'Forrest Gump on a tractor.'

Those five words are probably my favourite film review ever. More importantly, they constitute the most damaging hatchet job I ever encountered, managing to do something I had often argued was impossible – to kill a movie stone dead. I didn't read them in a newspaper or on a blog, I didn't hear them on the radio or television; rather, they were whispered in my ear by a trusted friend and colleague, David Cox, as the house lights went down on a screening of David Lynch's *The Straight Story*.

I'd been really looking forward to that movie. I've been a huge Lynch fan ever since being blindsided by a late-night screening of *Eraserhead* at the Phoenix East Finchley in the late seventies. I'd wept buckets at *The Elephant Man*, taken several runs at *Dune* (it still doesn't work), been both out-raged and strangely exhilarated by *Blue Velvet*, swooned at *Wild at Heart* and even argued that *Mullholland Dr.* 'makes perfect sense'. Now, there was something illicitly thrilling about the fact that the high-priest of weird had pulled the most audacious trick of all – he'd made a 'straight' movie, a film praised for its simplicity, lack of outlandish visual and aural experimentation, and almost wilful adherence to strict narrative linearity. Like Johnny Rotten turning up in a suit and tie, this was the one thing Lynch aficionados didn't expect, a movie with a beginning, a middle and an end – and in that order. And what about that title? Initially everyone assumed it to be ironic, but reports from those who had seen *The Straight Story* were that it was anything but. This was Lynch's masterstroke, like that line in *The Usual Suspects* about the devil's greatest trick being to convince people that he didn't exist. Was this Lynch as the devil in disguise? Or had he finally followed Laura Palmer to take his place amongst the angels?

All these questions were rushing through my head as we sat there in the Curzon Soho, quivering with anticipation. I was ready of spirit, willing of heart, and open of mind. I wanted only to be ravished. Instead, I was rubbished, brought low from the lofty heights of expectation by five words that sucked all the life out of the movie and left it writhing in silent space before the curtains had even opened. That poor kid hearing that Shoeless Joe Jackson's team-mates had thrown the World Series ('Say it ain't so!') couldn't have suffered any more crushing a sense of loss and disappointment than I did when David Cox slipped that insidiously low-key invective into my loppylugs and let it crawl like a radioactive earwig into my cerebral cortex, where it sat, pustulent, eating its evil way into anything that vaguely resembled hope, admiration or generosity. Instead, I found myself possessed only of the spirit of sneering cynicism as I endured the next two hours in which an old man swapped homely platitudes with folksy caricatures whilst making his extremely slow way across America in the absence of a full driving licence.

Forrest Gump on a fucking tractor indeed.

What's particularly evil about the effect those words had on my state of mind is that I actually really like *Forrest Gump* (and I'm quite partial to tractors too – although what Richard Farnsworth actually drives in the movie is technically a lawnmower). While many other lazy left-leaning liberals – of which I am one – were merrily slagging off Bob Zemeckis's Oscar winner as some kind of right-wing Reaganite wet dream, celebrating old-fashioned down-home stupidity over disruptively rebellious intelligence, I always thought (as does Danny Boyle) that the outlook of any film starting with a single mother having to have sex with a headmaster in order to ensure a decent education for her special-needs son was anything but rose-tinted. For me, seeing *Forrest Gump* as some kind of neo-con tract was a perfect example of what happens when film theory gets in the way of film-viewing; when people start *reading* movies rather than watching them. If you really want to judge something by what it looks like on the page, go read a book. As for cinema, it's a slippery audio-visual medium which, at its best, is ill served by mean-spirited reductionist critiques.

Yet as wrong-headed as they may be, mean-spirited reductionist critiques can be really funny, particularly if served up in a pithy one-liner that pierces the heart of the movie and bursts its shimmering creative bubble, like 'Forrest Gump on a tractor' – the best/worst film review I ever heard. Today, David Cox says he wishes he'd never uttered the five words I have carried around with me ever since. He insists he didn't mean anything by them, that it was just a silly joke, not to be taken seriously, and certainly not to be held up as a reason to hate Lynch's low-gear road-movie. Hey, according to David, he really likes *The Straight Story* and if he can get over that damned phrase, why the hell can't I?

The answer is simple: no matter how much you love a film and how many good notices it gets, it's the bad reviews that stick. Always. I have first-hand experience of this phenomenon. I am a film critic, and for all the movies I love and praise and try to get other people to be enthusiastic about, it's the ones I hate that people remember. Take a look at my reviews on the Kermode and Mayo YouTube channel, where the numbers speak for themselves. No matter how upbeat and excitable I may be about any number of films, the reviews to which people are drawn are my bilious rants – *Pirates of the Caribbean*, *Sex and the City 2*, the complete works of Michael Bay – the angrier the better, apparently. Sometimes, listeners to the BBC Radio 5 live *Film Review* show actually get disappointed if I don't get angry enough, feeling let down by the expectation of hearing a movie get a really good spittle-spewing kicking only to be fobbed off with an uninterested dismissal or (more disappointing still) a few words of measured praise. For better or worse, those who read or listen to film reviews have a fondness for vitriol, a sobering truth not lost on critics themselves; no wonder Dorothy Parker's theatrical assessment of Katharine Hepburn running 'the gamut of emotions from A to B' remains perhaps the most oft-quoted review in vicious critical circles – a killer line we all wish we had written, even if few of us agree with its sentiment.

I once asked viewers of my BBC video-blog, Kermode Uncut, to let me know their own favourite celluloid massacres, the pithier, funnier and nastier the better. The response was typically overwhelming – in under forty-eight hours I received well over a hundred suggestions of succinctly splenetic put-downs, which provided hours of sour-spirited delight. In the blog, I had cited the now infamous reviews of *Psycho* ('Sicko') and *I Am A Camera* ('Me No Leica'), both of which adorn the front cover of popular film critic Chris Tookey's compendium of film writing savagery through the ages, both being notable for their economy of wordage, if not their critical judgement. Inspired, blog commenters proffered a number of one- or two-worders, such as Leonard Maltin's verdict on *Isn't it Romantic?* ('No'), *Empire* magazine's punning assessment of *Battleship* ('Miss'), and the advice offered severally regarding the live-action *Flintstones* movie ('Yabbadabba-Don't'). After three hours of watching *Exodus*, Mort Sahl delivered the succinct critical *cri de coeur* 'Let my people go!', which is good, but isn't quite as funny as his summation of *Ben-Hur* – 'Loved him, hated Hur'. *Telegraph* writer Robbie Collin proved that his years at the *News of the World* had made him the master of the pithy tabloid pun (an underrated art form) when he tweeted a preview of his review of Clint Eastwood's latest which read simply: 'J. EDGAR? J. Arthur.' Titular putdowns proved popular, with special mention due to Nev Pierce who brilliantly dubbed Mel Gibson's torture-porn-inflected biblical epic *The Passion of the Christ* 'Jesus Christ: Splatterstar'. Over at *Rolling Stone*, Peter Travers was one of many to review the unfunny *Twilight* spoof *Vampires Suck* with variations on the words 'this movie sucks more', while umpteen sources are credited as being the first to write of Alex Proyas's *Knowing* that 'You're better off not'. The best titular pun I ever encountered was coined by John Naughton, with whom I first worked back in the days of Manchester's *City Life* magazine, and who would later become the film editor of *Q*, where he memorably dubbed Kevin Costner's disastrous end-of-civilization epic *The Postman* 'Post-Apocalyptic Pat'.

As for 'Eyes Wide Shit', that poignant pun appears to have occurred simultaneously to everyone who saw Stanley Kubrick's piss-poor final film, becoming as ubiquitous as 'a film by, for, and about dummies', which adorned more than one review of *Mannequin* and, more recently, the living-doll slasher remake *Maniac*. Of the latest drubbings, my favourites include Kate Muir of *The Times* describing Madonna's execrable *W.E.* as 'Mills and Boon meets *Homes and Gardens* with offcuts from the History Channel' and Larushka Ivan-Zedah of *Metro* likening *A Good Day to Die Hard* to 'an explosion in a stupidity factory'. Less aggressive, but no less elegant, is Tim Robey's delicately damning *Telegraph* verdict on Joe Wright's stagey adaptation of *Anna Karenina* which included the delicious phrase 'Wright [has] this unashamed love of the proscenium, but did it need to be so arch?'

Several writers turned up time and time again, such as Vincent Canby, who observed that watching *Heaven's Gate* is like taking a 'forced four-hour walking tour of one's own living room' and suggested that the price of the success of *The Deer Hunter* had been for director Michael Cimino to sell his soul to the devil, who had now come to collect.

Judith Crist memorably dubbed the sixties drama *The Agony and the Ecstasy* as 'all agony, no ecstasy'; the *Village Voice* dismissed the seventies Streisand–Kristofferson remake of *A Star is Born* under the headline 'A Bore is Starred'; and Pauline Kael elegantly trashed the 1990 Oscar winner *Dances with Wolves* with the phrase 'Kevin Costner has feathers in his hair and feathers in his head; the Indians should have called him "Plays with Camera".' Here in the UK, the *Guardian*'s Peter Bradshaw was hailed as the 'Shakespeare of film criticism' for his scathing reviews of stinkers such as *Sex Lives of the Potato Men*, a Lottery-funded national embarrassment which raised the question for the British film industry of 'whether to put the gun barrel to our temples, or in our mouths for a cleaner kill'. Of the undiverting romcom *Leap Year*, Bradshaw wrote: 'The only "leap" I felt like making was off the motorway gantry into the fast lane of the M25.' This made me chuckle, which was more than the movie managed, although I must confess that my real unexpected guffaw moment came when reading John Patterson describing Disney's animated *Treasure Planet* as being 'Like watching Robert Louis Stevenson being sodomised by Michael Eisner in front of a class of 10-year-olds'. Ha!

Of the somewhat wordier favourites, the great American critic Roger Ebert naturally scored high, with several people citing his untrammelled loathing of Rob Reiner's *North* as a particularly splendid example of comedy through repetition. 'I hated this movie,' wrote Ebert. 'Hated, hated, hated, hated, hated this movie. I hated it. Hated every simpering stupid vacant audience-insulting moment of it. Hated the sensibility that thought anyone would like it. Hated the implied insult to the audience by its belief that anyone would be entertained by it.' While this is all well and good, personally I'd opt for Ebert's withering assessments of Vincent Gallo's abominable road movie *The Brown Bunny* ('I had a colonoscopy once, and they let me watch it on TV. It was more entertaining') and John Travolta's Scientology-based sci-fi debacle *Battlefield Earth* ('like taking a bus trip with someone who has needed a bath for a long time') as funnier and therefore better. Ebert had a nice line in anti-analogies (*The Spirit* – 'To call the characters cardboard is to insult a useful packing material'; *The Village* – 'To call it an anti-climax would be an insult not only to climaxes but to prefixes') and a special talent for absurdist hyperbole (*Freddie Got Fingered* – 'doesn't scrape the bottom of the barrel. This movie isn't the bottom of the barrel. This movie isn't below the bottom of the barrel. This movie doesn't deserve to be mentioned in the same sentence with barrels.'). But my own Ebert favourite came from his review of Michael Bay's catastrophically poor World War II barf-fest *Pearl Harbor*, the film which (along with *Gigli*) helped put Ben Affleck's career so deep in the dumper that he would later have to thank Hollywood for giving him 'a second chance' when accepting an Oscar for *Argo*. *Pearl Harbor* was horrible, but may have been worth it for giving Ebert the opportunity to describe it as 'A two-hour movie squeezed into three hours, about how, on Dec. 7, 1941, the Japanese staged a surprise attack on an American love triangle.' Pure genius!

As for myself, I received a few honourable mentions (of course I did; after all, it's my bloody blog) for describing *Movie 43* as 'the cinematic equivalent of herpes' and *Marley & Me* as 'less fun than having a real dog put down'. There were also nods for the phrase 'Eat, Pray, Love, Vomit' (of which, I confess, I am pathetically proud) and the inevitable resurrection of the spectre of my reviews of *Sex and the City 2* ('consumerist pornography') and *Pirates of the Caribbean: At World's End* ('The IMDb says they started without a completed script – no, they *finished* without one'), for which I am now far better known than for anything nice I ever said about a film. Ironically, I was also reminded that in berating David Fincher's self-regarding, life-lived-backwards boreathon *The Curious Case of Benjamin Button*, I had airily dismissed the movie as '*Forrest Gump* with A-levels'.

Occasionally, words have failed me, leaving only violent self-harm to do the job. My online review of Michael Bay's *Transformers 2: Revenge of the Fallen*, for example, consisted entirely of a short film of me banging my head against a number of hard objects, including a concrete post, a metal table, and an iron railing, before hurling myself enthusiastically at a wall. Recent news of the green-lighting of yet another *Transformers* flick would be met with a video of me breaking a laptop with my face. I also whacked myself hard across the bridge of my nose (for real) with a large hardbound copy of the *Oxford English Dictionary* to see if doing so was actually more fun than watching *Keith Lemon: The Film*. It was – and a lot shorter. At some point, I'm probably going to have to shut my hand in a car door or cut off my thumb in a waste disposal unit to prove that such everyday domestic accidents really do have more entertainment value than sitting through *Pimp* or enduring *Little Man*, as I have often claimed. And I'm sure if I do, the YouTube viewing figures will go through the roof.

Whether or not you agree with any of these value judgements matters not a jot; what matters is that you remember
them. I may love Hal Ashby's sublime black comedy *Harold
and Maude*, but the only review of it I can remember is the
one in which the critic from *Variety* described it as contain-
ing 'all the fun and gaiety of a burning orphanage'. Why?
Because it's nasty – and funny. The best hatchet jobs are
not only amusing, but lasting, and the more amusing they
are the longer they last. No surprise, then, that when Roger
Ebert died in early 2013, it was his scathing put-downs
rather than his ebullient praise of movies which were quoted
in memoriam.

It's not only critics who like to deliver the killer blows; film-
makers themselves have long appreciated the art of being
spectacularly nasty about their fellow craftspeople with a
splendid disregard for any sense of 'community'. Despite
being hailed by Woody Allen and Steven Spielberg et al. as
perhaps the world's greatest living director (Spielberg said
'his love for cinema almost gives me a guilty conscience'),
Swedish maestro Ingmar Bergman proved that he could be
fulsomely mouthy when it came to damning the work of his
canonical contemporaries. In an interview with the Swedish
daily *Sydsvenska Dagbladet*, for example, he told journalist
Jan Aghed that Orson Welles was 'just a hoax . . . an infinitely overrated film-maker' whose greatest work, *Citizen
Kane*, is 'a total bore. Above all, the performances are
worthless. The amount of respect that movie's got is
absolutely unbelievable.' He was even more damning of
Antonioni, a couple of whose pictures he admired, but

who was ultimately 'suffocated by his own tediousness'. (Kim Newman points out that since Antonioni outlived Bergman by eighteen hours, he was 'indisputably the world's greatest living director for less than a day'.) On the subject of Jean-Luc Godard, Bergman merrily admitted that 'I've never got anything out of his movies. They have felt constructed, faux intellectual, and completely dead. Cinematographically uninteresting and infinitely boring. Godard is a fucking bore. He's made his films for the critics. One of his movies, *Masculin féminin*, was shot here in Sweden. It was mind-numbingly boring . . .'

Orson Welles, for whom Bergman had such contempt, was similarly snippy about Godard. 'I just can't take him very seriously as a thinker,' he said wryly, 'and that's where we differ. Because he does.' Even Werner Herzog has got in on the act, famously declaring in his trademark Bavarian deadpan drawl that 'someone like Jean-Luc Godard is for me intellectual counterfeit money when compared to a good kung-fu film'. Godard seems to have taken all this on the chin, if anything going out of his way to make even more terrible movies just to annoy his detractors. Certainly, no one who managed to stay awake through the inter-minable sludge of *Film socialisme* should have been in any doubt that the director was taking the piss – hence my own verdict when the film premiered at Cannes that 'it's not just a case of the emperor having no clothes, but of the emperor running naked down the street waving his *nouvelle vagues* in your face'. Indeed, the most remarkable thing about that movie (for which Godard opted to provide gnomic 'Navajo' subtitles to make it even more wilfully incomprehensible) is that a lot of it was filmed on the *Costa Concordia*, a vast

and imposing cruise liner that would go on to make horri-
fying real life headlines when it became shipwrecked off the
western coast of Italy in January 2012.

Godard himself has made a habit of badmouthing everyone who isn't Godard, particularly if they are American, and
especially if they've had hits. On the subject of Quentin
Tarantino, whose 'Band Apart' production company appears to have been named in homage to Godard's *Bande à
part* (boom, boom), he moaned that 'he named his production company after one of my films. He'd have done
better to give me some money'. Having trashed Spielberg's
Schindler's List with the three-word put-down 'du Max
Factor', Godard preened (without the slightest hint of professional jealousy): 'I don't know him personally. I don't
think his films are very good.' (Alejandro Jodorowsky was
funnier, describing Spielberg as 'the son of when Walt
Disney fucked Minnie Mouse'.) As for fellow art house
darling Jacques Rivette, he said of *Titanic*: 'It's garbage.
Cameron isn't evil, he's not an asshole like Spielberg. He
wants to be the new DeMille. Unfortunately, he can't direct
his way out of a paper bag' – which is a bit rich coming from
Rivette.

And then there are the feuds. After Spike Lee complained that Clint Eastwood had whitewashed the role
played by African Americans in World War II with *Flags
of Our Fathers*, Eastwood growled that 'a guy like him
should shut his face', causing Lee to reply, 'First of all, the
man is not my father, and we're not on a plantation either.'
Lee, who has picked fights with almost everyone in the
business, has also taken multiple pops at Tarantino for his

love of the 'N' word, causing Quentin to bleat that Lee 'would have to stand on a chair to kiss my ass'. Classy.

When *Clerks* director (and notorious critic-hater) Kevin Smith suggested that Tim Burton had lifted a scene in his *Planet of the Apes* reboot from one of his comic books, Burton demurred that 'anybody who knows me knows I would never read a comic book, and I would certainly never read anything written by Kevin Smith', to which Smith snarked back, 'Which, I guess, explains *Batman*.' Meanwhile, one-time critics' darling David Gordon Green had this to say about Smith: 'He kind of created a Special Olympics for film. They just kind of lowered the standard. I'm sure their parents are proud, it's just nothing I care to buy a ticket for.' Which, as UK blogger Stuart Barr brilliantly points out, is ironic because DGG said that 'just before he turned into Kevin Smith'.

Werner Herzog took the high road after Abel Ferrara cursed him for agreeing to helm a New Orleans-set remake of his raw-as-hell New York fable *Bad Lieutenant*, simply telling the press, 'I have no idea who Abel Ferrara is. Is he Italian? Is he French? Who is he? I have never seen a film by him.' Those who did know Ferrara weren't much kinder. 'He was on so much crack when I did *The Funeral* he was never on set,' remembered actor-turned-worst-director-in-the-world Vincent Gallo, who has pretty much burned all his bridges over the years, earning himself an enviable reputation as cinema's most cantankerous big mouth. 'I wouldn't work for Martin Scorsese for ten million dollars,' he boasted, at a time when the chance of being offered work for ten dollars was slim-to-none. 'He hasn't made a good film in twenty-five years. I would never work with an egomaniac has-been' – a statement which, presumably, means that if Vincent Gallo asked himself to star in one of his own movies, he'd be morally obliged to say no. And it continues. 'He's the biggest fraud out there,' Gallo opined of Spike Jonze, who appeared to have committed the unforgiveable crime of partnering up with Sofia Coppola. 'She's a parasite, just like her fat pig father was.' At which point, it seems appropriate to remind ourselves that whilst Sofia directed *The Virgin Suicides* and *Lost in Translation*, and Francis helmed *The Godfather* and *Apocalypse Now*, Vincent Gallo remains best known for making the film Roger Ebert memorably described as less fun than taking a guided tour around the inside of his own arsehole. (Gallo later recut the movie, causing Ebert to revise his opinion. I think he was right the first time . . .)

And on it goes. W. C. Fields once described Mae West as 'a plumber's idea of Cleopatra'. Tony Curtis said that kissing Marilyn Monroe was 'like kissing Hitler'. Alex Cox said Spielberg wasn't a film-maker but 'a confectioner'. Megan Fox likened Michael Bay to a fascist dictator (although she may have meant it as a compliment). Burt Lancaster said, 'Kirk Douglas would be the first to tell you that he is a very difficult man. And I would be the second.' Upon hearing that Joan Crawford had called him 'a man who loves evil, horrendous, vile things', Robert Aldrich replied, 'I am very fond of Miss Crawford.' And Bette Davis once drawled, 'You should never say bad things about the dead, only good. Joan Crawford is dead. Good.'

It's not just individuals; entire nations have been on the receiving end of the wit and wisdom of embittered film-makers, with Truffaut snottily mooing that there is an incompatibility between the words 'British' and 'cinema', while Akira Kurosawa once dismissed Japanese cinema in general as 'rather bland in flavour, like green tea over rice', a barely veiled dig at the title of a much-loved film by Yasujiro Ozu. Closer to home, the always entertainingly garrulous Alan Parker called the work of acclaimed British auteur Peter Greenaway 'a load of posturing poo-poo', while Ken Russell (who was constantly on the receiving end of stick from his fellow countrymen) concluded that on the evidence of Greenaway's movies 'he's more interested in shit than soul'.

All this meanness is entertaining and memorable, but what does it prove? First, that being entertainingly negative can help a critic build their career and make a name for themselves in what remains a cut-throat profession. Second, that there is no honour among thieves in the so-called film-making fraternity, a fact that film-makers would do well to remember the next time they feel like complaining about how nasty critics can be about their work. When it comes to being eye-wateringly bitchy and backstabbing about movies, those who make them should remove the planks from their own eyes before whining about the ocular slivers which afflict those who write about them. For all their carping and whingeing about the vindictive nature of negative reviews, the film-making profession as a whole has very little to be proud of when it comes to treating one another with dignity and respect. I once interviewed an A-list British actor who had played a major part in an on-going Hollywood sci-fi franchise, whose comments about his leading lady were so candidly unguarded that I actually stopped the tape and advised him to reconsider his words, since I could not in good conscience broadcast what he had just said – not for her sake, but for his. This was an actor whom I liked very much, and who had agreed to do the interview as a favour to me due to a labyrinthine personal connection which I felt duty bound not to exploit. I still think it was the right thing to do, although there's no denying that the unexpurgated version would have got more coverage. Similarly, when we were editing the Channel 4 documentary *Burnt Offering: The Cult of the Wicker Man* in 2001, film-maker Andrew Abbott and I chose to omit some of the more scabrous comments made about director Robin Hardy by certain members of the cast and crew. After all, whatever anyone said, Hardy had helmed one of the most important British movies of the seventies, hailed by *Cinefantastique* magazine as 'the *Citizen Kane* of horror'. Sometime later, I read an interview with Hardy in which he offhandedly dismissed our documentary as failing to appreciate the true merits of *The Wicker Man* and complained about how awful it was to have his masterpiece dismissed as a mere 'horror film' (perhaps we should have left the scabrous stuff in after all).

Like it or not, negativity is noteworthy, and – to invert a popular adage – 'good news is no news'. Everyone who has ever worked in film journalism knows that there's far more chance of grabbing a headline by getting an actor to admit how much they disliked a particular director or hated working on a certain film than there is if they simply tell you how marvellous the whole experience was, and how much they'd love to be given the chance to do it all again as soon as possible. In general, anyone involved in the promotion of a film is contractually required to be positive about it, hence the incessant repetition of all those 'it was wonderful' mantras trotted out by stars and directors discussing any movie during its initial release window. Sometimes, the stars will flatly refuse to promote a movie, which tells you everything you need to know about their view of the finished product. Daniel Craig, Rachel Weisz, and director Jim Sheridan, for example, were all unavailable to talk up the release of the psychological thriller *Dream House* in 2011 after the studio Morgan Creek (who have a reputation for butchering their own movies) took the film away from the director and re-cut it against his wishes. 'The movie didn't turn out great,' Craig later admitted, 'but I met my wife. Fair trade.'

The great get-out for actors when asked about films of which they are not proud is the phrase 'I haven't seen the movie'. This is generally accepted code-speak for 'I saw it and hated it but I'm not allowed to say that . . . yet', and is usually accompanied by the caveat 'I've just been too busy', which lets everyone else in the industry know that you've put the stinker behind you and moved on. Thus when asked 'Why?' in relation to his starring role in that festering cinematic sore *Movie 43*, Richard Gere was able to tell Simon Mayo on Radio 5 live that he 'didn't see it', and to act as if he had no knowledge of scenes in which he places his fingertips into the vagina of a life-sized iPod doll (and no, I'm NOT making this up) only to have them snagged by a swiftly rotating fan. 'Now I understand . . .' says Gere on screen, whilst pretending off screen to do no such thing. Similarly, Gary Oldman disavowed any knowledge of *Tiptoes* when I asked about the film in which he plays Matthew McConaughey's dwarf brother – on his knees. Directed by Matthew Bright, who made the splendidly outré revisionist Red Riding Hood romp *Freeway*, *Tiptoes* disappeared from trace immediately upon completion, with everyone involved in the project apparently feeling as embarrassed about it as Jerry Lewis does about his as-yet-unreleased Holocaust tragi-comedy *The Day the Clown Cried*. *Tiptoes* has since re-surfaced on video where unsuspecting viewers fancying a romantic comedy starring Gary Oldman and Kate Beckinsale (which is how the cover sells it) have been left gobsmacked by its ill-judged existence. I can't speak for Oldman, but if you'd spent a number of months doing an impression of José Ferrer playing Toulouse-Lautrec and the end result was now cluttering up supermarket shelves, you'd probably stump up £4.99 out of sheer curiosity, wouldn't you? So when Oldman told me he had 'never seen' *Tiptoes*, what I actually heard was: 'Oh, please don't bring that up, it was a bad time and I still don't want to talk about it, even after all these years . . .'

If actors and directors will often demur when it comes to slagging off movies for fear of damaging their careers, the opposite applies to critics, for whom it is often more expedient to dish out a few blood-splattered hatchet jobs rather than waste time attempting to explain why they really liked a movie. And while there is (as we have seen) genuine beauty, grace and craft involved in the fine tuning of a properly poisonous one-star review, most of us know there's a lot more at stake when you stand up for a movie than when you knock one down.

Take, for example, the case of the *Twilight* movies, which are widely regarded within the critical community as fair game for the literary equivalent of hunting with dogs. For the most part, very few reputable critics have dared to put their head above the parapet and admit to tolerating, let alone actually liking, this massively popular teen-orientated franchise. Nor is this scorn limited to critics – on the contrary, it has become popular currency amongst a wide range of naysayers, including film-makers themselves. Back in 2008, director David Slade, the rising star behind the edgy horror-thrillers *Hard Candy* and *30 Days of Night*, made some casually disparaging remarks ('*Twilight* drunk? No, not even drunk. *Twilight* at gunpoint? Just shoot me . . .') about what he called the 'repressed hormone teen vampire' series. He would later retract those comments ('I think I've eaten more than enough humble pie,' he told me), stating that they were made before he'd ever read Stephenie Meyer's novels about a young woman whose affections are divided between a vampire and a werewolf, or seen the blockbusting movies they spawned, all of which turned out to be far more interesting, intelligent and inspiring than he had ever imagined. Cynics dismissed this retraction as a contractual *mea culpa* by Slade who had ironically just signed on to direct the third *Twilight* film, *Eclipse*, but it has about it the ring of truth. The world is full of people (many of them middle-aged men) who feel duty bound to be sniffy about *Twilight* without having seen the films, read the books, or attempted to understand why they mean so much to so many.

For me, an unabashed *Twilight* movie fan, the collective critical belch which greeted the arrival of each new screen instalment said more about how out of touch the film-reviewing fraternity were with a certain section of the movie-going audience than it did about the films themselves; the sight of stuffy, bespectacled greying men berating movies aimed primarily at teenage girls is as farcical as it is depressing. In a *Guardian* blog in 2011, critic and writer Anne Billson correctly noted that '*Twilight* attracts a lot more vitriol than any other nonsense aimed at the young male demographic' and pointed out that, love it or loathe it (and she was not particularly fond of it herself), the series catered to a market otherwise sorely unserved by the 'young adult fantasy genre that inevitably reduces females to also-rans and decorative sidekicks'.

Whilst this may be true, the idea that you have to be a teenage girl to 'get' *Twilight* is equally off the money – and I say that as a stuffy, bespectacled greying man who has enjoyed the *Twilight* movies a lot. The first instalment is a very decent tale of high-school angst and teen alienation given an alt-lite grungy edge by *thirteen* director Catherine Hardwicke, who did far better with the words of Meyer in *Twilight* than she did with the word of God in *The Nativity Story*. OK, *New Moon* sags somewhat in the middle (a season-changing montage in which Bella appears to mope in a swivel chair for an entire year has become something of a standing joke) but at least it's enlivened by Michael Sheen lasciviously licking the quasi-papal scenery – although you have to wait until the fifth and final movie to hear his maniacal battleground cackle, a cross between Kenneth Williams and Satan himself, which is weirdly wonderful and just a little bladder loosening – in a good way. For my money, *Eclipse* remains the best of the series, with Slade placing Kristen Stewart's heroine firmly in the narrative driving seat, emphasizing her right to choose her own destiny, and giving the movie real bloodsucker bite. My main regret about *Breaking Dawn* is that no one offered it to David Cronenberg, the vampire-pregnancy narrative swerving so insanely from the sentimental to the psychotic that it positively cries out for the director of *The Brood*. As it was, safe-pair-of-hands Bill Condon did his best to keep things on the right side of respectable, although I struggle to remember another 12-certificate film being quite this twisted. Even the Twi-hardest fans of Meyer's fourth novel accept that there are huge narrative problems with the final confrontation, something Condon and screenwriter Melissa Rosenberg opted to solve with an audacious *Dallas*-style device that had audiences laughing, gasping, groaning, and generally WTF!?-ing, all at the same time. It is ridiculous – but it knows itself to be so, inviting us to laugh with it, rather than at it, although most audiences probably did a bit of both.

I said all of this in an article for the *Observer*, to be published on the eve of the release of *Breaking Dawn: Part 2*. Having never made a secret of my fondness for *Twilight*, and in fact become something of a flag-waver for the series, I filed the piece and promptly forgot about it. Then, on the evening of Saturday 10 November 2012, I was propping up the bar at a local village hall when two unexpected text messages popped up on my mobile phone. I remember these messages very well because I was wearing the distinctive attire of George Cole during his 'Flash Harry' fifties Ealing

Comedy period and the mobile seemed anachronistic. The reason I was dressed as George Cole was that I was at a birthday party which, at the last moment, I noticed had a 'movie characters cos-play' theme. Stuffy as I may seem, I have never been above a bit of theatrical dressing-up, and having made no prior preparations I had to make do with whatever was in the wardrobe. As it happened, this was a collection of drape coats I had lovingly acquired over the years (once an old ted, always an old ted), with which I could have kitted out the entire cast of a Showaddywaddy revival show had the band planned a gig in the New Forest and then turned up *sans* costumes – which they hadn't. Sadly, Showaddywaddy weren't movie characters, which was a shame because that would have solved a lot of problems. I had a fleeting hope that they'd done a cameo in *Never Too Young to Rock*, but of course that was the Rubettes, who all dressed as Robert Redford from *The Great Gatsby* (the Clayton version, not the Luhrmann extravaganza). And if I was going to attend a movie-character cos-play party dressed as the Rubettes dressed as Robert Redford from *The Great Gatsby*, then I might just as well go as Robert Redford from *The Great Gatsby*; though of course I couldn't because I didn't have the trademark white cap which was the one thing that made the Rubettes look even remotely like Robert Redford from *The Great Gatsby*, although disappointingly Redford hardly wears the cap in the movie. What I did have was a cardboard 'Gatsby' cap that came with the first Rubettes album, punningly entitled 'Wear It's 'At' (geddit?), but this didn't actually look like the cap which Redford didn't really wear in *The Great Gatsby* – it just looked like a piece of cardboard.

In desperation, I googled 'people in drape coats in the movies' and came up with a picture of George Cole from *The Belles of St Trinian's*. I donned a moth-eaten grey drape, stuck a load of grease in my hair, and drew a pencil moustache on my upper lip. *Et voilà* – I was in character. Until my mobile phone went off and destroyed the carefully constructed illusion of post-war British black-and-white cinema – which is where we came in.

So there I was in a village hall in the New Forest, dressed as George Cole, supping an entirely in-character half of pale ale, when I got a text from Simon Mayo about the other George (Entwistle) who had just stepped down as head of the BBC, and a second text which simply read: 'Have you seen the *Guardian* message board? Scary crazy people!' This seemed like old news; all message boards attract a percentage of sociopaths, something everyone just accepts. The text referred to the comments rapidly piling up beneath my *Twilight* piece, posted online earlier that day, twenty-four hours ahead of Sunday's print publication of the *Observer*. Some of these comments were simply blank dismissals of the entire *Twilight* saga questioning my critical judgement and the honesty of my defence, claiming that I was only saying I liked *Twilight* to be provocative. (This is standard practice – pronouncing that someone you disagree with is only saying something 'for effect' rather than engaging and arguing with what they actually said.) Others took umbrage at my declaration that I've had more fun watching and debating the adventures of Bella, Edward and Jacob than I've ever had from the *Star Wars* movies. This casual aside, picked up by the headline writers and given rather more prominence in the piece than I had perhaps intended, invoked the wrath of the multitudes of Lucas fans still coming to terms with the fact that Disney had just bought the rights to their beloved franchise. Looking back on the piece now, I think the *Star Wars* jibe was a cheap shot; although I've never been a fan of that narratively hobbled space opera, I understand that it means a lot to some people, striking a chord with the core audience in exactly the same way the *Twilight* movies connect with the Twi-hard fans. Having grown up a fully-paid member of the horror 'bat pack', and cut my critical teeth writing for *Fangoria* magazine, I'm well aware that sneering at fans is, like patriotism, the last refuge of a scoundrel, and I've always been deeply suspicious of those who dismiss fan culture as somehow inherently laughable and foolish. If you've ever found solace in fan-driven fantasy films, you'll be well aware of the transformative power of oft-belittled genres like science fiction and horror, and the strange personal connection which those genres can make with audiences for whom weird narratives are the only things that make any sense. As a child, my only real friends were movies – not a cue for you to all go 'Aaah', because I was really happy about that situation, since movies, like dogs, are for life, not just for Christmas. Over the years, people have let me down plenty, but my favourite movies have always been there, steadfast, loyal and true. Taking casual swipes at *Star Wars*, then, is probably something I should stop doing forthwith. And to be honest, on the evidence of *Star Trek* and *Super 8*, I'm actually quite keen to see what incoming helmsman J. J. Abrams will do with the series. If anyone can make me love *Star Wars*, it'll be him.

So, in the first of many apologies in this book, let me say

for the record that I'm sorry to anyone whose nose I put out of joint with lazy Jar Jar Binks jibes – I understand your annoyance. Really. I also appreciate the feedback from those who disagreed with me (some vehemently) about *Twilight* and wanted to explain why they thought I was so wrong; robust conversation is an important element of film appraisal and debate. What I didn't understand or appreciate were the startlingly personal insults accusing me of being everything from a prat to a pervert, screaming abuse about my unfitness as a film critic and a father, lecturing me obscenely on the obscenity of my views. So toxic and unhinged were these comments that they were promptly deleted by the website's official moderator. If you think I'm exaggerating, go check the article yourself, where the rash of 'this comment was removed because it didn't abide by our community standards' announcements still stand like electronic acne scars on the face of civilized discussion.

As I read those comments it struck me that in all my time as a bitter and twisted critic, my negative reviews have never provoked responses as rabidly hostile as the positive ones – unless it's from the film-makers themselves (more of which later). For years I have merrily slagged off movies loved by millions, but only when I go out to bat for something do the knives really come out, as had happened here. But why did these people get so cross? And why were their responses so personal?

The reasons, I believe, are two-fold. The first is that the anonymity afforded by online communication clearly brings out the worst in some people, allowing them to say things they would never otherwise repeat in public. The Austrian-born film-maker Fritz Lang once commented that, although he was an atheist, he supported religious education because 'if you do not teach religion, how can you teach ethics?' Having fled the Nazis in the thirties, Lang had seen both the best and worst of humanity, and became convinced that a belief in the accountability of our words and actions is crucial to civilized behaviour. The problem of anonymity, and the lack of accountability which it enables, is a larger issue for the Internet in general, and in the course of this book I will attempt to examine its particular ramifications for criticism in the twenty-first century. For the moment, let us merely note that in the digital age the questions 'Who is saying this?' and 'Why are they ashamed to put their name to it?' are particularly relevant.

The second significant factor is that liking something involves a level of personal investment and vulnerability which will always leave one open to ridicule. In terms of individual risk (to reputation, to dignity, to pride) it's invariably safer for a critic to laugh than cry – to reach for the hatchet rather than the garland, no matter how good or bad a particular movie may be. History (and 'Forrest Gump on a tractor') proves that the killer punch endures, and it's easier to attack someone for admitting to being moved and affected by a film than for cynically slapping it down – in playground terms, the equivalent of telling someone you like them rather than hitting them with your satchel. We've all experienced the adolescent pain of puppy love, being laughed out of school by our shrieking classmates, thereby learning an important life lesson that whilst jeering is done in public, admiration and affection are best kept strictly private. On some level, saying you love a film is a bit like admitting you have a crush on someone – it opens you up to accusations of foolishness, setting you up for inevitable heartbreak.

None of which matters, of course, if no one knows who you are, hence the recent rise of unattributed endorsements which increasingly adorn movie posters in the consequence-free age of social media. Giving a movie an enthusiastic thumbs up without the possibility of repercussion (personal or professional) is the equivalent of what Erica Jong called 'the zipless fuck' – the no-strings-attached casual sex of film criticism. ('Sex without love is an empty experience,' Diane Keaton tells Woody Allen in *Love and Death*, to which Woody memorably replies, 'Yes, but as empty experiences go it's one of the best.') Only if you have something to lose – something valuable, such as your heart, your reputation, or your job – does a declaration of love become anything other than simply talking dirty.

For a critic's opinion to have value beyond the mere joy of the savage put-down or the well-constructed defence, I believe they must have something personal at stake, something about which they care, and are in danger of forfeiting. Whether praising or damning a movie, it is the risk to the critic's reputation and livelihood which ultimately lends weight to their words and ensures the integrity of their review. And if no one knows (or cares) who you are or what you have done, then what have you invested in your review? What do you have to lose?

When I started writing this book it was with the gnawing anxiety that the profession to which I had devoted my working life was in danger of losing its identity, of becoming somehow anonymous, and therefore weightless. Part of this change has been due to the rise of amateur online reviewers, their growing presence turning what was once an elitist profession into a more all-inclusive pastime. For some this may seem like a positive change; the declining dominance of a few 'name' specialists who make their living commentating upon movies in favour of a new democracy in which everyone can be a critic. As the marketplace widened exponentially, so criticism itself seemed to be mutating, transforming from a trade into something more like a hobby, shifting from the ephemeral to the inconsequential – in the sense that reviews could now be published by anyone, without consequence.

It may well be that this is the format of the future, and if that is something with which you are happy, then good luck to you – you are surely more in tune with the zeitgeist than I will ever be. Personally, when it comes to critics I want to know who they are, what they know, where they come from, and what they have to lose; an old-fashioned notion, perhaps, but one to which I find myself utterly wedded. So, before we go any further, let me say that however foolhardy and out of date the opinions expressed in this book may be, they represent all that I have as a professional critic, and for better or worse I am willing to put my name to them, to stand by them, and to stake my reputation upon them. Everything in this book was written by me (except for the quotations, obviously) and you should bear this in mind at all times, especially when assessing whether any of it has any validity or not. Every judgement and curmudgeonly gripe has been written by a middle-class, self-employed white man rapidly approaching his fiftieth birthday with a tangible investment in protecting the peculiar job which has served him so well for over twenty-five years, and to which he does not yet wish to say goodbye, thanks very much. It is the heartfelt testimony of someone who grew up in an age when computers were the stuff of science-fiction movies; who filed copy written on a typewriter and was baffled by a fax machine; and who is (in popular parlance) an immigrant in the Internet age rather than a digital native. It is the work of someone who clearly has their own interests to protect, and as such it is personal and partisan. If you don't like it, feel free to stop reading it; if you hate it, you can petition those who publish and employ me to stop doing so forthwith. I am not going to badmouth anyone and then disappear into the ether – on the contrary, I'm going to be right here, awaiting your response. If you suspect that I have said anything, in this book, or elsewhere, for improper purposes (as a result, for example, of a bribe or a backhander) and you have evidence to back it up, then you can probably have me hounded out of a job in less than six months. Almost everything I have written or broadcast over the last ten years (and more) is now available online at the click of a button, so critically speaking, you can do a credit check on me any time you like and discover all my petty weaknesses, mistakes, cockups and blind spots. Hell, someone even posted my PhD thesis online, so if you feel like trawling through that to see how stupid I was at college, be my guest!

I love *Mary Poppins* and *Dougal and the Blue Cat*, I hate talking in the cinema and substandard projection, I am overly forgiving of reprehensible seventies exploitation pictures, and overly judgemental of modern comedies for which I apparently have a tin ear. I love British skiffle and American jug band music and I once walked out of a radio broadcast because someone insulted Elvis. I have a stupid name and a stupid haircut, am slightly overweight, and apparently my voice can annoy people at fifty yards. I am given to repetition, and I am also given to repetition. I once got shot at with Werner Herzog and told off by Helen Mirren. I am not related to Frank Kermode. In the eighties I was on the cover of the Manchester magazine *Gay Life*. I used to play bass in the house band for Danny Baker's TV show *After All*.

I (still) think *The Exorcist* is the greatest movie ever made.

There you have it. Professionally speaking, you know where I live, what I have done, what I am doing, and what I have invested in doing it. In short, you know who I am and what I have to lose.

Now, tell me – who are you?

CHAPTER ONE

THE WHIPPING BOY

Ken Russell's funeral was a strange, melancholic, end-of-an-era affair. Held at Bournemouth crematorium on an overcast December afternoon in 2011, it brought together the various disparate strands of his splendidly unruly life: the partners, the children, the friends, the colleagues, none of whom could really believe that he was actually gone. Ken's lifelong champion Humphrey Burton spoke elegantly of his extraordinary artistry, whilst actors Glenda Jackson and Georgina Hale conjured some of the creative passion for which Ken had become legendary. Hymns were sung with gusto, lusty and rambunctious, and the strains of Elgar's 'Nimrod' echoed around the crematorium, all to Ken's very specific instructions.

At the centre of it all was the coffin, a fittingly splendid widescreen creation designed by Lisi Russell (*née* Tribble), who had been Ken's wife and soulmate for over a decade, and who had nurtured and supported him through turbulent times with the unswerving care and devotion of one who is utterly and completely in love. Swathed in ripe red roses which spilled over onto the wooden floor, the sides of the coffin were decorated with views of Russell's beloved Lake District, the green of the earth blending into the azure blue of the sky, an explosion of pastoral ecstasy. At the foot of the coffin was the image of a rising sun with a man, arms outstretched, silhouetted in its ochre glow. The image had been taken from the final frames of *Tommy*, Ken's celebrated screen adaptation of The Who's pinballing rock opera, which pretty much set the template for the modern pop-video that followed swiftly in its wake. Brilliantly, Lisi had digitally altered the image of the lithe, tiny Roger Daltrey to give it more bulk and heft, all the better to resemble Ken, who was something of a giant in terms of both bodily and psychological stature. Whichever way you looked at it, he was a big man; he filled a room with ease – vocally, physically and spiritually.

A few months later, Ken's ashes would be set asail in the Solent on a replica Viking ship over which arrows were fired as it was engulfed by flames, Ken's soul ascending into the ether, presumably en route to wreak havoc in heaven. And make no mistake, that's where Ken was going, whether it existed or not. He'd told me so on several occasions, pointing to the collection of plastic icons (Betty Boop, the Virgin Mary) which surrounded his living spaces, and observing sombrely that the Almighty clearly had a sense of both fun and (more importantly) kitsch. On the eve of his conversion to Catholicism several decades earlier, Ken had been asked by his priest whether he had any questions, or unresolved issues. 'Just one,' he'd replied. 'Sometimes, I'm not sure whether I actually believe any of this stuff.'

'Join the club!' replied the priest.

And so he did . . .

Ken's relationship with religion was sparky, controversial, constantly conflicted, and often oddly creative. At the risk of sounding flippant ('What's wrong with flippant?' Ken once asked, aghast) I think his relationship with critics was somewhat similar. Most of the time, Ken professed an almost pathological lack of interest in what critics said or wrote about him, a result – at least partially – of having spent so many years as what he termed 'the whipping boy of the British press'. This was not much of an exaggeration; after a period of adulation, when films like *Women in Love* and *The Music Lovers* were fêted around the world, Ken fell out of favour with some of the country's most high profile critics. The perceived excesses of *The Devils* provoked acclaim and outrage in roughly equal measure. In the wake of *Lisztomania*, which portrayed the classical composer as a latter-day pop star and featured staged set-pieces involving gigantic breasts and huge hydraulic penises, it became *de rigueur* to dismiss Russell as a self-conscious scandalmonger, an OTT parody of his own flamboyant reputation. While Ken played up to this in public (he loved nostalgic saucy seaside humour and was a fan of Benny Hill), he grew weary of seeing his cinema works dismissed as 'mere exhibitionism' and opted to rise above his critics by either ignoring them or, more regularly, laughing at them. Indeed, in the latter period of his life, I think he took an active pleasure in annoying and antagonizing them wherever and whenever possible.

I fell in love with Russell's movies at about the same time that others in my profession had fallen out of love with them, and this particular twist of fate made some of my more obvious proclamations ('Russell is Britain's greatest living director'; '*The Devils* is one of the ten greatest movies ever made') sound wilfully contrary. Ken was fantastically grateful for the support, but in truth he had no reason to be. In Europe, directors like Fellini (once described as 'the Italian Ken Russell') are revered and applauded and celebrated as national heroes long after their most internationally acclaimed work has been done. Here, we merrily consign our film-heroes to the dustbin of history, where scavenging fanboys like myself can somehow become their most vociferous champions. It was not without a sense of bitter irony that I read the many tributes to Russell following his death in which British film critics unanimously hailed him as an ill-treated genius and heralded *The Devils* as his enduring misunderstood masterpiece. Where, I wondered, had all these writers been for the past ten years while Ken was virtually begging Warners to release his director's cut of *The Devils* – still unavailable to this day due to the studio's pitiful anxieties about its untrammelled fiery power?

None of which is to say that no one had the right to criticize Ken. On the contrary – and somewhat to Ken's displeasure – I always felt that his staunchest critic, Alexander Walker, was a useful thorn in his side. Walker was a strange and enigmatic man whom I did not know well, even though I spent two days a week for donkey's years sitting with him in a darkened room watching the National Press Show screenings, a mainstay of the film critic's working life. I had once met him, quite by chance, at a hotel in Donegal on the west coast of Ireland where I recognized him sitting alone at a dinner table and went up to say hello, surprised to see a familiar face. As always he was immaculately dressed in shirt, tie and jacket, a handkerchief plumped handsomely in his breast pocket, his thick white hair perfectly coiffed. He was polite and charming, joining us for small-talk over coffee, asking after my well-being, complimenting my children – a perfect gentleman. He was also thrillingly mysterious; having told him that we were in Donegal on holiday with friends, I asked what he was doing there, to which he replied with a raised eyebrow:

'I am here on political business, of which we shall not speak.'

It was a fantastic turn of phrase, at once drawing a line under any further enquiry whilst simultaneously hinting at a glamorously enticing world of intrigue, adventure and amazement. It was the perfect arrangement of those words, 'of which we shall not speak', that made me desperate to know more, to *hear* more of that deliciously fruity theatrical drawl for which he became infamous. Of course, it was better for all of us that I should discover nothing further because politically Alexander Walker and I were at the very opposite ends of the spectrum. An Ulsterman of outspoken opinion, Walker had made the national news some years earlier by heckling a discussion at the Cannes film festival where Ken Loach's allegedly pro-IRA (and, let's be honest, not very good) *Hidden Agenda* had played to rapturous applause. Walker was furious that the film, which he found actively offensive, was being taken seriously by audiences who knew nothing of Northern Ireland, and his barracking of those who had backed and made the movie was a fearsome and slightly unhinged tirade, mighty and weird to behold. He might have sounded as mad as a box of frogs, but at least he sounded as though he meant it.

As a former student Trot turned wishy-washy bleeding-heart liberal, I really didn't want to get into a political argument with Walker. Some years later I would incur his ire when I penned an article for *Sight & Sound* magazine detailing the campaign by Associated Newspapers to ban David Cronenberg's brilliant *Crash*, in my opinion a near-perfect movie. Walker had seen the film in Cannes and had hated it, writing a scathing review which appeared in the London *Evening Standard* under the banner headline: 'A Movie Beyond the Bounds of Depravity'. In his review, Walker claimed that *Crash* would test the mettle of the British Board of Film Classification, an organization whom he often berated for being too lenient in their classification of films which he found offensive. In one memorably bonkers review of Takashi Miike's Japanese shocker *Audition*, he actually called upon the police to investigate the circumstances of the film's production, so outraged was he by what he (thought he) saw. In the case of *Crash*, Walker's review sparked a controversy which culminated in Westminster Council banning the movie outright. Meanwhile the *Daily Mail*, whose film critic Christopher Tookey despised *Crash* even more than Walker, launched a campaign urging its readers to 'Boycott Sony'. In the *Sight & Sound* article entitled 'Road Rage', co-author Julian Petley and I made much of the fact that the *Standard* and the *Mail* were both Associated titles, and implied some form of collusion at management level in the papers' attacks on Cronenberg's adaptation of J. G. Ballard's novel. It was this which had infuriated Walker – a fact which I don't think I really appreciated at the time. A one-time governor of the British Film Institute, the body publishing *Sight & Sound*,

Walker had read the article not as an account of his role in the *Crash* controversy but as something far worse – an accusation that his critical faculties had been influenced by industrial forces. The day the article appeared, I got a phone call from *Sight & Sound* editor Nick James warning that Walker was 'on the war-path' and seeking reassurance from me that there was nothing factually inaccurate in the piece. There wasn't – Julian and I had fact-checked it obsessively. In addition, I had specifically removed any emotive phrases and adjectives favoured by the more outspoken Julian, believing that the bare facts spoke for themselves. As such, Walker was unable to demand a retraction – there was nothing to retract. It's only looking back at the piece now that I think I can finally understand what had rattled him so much. He wasn't cross at our suggestion that his opinions about *Crash* were wrong-headed, ill-informed, intemperate, and, as it turned out, inflammatory. What he was cross about was the suggestion that they weren't *his* opinions.

Over the years I have come to realize that there is a valuable lesson to be learned from what thankfully turned out to be only a fleeting run-in with Walker. I'm fairly sure that it was this briefly explosive confrontation which first cemented my view that critics slagging off other critics is, as the *Telegraph*'s reliably insightful Tim Robey puts it, 'not a good look'. I disagreed with pretty much every word that Walker wrote, not only about *Crash* but also about other movies which I loved and cherished and wanted to defend. His politics were diametrically opposed to mine, his views of art and culture made me want to scream, and his ability to look and sound ridiculous often rivalled even my own.

But what I cannot fault is the passion, sincerity, and sense of total personal responsibility with which he expressed those views, nor the seriousness with which he took the craft of film criticism, a career to which he devoted himself wholly and utterly for a good portion of his working life. And if that *Sight & Sound* article implied anything to the contrary, then that is something I regret very deeply.

Alexander Walker never cared a fig about what anyone else thought of his opinions, least of all other reviewers. But he did care that his reputation as a critic of professional conduct and independent personal opinion was sacrosanct, and on this level I concur with him wholeheartedly. If integrity and risk are indeed intertwined as I suggested earlier, then Walker (for all his deeply conservative opinions) was one of the riskiest critics around, saying exactly what he believed, no matter how contrary, even when doing so made him look foolish, and opened him up to attack. The same is true of Chris Tookey, whose views often seem to me outrageously misguided, but whose track record as a professional film critic is beyond reproach. I may think Chris is wrong wrong wrong about loads of movies (and he surely thinks the same about me), but I would never accuse him of breaking any of the core tenets of 'proper film criticism', such as reviewing a film he hadn't seen – he just wouldn't do it. Ever. Nor would any of the critics with whom I still regularly share those National Press Show screenings, week in, week out, year after year. This is the base line for professional film criticism – a standard below which one simply does not fall.

Ken Russell felt rather differently about Alexander Walker's professionalism, and as a film-maker (rather than a film critic) that was, of course, his prerogative. Back in the seventies, Walker and Russell had enjoyed a spectacularly public falling-out which was broadcast nationally on live television and became something of a media *cause célèbre*. The source of their disagreement was Walker's *Evening Standard* review of *The Devils* in which he dismissed the movie as being little more than 'the masturbation fantasies of a Catholic boyhood', and charged the director with wanton sensationalism and lack of self-control. Russell took most of this on the chin, but objected to Walker's additional assertion that *The Devils* contained a shot in which we see Oliver Reed's testicles being crushed, something which is most definitely not in the movie. OK, so it's got everything else – violent enemas, wasps suckling purulent plague-victims, nuns masturbating with candles, stuffed crocodiles, etc. But crushed testicles? Nope. Sorry.

In Walker's defence, it's easy to see why he thought he'd seen it. In a scene in which Oliver Reed's Urbain Grandier is tortured by inquisitorial priests, there is a sequence in which his legs, having been placed in historically accurate irons, are smashed by having a wooden wedge driven between the knees by a hammer blow. The scene, brilliantly painful to watch, had given then-chief-censor John Trevelyan the heebie-jeebies, and he had insisted Russell make cuts in order to lessen its wince-inducing impact. As the scene went back and forth between the director and the censor, it became more and more oblique, with the actual shot of the hammer doing the damage to Grandier's legs becoming ever more elusive. In the final edit, that shot lasts for only a fleeting four or five frames – an almost subliminal flash, less than a fifth of a second long. Flinch and you'll miss it. And as far as I can tell, that's exactly what Walker did. He flinched; hardly surprising, considering the overwhelming power of the scene and the excruciatingly convincing reactions of Oliver Reed at the very top of his game. Having missed that crucial revelatory flash, which is intercut amidst gruelling longer shots of Reed from the waist up having something unspeakable (and un-seeable) done to him from the waist down, Walker's imagination simply filled in the blanks.

This is not the only time the censors' scissors have made something look worse in an attempt to make it look better. There is, to this day, much argument about whether what now appears to be an anal rape scene from Sam Peckinpah's *Straw Dogs* was in fact anything of the sort before the BBFC started cutting away at it, making everything more vague and 'interpretative' than originally intended. And, as horror directors have discovered throughout the history of cinema, if the audience is allowed to come up with something loathsome, putrid and sickening for themselves, they'll usually come up with something far more vile and repugnant than the film-maker could ever have shown – or even imagined.

Never underestimate the sickness of the average viewer's mind.

Anyway, having read Walker's unfavourable review of *The Devils*, some BBC producer or other decided that it would be a good idea to put the film-maker and his critic together on air and let them sort out their differences *mano a mano*. Never shy of publicity, both agreed. Exactly how the whole debacle played out is now a matter of recall rather than record; when making the documentary *Hell on Earth:*

The Desecration and Resurrection of The Devils, film-maker Paul Joyce and I attempted to track down the original recording of the Walker–Russell set-to, but no one in the BBC seemed to know if it still existed or, if it did, where it could be found. Instead, we had to rely on the testimony of those directly involved, namely Russell and Walker. According to Ken, Walker (who had previously praised *Women in Love*) refused to answer the director's questions about factual inaccuracies in his review, a copy of which Russell had with him on his lap. Walker not only remembered that copy of the *Evening Standard*, but also the exact number of pages in that particular issue, which was at the fatter end of the paper's publishing output. According to Walker, Russell became incensed when he pointed out that he was not alone in disliking *The Devils*, noting the rough ride given to the film by the American critics. Ken allegedly replied, 'Well, why don't you go and write for the fucking Americans?' Ken's memory differed, with the director simply insisting, 'You've lied, you've made it up, go on, admit it,' in relation to the aforementioned testicular inaccuracy.

What they both agreed upon was what happened next; rolling up his copy of the *Evening Standard*, Ken reached over and bashed Alexander Walker over the head with his own review.

The BBC switchboard went crazy.

According to Ken's associate producer on *The Devils*, Roy Baird, what made the event so memorable was that 'Walker had this kind of bouffant hairdo, and that sort of put a dent in it' – a plight with which I can identify. As for Walker, his main contention was that 'for all anyone knew, there might have been an iron bar in the newspaper' – a suggestion which Ken, once he heard it, regretted not having thought of first. Either way, national news was made by the spectacle of a grand British film-maker physically assaulting a critic on live TV, an episode which has since passed into legend.

Nearly thirty years later, infamously terrible German film-maker Uwe Boll (*Alone in the Dark*, *House of the Dead*, *Postal* – no, you don't need to watch any of them, trust me) invited his harshest critics to join him in the boxing ring for a few rounds of face-punching fun during which they could settle their differences. Several critics replied, some of whom were shocked to discover that the match wasn't just a harmless publicity stunt – Boll really did want to punch them in the face. Rich 'Lowtax' Kyanka from the website Something Awful, for example, declared that 'half of us hadn't even seen his movies', while Ain't It Cool News writer Jeff Sneider complained, 'I think [Boll's] a jerk. This might be PR, but I don't want to keep getting punched in the head.' In the wake of the so-called 'Raging Boll' event, Uwe has continued to make movies. They haven't got any better. Nor have the reviews. Hey ho.

When I first told Ken that I wanted Alexander Walker to appear in the *Hell on Earth* documentary to put forward his side of the story, Ken scoffed somewhat, clearly still smarting from what he considered to be the grave injustice of Walker's review. This didn't surprise me; for all his court jester reputation and riotous public facade, Ken took film-making very seriously and in many ways *The Devils* had been his most serious film, a trenchant statement about brainwashing and the unholy marriage of Church and State which summed up his heartfelt views about man's inhumanity to man. In a way I admired how sore he still felt because it suggested that his passion for his much-maligned masterpiece hadn't abated in the intervening years. In his mind, the film was still as fresh as the day the American Warner executives told him what a disgrace it was that he'd made 'this disgusting piece of shit' with their precious money. He was fantastically proud of *The Devils*, and was willing to defend it to the death.

Walker's response, however, *was* surprising. Having said very little to him since the *Crash* piece was published (an embarrassed silence now shrouded our brief encounters at the National Press Shows), I felt I owed him the right to reply in the *Devils* documentary, in which we were going to include the story of his on-air altercation with Russell. And so, as we were waiting for a Monday morning press screening to start, I sidled over to him, coughed apologetically, told him that I was making a documentary about a film he hated, and asked him whether he would do me the great favour of appearing in it.

Under the circumstances, I fully expected him to say no. After all, I was one of the journalists responsible for that *Sight &Sound* article. Moreover, he knew I was a close friend of Ken's, and that I had gone into print declaring *The Devils* to be one of the greatest films ever made. He also would have been aware that 'making of' documentaries tend to be broadly positive about the movie in question (who wants to spend years making a documentary about a film they don't like?) and that I had the agreement and participation of all the surviving key players, including Vanessa Redgrave, Sir Peter Maxwell Davies, Dudley Sutton,

David Watkin, Georgina Hale and Murray Melvin. In short, this was a 'Team Ken' production in which dissenting voices would be hugely outnumbered by those in favour and his role would basically be that of fall guy.

As I said, if I had been him, I would have said no.

As it was, he said, 'Yes, of course,' smiling politely, warm and welcoming, just like back in Donegal.

He was as good as his word. On the appointed day, at the appointed hour, prompt and camera-ready, hair coiffed to perfection, he arrived at the church in London where we were shooting interviews, having both re-watched the film and re-read his review in preparation the night before. He was gracious and courteous to everyone on set, introducing himself to the camera crew, making no fuss about lighting or angles or microphones, ready to talk eloquently, precisely and honestly about his reaction to *The Devils*. He recounted his criticisms of the movie, most of which he stood by, although he did concede that on second viewing he had been struck by Redgrave's performance as 'a twisted icon', something with which he was now impressed. He reiterated his belief in the film's masturbatory overtones, summed up his problems with Russell's tendency for excess and then recalled in great detail the BBC altercation, describing it with forensic clarity. If it had been a courtroom and he'd been a star witness, the judge would have thanked him for his marvellous contribution. It was textbook good journalism.

And I disagreed with almost all of it.

Not long after that, Alexander Walker died, quite suddenly and unexpectedly, at the age of seventy-three. He had served for over forty years as the film critic for the *Evening*

Standard, and the paper struggled to find a replacement. For a while they opted for star signing Will Self to file the lead reviews, even though it had long been assumed that trusted film critic Neil Norman would be the natural successor to the throne. Since then, the column which Walker once made his own has boasted such talented writers as Andrew O'Hagan, David Sexton, and Derek Malcolm, the latter of whom was recruited to the *Standard* after decades of service as chief film critic for the *Guardian*.

I miss Alexander Walker; I miss opening the *Evening Standard* on the train home from Waterloo and being barely able to contain my apoplexy at the craziness of some of his more strongly held opinions. I miss his sense of critical unassailability, his literary aloofness, his undeniably snobbish manner, his rigorous code of dress. I miss the fact that, if a screening started even thirty seconds late, Walker would get up out of his chair and go and scare the life out of the poor PR person whose job it was to get things moving. And if anyone ever dared (heaven forbid!) to waste our time by running *trailers* before a press screening, well . . . Alex would march out and explain to them that he had a job to do and he was not here to watch adverts, thank you very much. I even miss the fact that he made a point of detailing exactly how much funding from the National Lottery (he disapproved of gambling) had helped produce the movies which incurred his wrath, a constant reminder to his readers that their money had paid for these stinkers in the first place. He may not have been around to witness it, but Walker would have been both proud and delighted by news of the demise of the UK Film Council.

Most importantly, I mourn the fact that Alexander

Walker was part of a dying breed whose like I feel we may never see again: a professional film critic who lived and breathed his work and put all his pent-up passions into his writing. In America they had Roger Ebert; here in the UK we had Alexander Walker – each a national institution. In this respect, Walker was not so unlike Ken Russell, though neither would've been flattered by that comparison. Both were great British eccentrics, both had a flair for the flamboyant and the theatrical, both were outspoken in their opinions, and both were – in their different ways – passionate about, and happy in, their work. Crucially, neither wanted the other's job; Walker didn't want to be a film-maker, and Russell would have hated being a film critic (when I lent him a DVD of *Audition*, he threw it out the window and then remonstrated with me about my sick and twisted tastes in movies – a reaction not dissimilar to Walker's). Both were exactly where they were meant to be – one making distinctive movies; one writing very personal film reviews; both at frequent loggerheads.

This is not to suggest for a moment that film criticism is on a creative par with film-making; it isn't. The former is journalism which at best aspires to art; the latter is art which at worst is shackled by industry. Yet in their purest forms both have validity and integrity when practised by people with no ulterior motive other than pursuing their chosen craft to the best of their abilities, entertaining and perhaps even enlightening the audience along the way. In one of his more recent hissy fits about the evils of film criticism, writer–director Kevin Smith declared that the only good critics were those who longed to be film-makers and were using criticism as a rung on the ladder towards achieving this ultimate goal. He specifically cited Roger Corman as an example of someone whose films he greatly admired, and whom he had been surprised to discover had been a filthy leeching critic in his time. Quite how a self-proclaimed movie geek of Smith's nerdy reputation got so far in life without knowing that Corman used to write reviews is somewhat baffling – along with Truffaut, Godard, Schrader et al., Corman's humble scribe origins are as well rehearsed as the fact that Roger Ebert once wrote scripts for tits-and-ass schlocksploitation merchant Russ Meyer. Smith's claim that the only worthwhile film criticism is practised by those who see it as a necessary evil on the road towards the greater movie-making good is balderdash of the highest order, but in a perverse way it perfectly encapsulates the slough of disreputable despond into which the profession has fallen of late. For Smith (who clearly never read Alexander Walker) there is nothing creative or craft-worthy about film criticism itself, nothing to aspire to other than outgrowing the format. Nor is he alone in such views; these days professional film critics are viewed as being on a par with child-molesters and pension-fund embezzlers in the popularity stakes, and the media is constantly tying itself up in knots in an attempt to 'get away from' the traditional values of proper film criticism.

Just look at that last phrase, 'the traditional values of proper film criticism'. Admit it – you sneered when you read it, didn't you? As if you'd come across an archaic reference to 'the traditional values of the British Empire' or 'the traditional values of the decent honest slave trade'. Look at it again and ask yourself, what exactly is so wrong? The word 'traditional', perhaps? Or the phrase 'proper film criticism'? Or, more generally, the overwhelming impression that anyone who would use language like that about a profession as frivolous and ephemeral as movie reviewing is a stuck-up fusty old throwback with an inflated sense of self-importance, a rose-tinted view of the past, and an utter inability to adapt to the all-comers-welcome information superhighway of the present? I understand such a reaction; heaven knows I've encountered it regularly enough. But the fact that those words do regularly provoke such revulsion reinforces my anxieties about the degraded perception of the film critic's trade and the staggeringly low esteem in which anyone who considers the job a profession is currently held.

To be clear, I am not talking about myself here. Many people think I'm a lousy film critic, and with perfectly good reason. They object to my rash judgements, my sweeping generalizations, my absurd prejudices, my pet peeves, and my general gobshiteyness, all of which they interpret (probably correctly) as flim-flam and filibuster to cover my underlying lack of basic film knowledge. They accuse me of getting things wrong, factually and interpretatively, of having a thick head for comedy and a soft eye for gore, and of damning one movie for the exact same thing for which I'd happily praise another. They find my jokes unfunny, my impressions annoying, my writing lacklustre, and my continued employment wholly unfathomable.

Fair enough. I can't say I like it, but hey, it's a free country; and as Orwell observed, if freedom of speech is to mean anything at all it must mean the freedom for people to say the things you don't want to hear. I merely wish to point out that I am not complaining about people who don't like or respect my reviews (get to the back of the queue, it's a very long line) but more generally about a growing body of opinion that considers film criticism itself to be somehow bankrupt.

Let me give you an example:

In an article for the *Guardian* dated 16 September 2010, respected arts critic and writer Mark Lawson wrote of the challenges facing Jay Hunt, outgoing controller of BBC1, in her new position at Channel 4. Talking of her recent high-profile travails, which included the much-publicized *Countryfile* ageism row, Lawson discussed Hunt's appointment of a 'generalist' to the presenter's chair of the long-running BBC1 review show *Film 2010* (as was) rather than someone with specialist 'film-literate' knowledge. (The rise of 'generalism' over 'specialism' would be further discussed in a high-profile Radio 4 series, helmed by Lawson and broadcast a few years later, debating the declining role of the critic in culture – both popular and otherwise.) The article partly caught my eye because I'd been at the centre of an unsightly media brouhaha when, following the departure of Jonathan Ross from the BBC, several newspapers made the definitive assertion that I had been lined up to replace him as presenter of BBC1's *Film programme* (as it is officially known). This was utterly untrue; not only was I not being lined up to replace Ross, but Hunt herself had specifically ruled me out of consideration because, in her own words, she wanted 'a programme which will celebrate films like *Avatar*' – and, let's be honest, I wasn't going to do that, now was I? On this issue, she had a point – at the very moment that the negotiations were going on to seal the deal for the *Film programme*'s new presenter, I was touring the country doing a ninety-minute onstage rant-cum-show that included an extended set-piece in which I explained at great and (in my opinion) comic detail exactly what was wrong with 3D in general and *Avatar* in particular. To this end, I employed three Smurf puppets hanging on bits of string, which I then attached to the end of a twenty-foot pole and dangled in the faces of the four or five front rows of the audience while singing, 'We are the Na'vi! We are the Na'vi!' in a silly voice. OK, so you probably had to be there to find it funny, but I have to say I never tired of that joke and took some pride in the fact that the great Charlie Brooker ripped it off in his end-of-the-year *Screenwipe* special. (If imitation is indeed the sincerest form of flattery, then I take that as the very highest compliment.)

As I had blithely mocked the two biggest-selling movies of all time (*Titanic* and *Avatar*-aka-*Smurfahontas* – both from director James Cameron, who clearly got the last laugh), I can perfectly understand why the head of a main-stream TV channel would want to put clear blue water between me and the station's perennially popular film show. Welcoming all-inclusive bonhomie has never been my stock-in-trade, and when it comes to television I tend to frighten the horses (a review of my 1998 *Exorcist* documentary *The Fear of God* noted that 'the scariest thing about this programme is the presenter'). Yet there were plenty of other professional film critics, male and female, young and old, who had impeccable presenting credentials on radio and television, who were far more 'mainstream friendly', and who really liked *Avatar* (which was, in fact, generally fêted with the kind of rave reviews rarely bestowed on science-fiction films). As it turned out, many such seasoned critics would ultimately form an integral part of the show's ongoing success (one is now a co-presenter), ensuring that it retained its core credibility even as it broadened its audience. So what significance (if any) was there in the BBC's announcement that the *Film programme*'s famous chair would now be filled by a 'generalist' – albeit a very talented, popular and likeable one with wide experience in arts programming?

Pondering this issue in an *Empire* online article published in March 2010, film critic Damon Wise looked back to the appointment of Jonathan Ross in 1999, under whose helmsmanship he believed the *Film programme* 'went from being a TV show that *created* a TV personality to being a TV show that was fronted by one'. Although Ross had clear film credentials (he presented *The Incredibly Strange Film Show* for Channel 4 and had served time as a film critic for a national newspaper), Wise argued that his role on the *Film programme* differed fundamentally from that of the show's primary chair during its heyday in the seventies when 'the job was deemed to be a critic's job'. Back then, it was presented by Barry Norman, a brilliant orator and respected film buff who 'looked like a man who spent his time in screening rooms and at film festivals, which indeed he did'. Since Norman's departure, however, film literacy seemed to have become secondary to televisuality. 'In line with the rest of the media,' Wise concluded ruefully, 'the BBC has bought into the idea that film knowledge is somehow snobbish and elitist, and as a result film culture is really, really suffering.'

The thrust of that *Empire* online article chimed with a

growing anxiety echoing across the movie-going landscape, causing many professional film reviewers to fear for their livelihoods; the idea that, in the modern age, the 'real people' who love movies hate critics. Why? Because critics hate the movies real people love, and only love movies real people hate. This attitude was summed up perfectly in a recent parody in *Private Eye*, following the publication of *Sight & Sound*'s once-a-decade update of 'The Greatest Films of All Time', as chosen by film critics. In a break from tradition, and in a concerted effort to move with the times, *Sight & Sound* decided to 'abandon the somewhat elitist exclusivity with which contributors to the poll had been chosen in the past and reach out to a much wider group of international commentators'. Taking particular care to 'include among them critics who'd established their careers online rather than purely in print', *Sight & Sound* 'approached more than 1000 critics, programmers, academics, distributors, writers and other cinephiles', from whom they received a total of 846 top ten lists, in contrast with the 145 used in the previous poll. Regarding the term 'greatest films', editor Nick James told each contributor that 'We leave that open to your interpretation. You might choose the ten films that you feel are most important to film history, or the ten that represent the aesthetic pinnacles of achievement, or indeed the ten films that have had the biggest impact on your own view of cinema.'

The headline news from the 2012 poll was that, for the first time ever, *Citizen Kane* had been toppled from the Number One slot, with pole position usurped by Alfred Hitchcock's *Vertigo*. Quite what had caused this seismic shift is a matter of some debate; there is, in my opinion, an argument to be made that the widespread success of *The Artist* (which won umpteen Oscars including Best Picture) had inadvertently reminded people of the greatness of *Vertigo*, from which it lifts a large section of Bernard Herrmann's score. Indeed, in one of the most insanely vitriolic pieces of negative Oscar campaigning ever, *Vertigo* star Kim Novak somehow found both the will and resources to take out a full-page advert in the film trade bible *Variety* accusing the makers of *The Artist* of 'raping' her 'body of work'. This wasn't some casual slip of the tongue or pen; the piece actually opened with the words 'I want to report a rape', and the actress subsequently 'clarified' her statement by telling journalists, 'I had been raped as a child [and] I never told about it, so when I experienced this one, I felt the need to express it.' Blimey. Even by Academy Awards standards the attack was vicious. Yet while many felt that Novak's words were utterly inappropriate and their timing somewhat suspect, everyone agreed that *Vertigo* was indeed a work of genius to which *The Artist* could not hold a candle.

Whatever the reason, *Vertigo* was now the official critics' darling, closely followed by *Citizen Kane* and other top-ten regulars, such as Kubrick's *2001: A Space Odyssey* and John Ford's *The Searchers*, starring the solidly non-artsy John Wayne. Also featured in the list were F. W. Murnau's epochal silent classic *Sunrise*, Ozu's *Tokyo Story* (often cited as a filmmakers' favourite), Jean Renoir's *La Règle du Jeu*, Fellini's *8½*, Dreyer's *The Passion of Joan of Arc* and (perhaps surprisingly) Dziga Vertov's *Man With a Movie Camera*.

What's interesting about this list is that many (if not most) of those films were, to a greater or lesser degree, 'hit' movies, popular films which were well received by audiences around the world rather than simply being hailed as master-pieces by stuck-up critics. In fact, *Vertigo* replacing *Citizen Kane* at the top spot arguably represented the triumph of box office over abstract academia, for Hitchcock's thriller (although far from his most financially successful film) turned a moderate profit for Paramount, which is more than Welles's format-pushing feature debut did for RKO. In placing a Technicolor, Oscar-nominated, English-language Hollywood murder-mystery-romance (or 'genre' picture) with star names at the top of their hallowed pile, *Sight & Sound* could have been accused of playing to the stalls, courting the populist vote whilst turning their back on the magazine's more high-brow and proudly internationalist heritage.

So how did *Private Eye* parody the poll naming crowd-pleasing showman Alfred Hitchcock as cinema's greatest helmsman? Here's how: above a picture of Jimmy Stewart and Kim Novak engaged in a dramatic clinch (readable as either a struggle or an embrace) ran the spoof headline:

Those top ten films of all time as voted by the nation's most irritating film critics

Below the picture was the following list:

1 Black and white film
2 Black and white foreign film
3 Colour foreign film
4 Foreign film that no one has seen
5 Unfunny silent comedy film
6 Film noir
7 Film noir et blanc

8 Japanese film with German subtitles
9 Turkish film that doesn't make sense even with subtitles
10 They flew to Bruges (*shome mistake surely?*)

Now, I don't know about you, but when I read that list I laughed so hard the coffee I was drinking came out of my nose and I spent the rest of the train journey with scalded sinuses. I love *Private Eye*, not simply because they have a splendidly egalitarian attitude towards their potential targets (they ridicule *everyone* to marvellously democratic effect), but also because their humour works by flying painfully close to the truth. Or – in this case at least – painfully close to the perceived truth, which is a slightly different matter. Everyone reading *Private Eye*'s list would recognize immediately the kind of accepted snobbery which finds critics allegedly lauding obscure films that no one else likes while raising their noses at the blockbusters that entertain the masses and keep the industry afloat.

Except, that's exactly the opposite of what happened in *Sight & Sound*'s 2012 poll. In fact, when asked to name their favourite films, the 'nation's most irritating critics' (and their global colleagues) came up with a list very much in keeping with the populist tastes of a century of worldwide cinema, albeit one somewhat unrepresentatively skewed towards English-language, post-sound productions. Five of the top ten films were either UK or US productions (that's half of them, in case maths isn't your strong point), and only three come from the pre-sound era. By way of comparison, let me offer my own parodic poll of what an allegedly non-snotty top ten list might look like:

Those top ten movies of all time as voted by the real people who go to the cinema

1 English-language Hollywood colour talkie made in the last 20 years
2 English-language Hollywood colour talkie made in the last 20 years
3 English-language Hollywood colour talkie made in the last 20 years
4 British colour talkie with period setting made in the last 20 years
5 English-language Hollywood colour talkie made in the last 20 years
6 English-language Hollywood colour talkie made in the last 20 years
7 English-language Hollywood colour talkie made in the last 20 years
8 English-language Hollywood colour talkie made in the last 20 years
9 English-language Hollywood colour talkie made in the last 20 years
10 *The Artist*

OK, so it's nothing like as funny as *Private Eye*'s offering, but my point is that the widely accepted perceptions of the different types of movies allegedly favoured by critics and audiences are pretty much baloney on both sides. My spoof list, for example, makes no sense at all if you appreciate that most of the world's cinema audiences do not speak English – at least not as a first language. Equally, the idea that all the good movies were made in the very recent past ignores the fact that the real heyday of cinema (in terms of popularity) came in the thirties and forties; to all intents and purposes we are now merely sifting through the wreckage of an art-form whose popular supremacy has long been superseded by the advent of television, video-games, and the Internet. The main reason studios are still frantically ramming 3D down everyone's throat is that they're terrified cinema is dying on its feet, and they think (wrongly) that stereoscopy may offer some form of life-support system, a novelty to help them cling onto those dwindling teenage audiences who have grown used to downloading everything onto their phones.

For free.

No, my clumsy spoof bears no relation to the reality of mainstream movie-going habits, just as *Private Eye*'s entirely superior parody has little or nothing to do with the profoundly un-snobbish enthusiasms actually evidenced by 'the nation's most irritating film critics'. In fact, even in that most rarefied forum of the *Sight & Sound* critics' poll, it appears there's an enormous crossover between the kind of movies critics and audiences like, particularly when one takes into account the fact that cinema exists outside of Britain and America, and that people have been making movies since the turn of the twentieth rather than the twenty-first century. With these elements duly factored in, one could easily mistake that *Sight & Sound* poll for a century-long audience survey.

Incidentally, and speaking as one of 'the nation's most irritating critics', here's my own top ten contribution:

The Exorcist
A Matter of Life and Death
The Devils
It's A Wonderful Life
Don't Look Now
Pan's Labyrinth
Mary Poppins
Brazil
Eyes Without a Face
The Seventh Seal

You'll notice immediately that none of my choices match the final top ten, meaning either that I'm an excitingly singular voice or (more likely) that I don't know what I'm talking about. But proud as I am of my list, loads of things about it perfectly exemplify my failings as a professional film critic. For a start, the prevalence of English-language movies (seven out of ten) suggests my knowledge of world cinema is lacking. Worse still, despite the fact that I play in a band which provides live musical accompaniment for silent movies, every single one of my top ten choices comes from the age of sound – an unforgiveable oversight. And although I've updated my choices from ten years ago, with the inclusion of *Pan's Labyrinth* from 2006, there's nothing that pre-dates World War II, leading one to conclude that while I may be reasonably open-minded about modern cinema, I know next to nothing about the first half-century of movie-making. All of which could rightly have me drummed out of the critical fraternity forthwith, but should – according to 'perceived truth' – make me a big hit with the allegedly dumb multiplex crowd. It's also worth noting that my favourite movie of all time was, in its day, the biggest money-spinning blockbuster ever, a film which played in cinemas around the world for two whole years, and which is still regularly voted the most popular horror movie of all time by people for whom the multiplex is not a foreign country. So much for critical snobbery.

Alexander Walker's list for *Sight &Sound*'s top-ten poll back in 2002 was much more impressive than mine, with *Citizen Kane* taking second place to Antonioni's *L'Avventura* (a very erudite choice), and skipping nimbly between Scorsese's *Taxi Driver* and Fellini's *La Dolce Vita* via Visconti's *The Leopard* and Billy Wilder's *Some Like it Hot* (Doh! I didn't have any comedies in my list either!). The inclusion of not one but two Kubrick titles (*Dr Strangelove* and *2001*) may come across as a little on the fanboy side (Walker was one of the very few film critics whom Stanley apparently counted as a close friend), but in general Walker's list bespeaks a breadth of knowledge and an idiosyncrasy of personal tastes – essential tools of the trade. It doesn't matter that none of my choices match up with Walker's – I can be impressed by his list even if I don't agree with it. Whether he would have felt the same about mine, which featured a couple of movies he actively detested, is another matter. But judging by the way he conducted himself during the *Hell on Earth* documentary shoot, I'm pretty sure he'd have been respectful and polite, even if underneath he thought I was the biggest fool on earth.

As for Ken Russell, we can only guess what his top ten might have looked like; sadly, he wasn't around to contribute to *Sight &Sound*'s 2012 poll of directors, including such luminaries as Martin Scorsese, Terence Davies, Francis

Ford Coppola and Agnieszka Holland. But being the mischief maker that he was, Ken would probably have chosen a list packed with solidly non-canonical trash (including 'that film with the giant undersea octopus', the name of which he could never remember but which had freaked him out as a kid) just to prove what a bunch of know-nothing assholes all those pretentious knobs at *Sight & Sound* (myself included) really were.

As I said earlier, Ken really didn't care much for film critics, and he certainly wasn't interested in doing anything to impress them. As far as I can tell, the only critic to whom he paid any attention at all was his mother, who would use the phrase 'a British picture' to describe movies that were really drab and boring and well behaved – exactly the kind of movies that Ken strived so hard never to make. As for the reviews, I'm inclined to think the bad ones did as much to spur him on as the good ones, possibly more. Despite his understandable disdain for negative notices, there's no indication that Russell was ever hampered or confined by the snipings of those who accused him of being an unruly and excessive film-maker; such claims merely seemed to light a fire under him, encouraging him to be more adventurous, more risk taking, even more contrary. At one point in the seventies, Russell was in the unique position of having no less than three feature films playing simultaneously in London's West End, each of which had attracted a couple of high-profile critical slatings. Did it slow Ken down? Not in the slightest.

In the end, critics (or, at least, good critics) don't write their reviews for film-makers, just as great film-makers shouldn't make their films for critics. Film-making and film-criticism are separate disciplines – not equal, but definitely different, both with their own audience to whom, ultimately, each is solely answerable. Yet today it has become strangely fashionable to sneer at both, to imagine that anyone working in either profession who views their medium as a creative forum is somehow out of step with the times. Over the main doors at Zentropa film studios in Denmark (the home of the Dogme revolution) there hangs a sign which reads: 'No artistic integrity beyond this point' – something which seems less like a pointedly post-modern joke than a straightforward sign-post to the future.

In the later years of his life, despite his extraordinary body of work, Ken Russell found it almost impossible to get funding for his films. Holding court in either the Turf-cutters Arms or the Fisherman's Rest (his two favourite pubs), he would regale all-comers with tales of his now infamous meeting with one UK film-funding body at which a twenty-something office-boy asked to see some examples of his work and Ken responded by dumping a Tesco's shopping bag on his desk stuffed with VHS copies of *Women In Love*, *Mahler*, *Tommy*, *The Music Lovers*, *Altered States*, etc. Eventually, Ken simply gave up trying to explain himself to the people who funded films like *Sex Lives of the Potato Men* and simply took to his shed to make a string of 'garagiste' independent movies, shot on digital video, edited on home computers, and distributed (largely) via the Internet. As Glenda Jackson observed in the wake of his death, it is a shocking indictment of the state of the 'British film industry' (whatever that may be) that a man of his matchless talent and track record was effectively side-lined and shunned by the industry he revolutionized for so long.

As for Alex Walker, although he held onto his job at the *Evening Standard* for more than four decades, he must have been aware that the profession which he so loved was faltering and stumbling all around him. The sight of Russell and Walker having a ding-dong was prime-time television back in the seventies; by the nineties neither of them could get much meaningful exposure on TV. Having signed up for *Celebrity Big Brother* in 2007, Russell realized his mistake and walked, insisting that he'd rather be impoverished and ignored than humiliated and enraged. As for Walker, he had piloted a film show with that other stalwart of British film criticism, Derek Malcolm, on which the two debated the new cinema releases in intelligent but combative form, like Siskel and Ebert in the US. Sadly, the show failed to capture the popular imagination at a time when no one wanted to watch film critics talking about films. What they wanted was 'real people', hence the success of Channel 4's *Moviewatch*, in which ordinary punters would talk about movies, with talented broadcaster and notorious quick wit Johnny Vaughan in the presenter's chair. Vaughan would later become the subject of a low-level (non-) scandal when *Guardian* writer James Silver raised questions about whether he had actually watched all of the films he reviewed in his role as resident film critic for the *Sun*. This could have been interpreted as a serious suggestion of professional misconduct, but in a world in which film criticism was being taken less and less seriously every day, nobody saw it as such. Rather than issuing a writ, Vaughan's spokesman jovially replied that Johnny was lucky enough to have super-special private screenings, which explained why he hadn't been seen sitting with the rest of the critical rabble when a particular movie was screened to the press. Meanwhile, radio-presenter Richard Bacon recently took some pride in revealing how he managed to file film reviews for the *People* for several years without either watching the films or indeed writing the copy. In his hilariously frank 2013 memoir *A Series of Unrelated Events*, Bacon recounts finally being caught out by a film publicist who was working on the Keanu Reeves and Sandra Bullock stinker *The Lake House*. When he told the publicist that he would 'definitely try and see *The Lake House*', she replied that he had already reviewed it in a national newspaper, and indeed hated it – something of which he had no knowledge because not only had he neither seen the film nor written the review, he hadn't even bothered to read the column which proudly bore his name. When Bacon left the *People* after five years of service, he moved to *Loaded* magazine where he promptly became their resident film columnist 'using an identical modus operandi'.

How did we get to the point where 'proper film criticism' is held in such low standing? How did it become unremarkable for the film critics of national newspapers to be casually charged with not actually watching the films they review, or for them proudly (if entertainingly) to fess up to such practices as if they were of no consequence whatsoever? How did the profession fall into such disrepute that film critics are no longer considered for the ever-diminishing pile of film-reviewing jobs that are still out there? And what kind of parlous state must we be in when an official YouGov poll reveals that I am the most 'trusted' film critic in the UK (a shocking enough thought on its own), with a public approval rating of less than 3 per cent!

What the hell happened?

CHAPTER TWO

THIS TIME IT'S PERSONAL

So there I was at some film-related function – I forget precisely which one, but I think it was at the BFI on the Southbank in London – when a middle-aged man walked up to me and hovered uncomfortably on the border of what is commonly now referred to as one's 'personal space'. I didn't recognize him (this is nothing new – I don't recognize loads of people, even the ones I know), but he seemed to know me, and he looked like he had something to say.

So I turned to him.

'Have you got something to say to me?' he asked, bafflingly.

I was caught off-guard. 'Pardon?'

'Have you got something to say to me?' he repeated, this time with the merest hint of aggression.

I had no idea what this was about, so I did what I always do under such circumstances. I apologized. Contrary to the popular belief that I am an arrogant know-it-all who believes himself to be always right while everyone else is perpetually wrong, I actually spend most of my waking hours wracked with the suspicion that I am utterly mistaken and everything is actually my fault; thus I tend – in person, at least – to apologize first and ask questions later.

'I'm sorry,' I said.

'Sorry for what?' he demanded, not in a 'Hey, you've got nothing to be sorry about, it was me who started all this' kind of way, but in an altogether more angry 'I need to hear you say out loud EXACTLY what it is you're pretending to be so sorry about otherwise I won't believe that you are actually sorry about it at all' kind of way.

I decided to back-track.

'No, I mean "I'm sorry, I didn't understand what you just said",' I ventured, hopefully. 'You know, when you said, "Have you got something to say to me?"'

'Well, *have you*?' he insisted, that 'merest hint' of aggression now being replaced with a fairly definitive stamp of something unmistakeably abrasive, bordering on intimidating.

'Er . . . should I?' I floundered, feeling that I was really failing to get a grip on this conversation – again, not an uncommon occurrence.

'Well, yes, I think you *should*,' he said assertively, clearly realizing that I was on the back foot, and more than ready to indulge in what Mary Poppins would practically perfectly define in a disapproving manner as 'playing your advantage' (something Bert would never have done – which is, after all, why she loved him).

I was completely befuddled. I decided to apologize again.

'Look, I'm sorry . . .'

'You already said that,' he pointed out, unnecessarily. 'And I asked you what you were sorry about?'

He waited for me to respond.

Nope. I was still drawing a complete blank on this one.

He decided to change tack.

'Do you know who I am?'

Aaaah, the light was beginning to dawn. This was a simple case of mistaken identity. This man, whom I had never seen before, thought that I was someone who knew him, someone who clearly had something that they wished (or ought to wish) to say to him. Someone like Jesse Birdsall, perhaps, for whom I am frequently mistaken (see my first book, *It's Only a Movie*). Or Nick Faldo. Or that bloke off *The X Factor*. Or the hideous pasty-faced monster from the *Doctor Who* episode 'Waters of Mars' whom everyone keeps telling me looks exactly like me, only less ugly and scary, ha ha ha.

'Do you know who *I* am?' I offered genially (or so I thought), sure this would clear up the entire misunderstanding forthwith and bring our short-lived but nonetheless discomforting confrontation to a swift conclusion, after which we could both smile and laugh merrily (but briefly) about what a funny old world it is, and then go our separate ways, amused and amazed by the way two completely different people can look so similar in the flesh.

'You're Mark bloody Kermode,' he replied, without a smile.

Bugger.

'And *you* are . . . ?'

'I'm . . .'

And he said a name that I did not, do not, and probably will not recognize no matter how hard I try. And so for the purposes of this story I'm going to call him 'Bert Schnick', which is my own personal version of 'Alan (or Allen) Smithee' – the name I use in the absence of a 'real name'. On the off-chance you're unfamiliar with the Smithee moniker, it's the pseudonym which for decades was officially accepted by the Directors Guild of America to signify a movie from which a film-maker, for whatever reason, has had their name removed. While the effect of critics' negative words on box office figures may be negligible, it is a generally held belief in Hollywood that irate film-makers can substantially damage the reputation of a movie by airing their artistic laundry in public. In such cases, it's often better for the film and film-maker simply to part company, limiting the potential harm to both parties. Hence the creation of the fictional 'Smithee', whose astonishing credits range from the unfunny romp *The Shrimp on the Barbie* to the equally unfunny *Stitches* and the unfunny/unscary *Ghost Fever*; the made-for-TV Hitchcock sequel *The Birds II: Land's End*; the action-adventure *Let's Get Harry*; the big-budget sci-fi epic *Solar Crisis*; and the bonkers erotic thriller *Catchfire* (later released on US TV in a director's cut renamed *Backtrack* to distinguish it from the version previously disowned by helmsman Dennis Hopper).

The 'Smithee' credit was first used in 1969, when neither Don Siegel nor Robert Totten wished to be named as director of *Death of a Gunfighter*, on which actor Richard Widmark had effectively called the shots. Conceding that the film did not represent the vision of either director, the DGA agreed for it to be credited to 'Allen Smithee' on the understanding that neither Siegel nor Totten would discuss the production difficulties in public – with which the studio concurred. In fact, having been disowned by both its directors, *Death of a Gunfighter* opened to decent critical notices, with Roger Ebert declaring that 'director Allen Smithee, a name I'm not familiar with, allows the story to unfold naturally. He never preaches, and he never lingers on the obvious. His characters do what they have to do.'

But as Smithee's credits grew, so did awareness of his pseudonymous status, meaning that the deflection of negative publicity became less and less viable. In 1997, *Basic Instinct* writer Joe Eszterhas penned and produced an ill-fated post-*Player* Hollywood satire entitled *An Alan Smithee Film* about a movie director whose real name is Alan Smithee, who attempts to disown a movie he's made only to discover that, under DGA rules, the said stinker must now be credited to . . . 'Alan Smithee' (Boom tish, here all week, tip your waitress). In a supremely ironic turn of events (interpreted by many as being so improbable that it just had to be a publicity stunt), director Arthur Hiller fell out with Eszterhas after he re-cut his movie with the approval of financiers Cinergi Pictures. Hiller was so displeased with Eszterhas's cut that he went to the Directors Guild and insisted upon having his name taken off the film, meaning that *An Alan Smithee Film* became, quite literally, 'An Alan Smithee Film'. At which point, the DGA started to think that this whole Alan Smithee business was getting out of hand. Shortly afterwards they gave up on it, giving *An Alan Smithee Film* the dubious honour of being the film that was so bad it actually killed Alan Smithee, making it officially 'worse than *Showgirls*'.

Certainly, the reviews for *An Alan Smithee Film* aka *Burn Hollywood Burn* weren't kind (although posters bear the legend 'Hilarious – *LA Weekly*'), but the worst critical hatchet jobs are nothing compared to the fury of a film-maker scorned. Producers understand this, and it scares them because, unlike critics, they actually have to work with directors. In fact, despite the endless cineaste stories about venal money-men stamping on the vision of creative geniuses, most financiers still believe that there's a bankable cache in the concept of the 'final cut', and they like to give movie-goers the illusion that what they're watching is pure art, raw hewn from the film-maker's imagination – even if it isn't. Directors, meanwhile, spend their time bleating about how badly they're being treated by the financiers, even when those who are bankrolling their exorbitant flights of fancy exhibit the deep-pocketed patience of Job.

Take the example of British film-maker Tony Kaye, who took out umpteen adverts in the trade press denouncing the released cut of his still strangely impressive feature debut, *American History X*. Having been refused permission by the DGA to use the Alan Smithee moniker because his 'public complaints about the movie had precluded that action', Kaye recalls that New Line were 'begging me to come back because for a small film like that it's disastrous to have the director himself discrediting it'. This despite the fact that Kaye had spent a year failing to edit the movie, and turning up to meetings armed with a priest, a rabbi and a monk, none of whom had seen the film, but whose presence the director felt would provide 'some help from God'.

In the end, the final edit was overseen by leading man Ed Norton, who was keen to work the phrase 'Tony Kaye's vision' into every promotional press interview, and who had long been a flag waver for his eccentric director. Around the time of the movie's release, I found myself in a Hollywood editing studio with legendary cutter Jerry Greenberg – whose credits include *The French Connection*, a masterclass in movie editing – who had worked with Norton on *American History X*. When asked for the inside story on Kaye's tales of artistic mistreatment, Greenberg repeated the familiar mantra that the director was indeed a genius, but stressed that Norton was guilty of nothing more than trying to finish an ambitious film about which Kaye appeared to have developed a self-destructive block. In Greenberg's opinion, the version from which Kaye ultimately failed to get his name removed was pretty much the movie he set out to make in the first place, but about which he seemed to have a terminal crisis of confidence when faced with the awful finality of actually locking the picture and handing it over to the public. This is a familiar scenario – the putative genius from whom such greatness is expected that they become unable to complete anything for fear of disappointing the audience, the critics and, most importantly, themselves. The irony, of course, is that the critics were generally very kind to *American History X*, which picked up an Oscar nomination for Norton and earned decent reviews despite Kaye's demands that, if it couldn't be an Alan Smithee picture, it should be credited as 'A Film By Humpty Dumpty'. I would have gone for 'Un film de Bert Schnick'.

I picked up the Schnick name (unwittingly) from Richard O'Brien's *Shock Treatment*, the sorely underrated sequel to *The Rocky Horror Picture Show* which failed to garner a cult following despite having been tailor-made for the midnight movie circuit. A horribly prescient tale of the rise of reality TV, the movie is, in the words of its creator, 'a total and utter mess'; it began life as one thing and was bent out of shape into something completely different, a classic example of a camel being a horse designed by a committee. According to O'Brien, the original pitch for *Shock Treatment* was a direct narrative follow-up to *Rocky* in which Frank-N-Furter was revived zombie-like from the grave to carry on his cross-dressing shenanigans anew. But having declared the original script to be 'perfect', director and co-writer Jim Sharman soon began asking for radical changes, prompted perhaps by the fact that key cast members (Tim Curry, Susan Sarandon, Barry Bostwick) were all proving unwilling or unable to participate. Hampered by industrial action, the film moved from US locations to UK studios, with the resultant hotchpotch drama being set entirely within the confines of a television studio. Enter Bert Schnick, a psychopathic TV psychiatrist played by Barry Humphries (after Jonathan Adams bowed out of reprising his Doctor Scott role), described by the actor as 'a highly expressionist character, a blind Viennese-born game show host' with Caligarian hair on his head and Jerry Springer's as-yet-untapped fire in his loins.

I first saw *Shock Treatment* on a late-night double-bill at the Phoenix East Finchley in 1984, some years after its initial dismal release, during which it had flopped more spectacularly than *The Rocky Horror Picture Show* (but without the caveat of going on to become an enduring cult favourite). The audience was minuscule and the atmosphere in the normally vibrant auditorium positively

71

funereal – of the twenty or so people who were there when the movie started, only a handful lasted to the end. But for reasons I'm still unable to fathom, I absolutely loved *Shock Treatment* – all the more so, I confess, because it seemed to be so wholly unloved by everyone else. In my subsequent career as a film critic I have often been accused of being a contrarian; of liking or disliking a movie simply to be out of step with everyone else. It's a supremely lazy accusation, generally made by people who haven't seen the movie in question and are unable to entertain the notion that a film may provoke a multitude of reactions, all of them honest and heartfelt. Yet even as I write this, I am aware of the normal and perfectly admirable instinct to feel protective towards the runt of the litter, to want to embrace something struggling to thrive in a world where natural law supports only the survival of the fittest. Everyone understands this, and I defy even the most clear-headed critic to tell me with hand on heart that such an instinct has never once coloured their view of an otherwise despised movie. Indeed, for every decent movie unfairly kicked around town by the critics, I would wager three or four have been lauded and championed by reviewers whose passionate sympathies have been aroused by a film's singular lack of success. Far from being a pack of baying butchers, critics sometimes have a perverse habit of tending to the sick and wounded on the cinematic field of battle, rushing in where angels fear to tread, even when the patient is clearly without a pulse.

The same is true of film-makers; ask any movie director to name the films of which they are most proud, and the chances are they'll name one of their biggest 'failures', perhaps invoking the age-old analogy that all their films are like children, with the flops becoming the recipients of particular parental protection and pride. William Friedkin attested for years that the Joe Eszterhas-scripted misfire *Jade* 'is certainly my most personal movie', while David Lynch retains a special place in his heart for the critically savaged *Twin Peaks: Fire Walk With Me* – the latter being one of my favourite films of the nineties. Meanwhile, Michael Cimino will probably go proudly to his grave as 'The Guy Who Directed *Heaven's Gate*', the film which sank United Artists but is now championed as his master-piece, even though it's rubbish.

Not so *Shock Treatment* – which isn't rubbish, although it is clearly 'an utter mess' of a movie. For whatever reason, it stuck in my mind and I found myself first renting the soundtrack album (this was at a time when record libraries would lend out vinyl discs like books) and then finally buying it (a major financial commitment) and recording it onto a C-60 cassette, which became an immovable resi-dent in the tape-player of my red Hillman Imp for the best part of five years. Honestly, I couldn't go anywhere without listening to that weirdie soundtrack; it was as much a part of driving as the noise of the engine and the squeaky creak of the plastic upholstery. I loved that car (which was called Horace) and I bloody loved that sound-track album too. Just thinking about it now is making me (in the incongruous words of Vinnie Jones in *Lock, Stock and Two Smoking Barrels*) 'emotional'.

Years later, I would invite Richard O'Brien to introduce a gala screening of *Shock Treatment* at the New Forest Film Festival, despite assurances from everyone (from my fellow festival organizers to O'Brien himself) that *Rocky* would do much better. That was kind of the point – everyone knows *The Rocky Horror Picture Show* inside out, but almost no one has seen *Shock Treatment*, which makes screenings of it all the more special. As, indeed, it was. Having jumped through the peculiar profit-participation payment hoops required to show the wretched thing (you'd think they'd make it easy, considering its chequered history, but nope), we screened *Shock Treatment* to a fairly packed house on a Friday night in September 2011, with an introduction by Riff Raff himself, who went splendidly off-piste during the post-screening Q&A session, reminding me exactly why I liked the movie so much despite everything that was so demonstrably wrong with it. And in the middle of this wonderful mess, there was 'Bert Schnick', a man whose name had stuck with me ever since that first viewing in the Phoenix back in 1984.

All this time I'd been merrily using the 'Bert Schnick' moniker, without consciously making the connection with *Shock Treatment*, wherever and whenever I needed a non-specific name to denote some disreputable personage involved in the screen entertainment industry, usually while recounting an entirely imaginary conversation about the origin of some lousy movie or other, more often than not in a silly voice. For example, if I'm attempting to describe the marketing fiasco leading to the rubbish science-fiction film *John Carter of Mars* becoming merely *John Carter* (** ****), it will be focus-group whizz 'Bert Schnick' who tells the assembled Disney managers that, 'According to our in-depth audience research, the problem with the movie is not that it is an utter stinker and everyone hates the whole muddy 3D thing anyway, but that it has the word "Mars" in the title, so we figure that if you take the word "Mars" out, then the movie will do just fine. Because, hey, there are *loads* of people out there who really want to watch a movie about some guy called "John Carter", they just don't want to watch it if it's about, y'know, Mars. So if we just call the picture *John Carter*, everyone will be really intrigued and go, "Just who *is* this John Carter guy? I don't know. Let's go see the movie and find out!" Whereas before they would have been, like, "Well, this John Carter person sounds really interesting but I just don't give a hoot about him now that I know he's, y'know, 'of Mars', so I'm gonna give that movie a swerve." Honestly, trust us, we've done all the tests and we *know* that *John Carter* will be a hit!'

Incidentally, a version of that conversation really did take place in the Disney offices in Hollywood, and that really is the reason the movie ended up with such a stupid, boring, unexciting title. Having noticed that *Mission to Mars*, *Mars Needs Moms*, and *Ghosts of Mars* had all tanked at the box-office, the people who caused William Goldman to observe that, in Hollywood, no one knows anything, concluded that the red planet (*Red Planet* flopped too) was toxic, 'title-wise', and thus changed the name of the movie from *John Carter of Mars* to just *John Carter*. According to their spreadsheets, this also had the added benefit of making it not sound like a science-fiction film, which was good because somebody had a graph proving that 'people don't like science fiction'. This may come as a surprise to George Lucas and James Cameron, both of whom made bazillions of dollars with their little-seen *Star Wars* and *Avatar* movies,

and is particularly ironic since Disney would end up purchasing the former franchise in an attempt to regain their
flagging Force. Yet still they managed to conclude that it
was better to attempt to dupe any movie-goer who hadn't
heard of the extremely famous Edgar Rice Burroughs
source material into imagining that John Carter was neither
science fiction, nor set on Mars. And if any such person
actually existed, just imagine their reaction twenty minutes
into the movie when the cowboy Carter gets knocked out
on the American plains and wakes up in a cave . . . ON
MARS! Doh!

If the man at the BFI, whom I had so far failed to
recognize, had told me that his real name was Bert Schnick
(or Alan Smithee, or even John Carter), I would have
known immediately why he was so pissed off. Think about
it; in a world in which there are real people named Moon
Unit Zappa, Paris Hilton and Boutros Boutros-Ghali, the
chances are that there are plenty of people out there whose
real name is Bert Schnick. Maybe you are one of them. In
which case, let me apologize unreservedly right now for any
offence I may have caused by accidentally bringing your
doubtless good name into disrepute.

It's important to make clear that, even though I have
given him a made-up name, the bloke who walked up to me
on the Southbank (or wherever it was) and demanded to
know whether I had something to say to him was very real
indeed – although at the time I wished he wasn't.

So, 'Bert' told me his name and waited for me to react.
I didn't, because I still had no idea who he was, or why he
thought I might have something to say to him – but I was
starting to get a creeping suspicion that I had at some point

said something terribly insulting about something about which he cared a lot. He knew exactly who I was and was clearly very angry about it (an anger now further fuelled by the fact that I couldn't remember who he was), and I started to suspect that he was a film-maker.

'I'm a film-maker,' he said.

Bollocks.

'Oh great!' I enthused, knowing full well that it was nothing of the kind.

A pause.

'I made a film,' he explained, somewhat redundantly; after all, if you're a 'film-maker', then by definition you will have made a film. Although, to be fair, I've met loads of people who blithely call themselves 'film-makers' who have never made a film in their lives.

'Oh great,' I said again, somewhat lamely.

'Yeah, it was,' said Bert. 'It *was* great.'

'Great,' I said again, clearly stuck in a groove.

'But that's not what you said about it, is it?' Bert insisted, clearly waiting for my veneer of encouraging small-talk to crack.

'Isn't it?' I asked. 'Sorry about that. What was the film called?'

'It was called . . .' And here he said the name of a film I don't remember either, though clearly I'd been disparaging about it – extremely so, judging by Bert's general demeanour.

'So go on,' said Bert.

'Go on what?'

'Say it to my face.'

'Say what to your face?'

'What you said about my movie. On the radio. On that programme you do with that bloke. The other bloke. That Steve bloke. Say it again, only this time, say it to my face . . .'

Now, whatever else had been a source of disagreement between us up until this juncture, I had to concede that, when it came to matters of the moral high ground, on this particular issue he had a perfectly valid and justified point. I have long been of the opinion that if you can't say something to someone's face, then you probably shouldn't say it all – at least not in public, on a radio or TV show, in print or on the Internet, or wherever else irately robust film-criticism is disseminated nowadays. As a critic you are at liberty to like or dislike any movie as much as you want, but if you choose to go slagging off those who have spent their time and money making the darned thing (all movies take a lot of effort to make, even the really rotten ones), then bear in mind that your comments will almost certainly reach those people and you'd better be ready to back them up in person should the occasion arise. Remember: Uwe Boll is not the only film-maker in the world who may come seeking satisfaction. This doesn't mean you have to tiptoe lightly around the subject of hating something; only that you should attempt to understand why you hated it, and be able to explain yourself, in person if need be. For example, if I ever meet any of the 'creative' team behind *Four Christmases* or bump into the perpetrators of *New Year's Eve* (an eventuality I cannot imagine happening in a million years), then I believe I would be morally required to tell them why I think their work is an active part of the end-game of all humanity; clearly, concisely, and – most important of all – politely.

Admittedly, not all film critics feel the same as I do about this code of conduct. I was recently introduced to the online comments of an aspiring blogger who took it upon himself to tell the world through the magical medium of Twitter how very much he hated me; not my writing, just everything about me, from my physical appearance, to my smug arrogance (that old chestnut), to the way I behave at screenings, which is – apparently – 'all about me'. This struck a strange note because although I may be a smug, arrogant, ugly bastard, I am, in fact, generally quite low-key at screenings – not least because of the increasing prevalence of thumb-happy tweeters from whom not even a retreat to the men's room provides an escape.

What was bizarre was that this bilious personal stuff was being written about me in a very public arena, in the apparent belief that its author would never be called upon to say it to my face. Although politicians and footballers may fail to grasp this fact, there's a key difference between emailing one's thoughts to a friend and publishing them on the Internet. And no matter how much a blogger may claim that their chosen medium is every bit as valid and vibrant as the printed word (which it may well be), some still seem to be genuinely surprised when someone actually reads what they have written.

A few weeks after this particular scribe had put his not-so-private feelings about me into the public arena, I walked into a screening room, and there he was, clearly recognizable from the beaming picture of himself posted on Twitter above the comments about what a twat he thought I was. I looked at him, he looked at me – but (perhaps unsurprisingly) he said nothing at all. We took our seats in the screening room, with him sitting a few seats away from me, talking loudly to a mutual acquaintance – still he passed up the golden opportunity to put his money where his mouth was. Later, outside the screening, he was talking to another journalist who waylaid me to ask what I thought of the film, and still the blogger who had been so boldly abusive from the safety of his Internet keyboard said nothing. So I decided to say it for him. 'Excuse me,' I asked politely, 'are you [name withheld]?' He looked ashen, and offered a mumbled assent. 'Do you mind if we have a quick word in private?' I asked, and walked a few yards down the road so that we might speak 'in camera'. I had no desire to have a public spat with this writer, nor to give him reason to feel embarrassed in front of his peers; for all I know, he may well turn out to be the next A. O. Scott or Anthony Lane. I merely wanted to give him the opportunity to call me a wanker to my face – which he still didn't. And so, quietly and calmly (but in a manner that was 'all about me', obviously), I told him that whilst I wished him all the very best in his future career as an aspiring film journalist, bad-mouthing other film journalists in public and making derogatory remarks about their personal life on Twitter did a disservice to his craft and indeed the entire profession. He agreed eagerly, making quietly co-operative noises in the manner of a chastised child. I restated my hope that his career would thrive, and bid him good-day. And as I turned away, he said rather feebly: 'I admire your work . . .'

I could verify this story by naming the blogger in question, but I believe that is a matter for his conscience alone. Also, from what I've read, he's a perfectly decent critic and I genuinely wish him well, regardless of his personal opinion of me.

Meanwhile, back at the BFI, Bert Schnick was similarly demanding that I repeat to his face whatever appalling slur I had cast upon his film. To be clear, the fault here was mine, not his. Not because I badmouthed his movie – I had every right to do so if I disliked it, which, by all the evidence, I did – but because I was now woefully failing to remember, let alone repeat, the insult to his face in the manner he quite justifiably demanded. And whatever I had thought/said about his film, I had to admit that my respect for this particular film-maker was rising by the moment, while my own self-respect was diminishing faster than public faith in seventies disc jockeys.

And so, flustered, I made a hideously botched attempt to do the right thing.

'Look,' I said, 'I'm really sorry, but I honestly can't remember what I said about your film, but it seems that you *can* remember – quite clearly by the sound of it – so if you just tell me what it is that I said, then I will of course say it to your face.'

There was a massively awkward silence during which all the air seemed to have been sucked out of the room by giant oxygen-stealing extraterrestrials, leaving us poor earthlings slowly suffocating in an ever expanding void of angst-ridden awful emptiness. Or as Woody Allen would have it: 'Wheat. Fields of wheat. Cream of wheat. A *tremendous* amount of wheat . . .'

'You *what*?!' said the film-maker, whose previously quiet and bottled-up rage had suddenly become so 'out' it was preparing to parade up and down the streets of San Francisco wearing nothing but a tutu and a bowl of fruit.

'It's just that—'

'You want *me*,' he interrupted in a voice that was now perilously close to shouting, 'to tell *you* what *you* said about *my* movie so that *you* can say it back to *me* . . . ?'

Put like that I have to admit that it sounded rather unusual, and not a little rude. But that, in a nutshell, was what I was asking him to do.

'Um, well . . . yes. If that's what you want.'

There was another gapingly hideous pause during which no birds sang.

'Isn't that what you want?'

'Are you taking the piss?'

'What? No, I'm not. Really. I'm just trying to do the right thing. Look, clearly I've insulted your movie, which has upset you, about which I am sorry – although I hope that I was also being honest – and you think I'm just some twatty critic who says terrible things about people's work without any thought for how that might affect them or how they may feel about it, but that's not the case. People have said terrible things about my work and I know just how much it hurts, and—'

'So have *you* ever made a film?' he cut in.

'What? No, of course not. I could never make a film.'

'Then what do you mean, your "work"?'

'I mean my writing, my reviews.'

His expression was a mixture of outrage and amusement.

'That's not "work",' he scoffed, 'that's just slagging off

somebody else's work. "Work" is making a film. Have you ever made a film?'

I thought I'd covered this point already, but since he was insistent, I repeated, 'No, I've never made a film and nor could I. I have zero talent in the film-making department. I am genuinely amazed that anyone ever gets a film made and if you have managed to do so, then you have done something that I could never do in a million years. The worst film I have ever seen is a million times better than anything I could do, so whatever you've done there's no possibility that I could have done better or even as well.'

This seemed to disarm him, but only for a moment.

'So what right have you got to judge my work?' he demanded.

'What do you mean, "what right"?'

'If you've never made a film, how can you judge someone else's work? What gives you the right?'

This was a common question, and one to which I always (annoyingly) give the same answer.

'I have no "right",' I said, 'but it's my job. I'm a film critic. That's what I do.'

'That's not a job,' he sneered. 'That's just getting paid for being mean about other people's work.'

Again, I thought we'd covered this already, but hey.

'Well, I don't think it's—'

'Like you were mean about my work.'

'Ah, right, which is where we came in. So, as I was saying, if you could just tell me—'

'What you said about my movie but now you can't even bloody remember?'

More wheat . . .

'Yes, exactly, and then I can—'

'*Say it to my face?!*'

Galaxies of wheat. A cornucopia of wheat.

'In a nutshell.'

'You said,' he said, bringing his face ever so slightly closer to mine that I might better appreciate his enraged disdain, 'You said . . .'

Here we go; what the hell had I said? That his film was the work of the devil himself and that every copy should be consigned forthwith to the fiery bowels of hell? That I would rather slam my face repeatedly against a wall than be forced to watch another frame of his pestilential abomination? That the film was so bad that I expected my intestines to leap out of my body and strangle my head in the manner of someone listening to a life-threatening recitation of Vogon poetry? That I had actually considered setting fire to myself rather than endure another moment of this fatuous claptrap? These are all things that I have said about films in the past, along with many other evocations of inhuman pain and torture which I have chosen to conjure up for dramatic effect whilst attempting to explain just how much I hadn't enjoyed a particular movie. In one case, I did indeed proclaim that the director of a movie was the Antichrist himself, sent to destroy cinema with his flaming sword of greedily corpulent putrefaction, a view I find holds up surprisingly well to sustained scientific scrutiny. In fact, when attempting to repeat this assessment in print, I ended up in an extremely strange correspondence with my former publisher's lawyers who wanted to know whether I could prove in court that the gentleman in question was actually 'the Antichrist' because if I couldn't, then they weren't too crazy about letting me say it in one of their books. An interesting legal point: the need to verify that what I was saying was neither wilfully malicious nor factually inaccurate in order to prevent any possible claims of defamation or damage to the good name and reputation of the Son of Satan – allegedly. The usual solution to such problems is either to drop the potential libel altogether (thereby undermining the dramatic effect), or – more clumsily – to surround it in qualifying phrases like 'in my opinion' or 'it seems to me'. This is somewhat tautologous because, as a critic, everything I write is clearly 'in my opinion' – otherwise I wouldn't have written it in the first place. But publishing lawyers are extremely jumpy about anything blurring the boundaries between 'fact' and 'opinion', and in the case of my writing that's pretty much everything. In fact, in the wonderful world of film criticism, there's almost nothing you can say about a movie that isn't utterly loaded with the all-too-personal opinion of the critic. Even such apparently immutable 'facts' as the date and title of a movie are a matter of opinion and debate.

For example, if you look up a movie on the IMDb (Internet Movie Database), you will find that the title will be accompanied by a year, such as: *The Last House on the Left* (1972), *A.I. Artificial Intelligence* (2001), or, more recently, *Margaret* (2011). If you were to write about these films, you might feel that the date and title as presented on the IMDb were pretty much definitive and choose to repeat these in print as 'fact'. But in doing so, you'd actually be expressing an opinion about the veracity of the information provided by the IMDb, which in all three of these cases turns out to be a matter of heated – occasionally furious – debate.

Let's start with those titles. Is Wes Craven's seminal seventies shocker called *Last House on the Left*, or should that title include a definite article: *The Last House on the Left*? Popular opinion holds that the former is correct, and indeed this is the title generally used by horror aficionados, Craven completists and those who have worried long and hard about the cultural and academic significance of an extremely nasty little movie mixing grotesque scenes of death by blow-job with ill-judged interludes of chicken-flapping comedy. Posters and publicity material often refer to it as *Last House on the Left*, and Craven himself has favoured the 'no definite article' option in interviews. But look at the opening sequence of the movie and you'll notice that the title superimposed upon the soft-core spectacle of the first bathroom scene is clearly '*The* Last House on the Left'. According to *Sight & Sound*, the 'correct' title of a movie is the title exactly as it appears on screen, and on that basis the first word of the official moniker is 'The'. Matters are complicated further by the fact that I have seen a print of the movie which bears the title *Krug & Co.*, a name acknowledged by the IMDb as an 'alternative title', but one not generally recognized as definitive. Meanwhile, the video sleeve for an eighties release of the most complete version of Craven's cult classic insists that the movie is called *Last House on the Left* but the label on the tape inside proudly bears the annoying definite article. So what's the movie called? You pays your money, you makes your choice. But make no mistake, it is your choice, however you call it.

The same is true of Steven Spielberg's melancholic sci-fi

movie *A.I. Artificial Intelligence*, which the director effectively inherited from the late great Stanley Kubrick (and to which we shall return in more detail later). Should that title include a semicolon, or a hyphen? And if so, what happens to the full stop after the capital 'I'? The movie's title sequence is no help, since at no point in those opening credits do we ever see the whole name of the film on screen. Instead, we have to make do with watching the words 'Artificial' and 'Intelligence' artfully passing across each other in a highly choreographed typographical dance, briefly forming the acronym 'A I' in the process without any form of punctuation, not even full stops. Having previously argued about the authoritative nomenclature of what the IMDb calls *E.T. the Extra-Terrestrial* (caps with full stops, no colon, lower case 't' on definite article, hyphenated final word/words), Spielberg devotees would already be primed for this kind of molecular-level investigation, but you will still struggle to find a consensus on what the movie's actually called and, in the end, you'll be forced to make a judgement call based on your own interpretation of the 'facts'.

A similar debate raged for months on the Internet regarding the correct title of J. J. Abrams's *Star Trek* sequel. By January 2013, more than 40,000 words had been written on Wikipedia's talk pages devoted to the single (and singularly divisive) issue of whether or not the letter 'i' should be capitalized in the title *Star Trek i/Into Darkness*. Since the title had no colon, advocates of the lower case 'i' insisted that 'into darkness' was not a subtitle but part of the main title, falling under the general style guide ruling that prepositions (particularly those of four letters or fewer) don't get caps. In the other corner were those who insisted that '*Star Trek* is a noun – a thing, not an action; you cannot "Star Trek into" anything', and who pointed out that the official Paramount website for the movie significantly capitalized the 'I'. After months of crazed discussion, in-fighting, and name-calling, Wikipedia settled (briefly) on what Daily Dot correspondent Kevin Morris called 'a compromise, a way to please everyone and no one – and at the same time make the encyclopaedia look rather ridiculous. The first line of the entry now reads '*Star Trek into Darkness* (usually written as *Star Trek Into Darkness*) . . .' When the film finally came out in May 2013, the entire title was capitalized on screen, with the phrases STAR TREK and INTO DARKNESS stylishly juxtaposed against a space-aged background, without punctuation. Meanwhile, the usually ultra-precise BBFC randomly inserted a hyphen into their certification card which opened all screenings of the film in the UK. Speaking to J. J. Abrams for *Kermode and Mayo's Film Review* on Radio 5 live, I asked if he cared to comment upon the titular hornets' nest which his movie had inadvertently stirred up. 'Well, I'd like to start with an apology!' he replied. 'I certainly didn't mean to cause such a problem. But the idea was essentially "Star Trek" as an entity was in itself going "into darkness". The idea of a trek *into* something doesn't necessarily mean to be taken literally . . . But yes, this film is a colon-free zone. Although we were talking for about twenty minutes about a semicolon. And we decided not to do that . . .'

Happy now?

As for the issue of dates, things are no clearer. Ask yourself this – to what exactly does the attributed date of a movie refer? Perhaps it is the date of 'registration', for decades used by the BFI as their official timekeeping tool. Maybe it's the date of the start, or finish, of principal photography. Or maybe it's the year of the movie's release, long preferred by the IMDb, which is often the year after the registration date and the date of filming. But how exactly do you mark the release date? If a movie is screened in December 2011 but not made generally publicly available until January 2012, in what year was it 'released'? Moreover, what happens to a movie which sits on a shelf for some time before finally finding its way out into the world, meaning that the production date and the release date are years apart? This is no hypothetical scenario; look, for example, at the recent case of Kenneth Lonergan's sprawling New York drama *Margaret*, about a young woman whose life intersects with that of a city-bus driver whose attention she catches just before he jumps a red light and kills a pedestrian. Lonergan, hailed as a genius in literary and theatrical circles, shot the film in 2006 with a starry cast including Anna Paquin, Mark Ruffalo, Matt Damon, and Matthew Broderick. But in the eighteen months which followed the completion of principal photography, the director spectacularly failed to complete a workable edit of his eagerly awaited masterpiece, despite the best (or worst) efforts of his financiers, who were desperate to get the film finished and released so that they could see a return on their investment. By 2009, with lawsuits flying, the film was effectively deemed unreleasable, although such luminaries as Martin Scorsese and his long-time editor Thelma Schoonmaker were ready and able to help Lonergan out, as was Broderick who stumped up his own money to help finance the apparently unending editing process. Finally, in 2011, a version with which the director was if not happy then at least reconciled emerged into the semi-public arena, with cuts of varying lengths appearing in the festival, theatrical and home viewing marketplaces over the next twelve months or so.

So, which date should we attribute to *Margaret*? 2006, when shooting took place? Or 2008, when the first edit was completed? Maybe 2009 or 2010, when the film was viewed by various outside parties? Or 2011, when it was finally 'released' to almost no fanfare whatsoever? Most people would go for 2011, which seems the obvious choice, but then what does that do to the filmographies of those who worked on the movie, and who went on to make several other movies in the interim before *Margaret* was finally released? Doesn't dating the film as 2011 actually misrepresent the chronology of their work? Some sources go for the oddly ambiguous 2006/11. Others just split the difference and call it 2009. Whichever way you cut it, in the end it's a bodge and – more importantly – it's a judgement call, a question of discretion, a matter of opinion.

Which brings me back to the whole 'Antichrist' business. Unsatisfied with simply repeating the phrase 'in my opinion' – redundant for all the reasons discussed above – I tried arguing that calling someone 'the Antichrist' was clearly a joke. 'The problem with "jokes",' came the lawyers' clearly well-practised response, 'is that they never sound funny in court.' Good point, well made. All right, how about I simply stand by my claim that the film-maker in question really is the Antichrist and have him attempt to prove otherwise – in court if necessary. Inspired by the legal balderdash of such enjoyably trashy horror titles as *The Exorcism of Emily Rose* (a 'true story' in which a belea-guered priest attempts to convince a judge and jury that a young woman has died as a result of demonic possession rather than professional misconduct) or *Audrey Rose* (in which a lawyer sets out to 'prove' that the titular young girl has reincarnated in the body of someone else's daughter), I pictured myself theatrically showing a series of terrible movie scenes to an increasingly distressed courtroom, each one labelled as a piece of evidence from some unspeakably hideous crime scene ('If m'learned friend would care to turn to Exhibit 7A – yes, your honour, I'm afraid the ladies and gentlemen of the jury do have to watch it, but perhaps they could take a short break afterwards . . . ?'). In closing, I could demand to have the film-maker's head shaven to reveal the 666 birthmark nestling Damien-like beneath his famously terrible haircut, a request with which he would doubtless refuse to comply (he's even more touchy about his hair than I am, apparently), thereby proving his guilt. Ha!

This idea, being at once both pompous and pathetic – my ideal combination – appealed to me enormously, and I had almost talked myself into following it through before my editor told me to stop being so stupid and just get on with helping the lawyers help me not to get my arse sued by a film-maker who would quite probably have enjoyed seeing me get kicked around a courtroom. After all, Jeffrey Archer may be a convicted liar and a terrible author, but he still serves successful writs on anyone who wrongly accuses him of handing envelopes full of money to prostitutes for sex (they were 'travel funds' handed over by an aide) and if Archer can achieve that sort of success in the British courts, then just think what the Dark Lord himself (aka 'He Who Must Not Be Named') could do.

In the end, I just caved in and took out the words 'the Antichrist' – clearly a sensible decision, but one which also highlighted my underlying cowardice, something about which I still feel a bit ashamed (although, as you will notice, not ashamed enough to name the director in question, thereby cementing my lily-livered reputation).

Anyway, back to the Southbank where, you will remember, I was still waiting to hear whatever terrible thing it was that I had said about the film-maker whose name I cannot remember (as opposed to the film-maker whose name I cannot speak), fully expecting to be appalled by the callousness of my words, which I had promised to repeat back to him – to his face.

'You said . . .' he seethed, almost unable to bring himself to speak the words, so poisonous was their nature, 'that it was . . .'

'Yes?'

'. . . that it was . . .'

'Yes?'

'. . . that it was . . .'

'That it was what?'

'"Amateurish and overlong".'

An entire cosmos of wheat.

'Pardon?'

'You said it was "amateurish and overlong".'

Oh, for fuck's sake.

'You're kidding?' I almost laughed.

He wasn't kidding. Or laughing.

'No, I am NOT kidding,' he said with indignation. 'I am *not* kidding, that's exactly what you said. "Amateurish and overlong." I remember it clearly. It's burned into my brain. My film, which I slaved away at for the best part of two years. "Amateurish and overlong."'

'Well, was it?'

'Was it what?'

'Amateurish and overlong?'

'Well . . .' he said, a little crestfallen, 'it was a bit long . . .'

'Aha!'

'But it was *not* bloody "amateurish". It looked fantastic. We had loads of people – *professional* people – who gave us their time and expertise for free. And everyone said how great the film looked. *Everyone*. They all said how *professional* it looked. Everyone except *you*!'

'Well, that's great,' I said merrily. 'Clearly I was in the wrong. Hey, what the hell do I know? Critics, huh?'

'So now you're changing your mind?'

'What? No, I was just saying that I don't know anything but it's great that everyone else thought your film looked really professional and I'm sure it did and I was wrong.'

'So you *are* changing your mind.'

And on the seventh day he rested, having made more than enough wheat.

'No, I was just saying that it's great that so many people loved your movie and hey, what do I know? Nothing! Clearly.'

'So you won't say it to my face.'

'The thing about it being amateurish?'

'Yeah. And "overlong".'

'But you just admitted that it was overlong.'

'A bit.'

'OK, "a bit", but "a bit *overlong*", right? We're agreed on that. Brevity was not its strength.'

'It could have been tightened up.'

'Exactly.'

'A touch.'

'My point entirely.'

'But it was not bloody "amateurish".'

'Clearly not.'

'But you want to tell me that it was?'

'If that would help . . .'

'Go on, then . . .'

'OK, it was "amateurish".'

'Righto,' he said.

And with that he turned and marched briskly away, disappearing into the crowd.

CHAPTER THREE

FOR WHOM THE BELL TOLLS

The best review I ever got was from Roger Ebert, who described me as 'fair, open-minded, very clear, and absolutely correct'. Believe me, I was every bit as shocked as you are; I've been called a lot of things in my time but 'fair' and 'open-minded' are not words with which my name is usually associated. In many ways, this minor accolade represented the high point of my career, for I (as with most others in this profession) had long walked in Ebert's shadow, inspired by his endless passion for cinema, enthralled by the grace and elegance of his writing, and thrilled by his ability (as we saw in the Prologue) to turn a really devastating sentence when a movie deserved a good kicking. I may have grown up wanting to be Barry Norman, but it was the standard set by Ebert to which I aspired, seeing his work as a constant reminder of everything that could be great about film criticism. Although I've not written or said anything as witty, insightful and intelligent as Ebert and probably never will, I still comfort myself with knowing that he once said something positive about my work – and that's all the encouragement I need to keep droning on. In fairness, Ebert wasn't endorsing my work in general, just a single video blog in which I complained yet again about the light loss issues associated with 3D, a format about which Ebert was famously unenthusiastic. But hey, a thumbs-up is a thumbs-up!

When Roger Ebert died in April 2013, his passing provoked an unprecedented outpouring of affection from all sides of the movie industry: film-makers, critics, viewers – even the President of the United States. 'For a generation of Americans,' wrote Obama in an official statement released by the White House on 4 April, 'Roger was the movies. When he didn't like a film, he was honest. When he did, he was effusive – capturing the unique power of movies to take us somewhere magical.' It was an extraordinary and deserved tribute from the leader of the most powerful country in the Western world, and crucially it seemed both heartfelt and sincere. It would be hard to imagine a more glowing display of admiration and sadness than that attending the news that Ebert had filed his final review – an appraisal of Terrence Malick's *To the Wonder*, describing its attempt to 'reach beneath the surface and find the soul in need'. Significantly, many of these tributes had an end-of-an-era edge, with Obama's statement that 'the movies won't be the same without Roger' echoing the thoughts of all who saw Ebert as the last great film critic, to whose noble lineage there was no heir apparent. Take as typical the article in the International Business Times headlined 'Movie Critic's Death Symbolizes the End of a Profession', which declared that 'Ebert was the last of a now-extinct breed; a professional movie reviewer whose opinion actually mattered' and concluded that 'when Ebert died, he took with him the very soul of his profession . . .'

This sense of finality about the ethics and value of film criticism had been brewing for some time. I described in Chapter One my own sense that something was coming to a close with the death of Alexander Walker back in 2003, but these general anxieties were nothing compared to the havoc about to be caused by the economic and techno-logical realities facing the profession in the twenty-first century.

Things really came to a head in March 2010, the month that Kathryn Bigelow made history by becoming the first woman to win the Oscar for Best Director at the eighty-second Academy Awards. (Just think about that; for the first eighty-one years of its existence, the Academy of Motion Picture Arts and Sciences had concluded that the very best work in cinema had been directed, without exception, by men – oy!) Fighting off heavyweight competition from James Cameron, her former husband, Bigelow also scooped the Best Film gong with the much-praised (but compara-tively little-seen) bomb-disposal drama *The Hurt Locker*. Fêted by critics, who applauded its intense atmosphere and nail-biting tension (Ebert called it 'a spellbinding war film . . . a great film, an intelligent film'), *The Hurt Locker* won a David and Goliath battle against the thundering behe-moth that was *Avatar*, a 3D sci-fi spectacular the catering budget of which would have covered all of its competi-tors' total costs several times over. Although TV stations moaned that the success of 'arty' movies like Bigelow's challenging actioner was Kryptonite for Oscar's audience ratings, the director's double-whammy triumph sent out a message to critics that they weren't as out of touch as everyone kept telling them. OK, so *The Hurt Locker* grossed shy of $20 million worldwide, making it (according to the IMDb) the lowest-grossing Best Picture Oscar winner ever, when adjusted for inflation. But the fact that the membership of the American Academy had followed the lead set by (amongst others) the British Academy in awarding Bigelow top honours meant that many, if not most, of those who had actually seen the film absolutely loved it. And while it was one thing for the haughty Limeys of BAFTA to go for a comparatively low-budget art movie, it was quite another thing for the middle-brow, octogenarian AMPAS membership (the people who once judged *Driving Miss Daisy* to be the very best picture of the year!) to come to the same conclusion. For a moment, all those critics on both sides of the Atlantic who had been telling their often uninterested readers and viewers that this really was something worth seeing (Richard Corliss of *Time* magazine went the extra mile and called *The Hurt Locker* 'a near-perfect movie') seemed temporarily vindicated. It was as if Oscar had gotten down from his golden pedestal, pulled his sword out of its hallowed film canister, raised it aloft and declared; 'Hey, guess what – those assholes were right!'

But film critics are unlikely kings of the world, and this fleeting moment of triumph was not to last. The very next day, the US entertainment industry bible *Variety* dropped a bombshell which saw the status of traditional print critics, for decades the backbone of the industry, fundamentally undermined. Todd McCarthy and Derek Elley, both long-standing high-profile film critics for the paper, were to lose their staff jobs (along with respected theatre critic David Rooney) as part of swingeing cost-cutting measures. 'It doesn't make economic sense to have full-time reviewers,' explained editor Tim Gray in an internal memo on 8 March, confidently predicting that 'Today's changes won't be noticed by the readers'. Perhaps not – after all, both McCarthy and Elley had been offered the opportunity to continue filing for the paper on a free-lance basis. Yet an outraged article published by IndieWire on the same day, boldly entitled '*Variety* Cuts its Life's Blood', made clear that some readers had indeed noticed the changes. Declaring that 'for three decades [McCarthy has been] the paper's biggest star and the main reason readers all over the world read the august trade', writer Anne Thompson argued that 'his reviews post first, and are the best-read thing in *Variety*, bar none'. According to Thompson, setting its most prominent writers loose was akin to the paper slashing its own wrists. Without McCarthy and Elley on staff, *Variety* would become a shadow of its former self, another victim of the growing online competi-tion to which traditional print media was still struggling to respond. Meanwhile, Roger Ebert blogged that 'Todd McCarthy is not a man *Variety* should have lightly dis-missed' and stated damningly: 'If *Variety* no longer requires its chief film critic, it no longer requires me as a reader.'

A few weeks later, respected *New York Times* critic A. O. Scott addressed a conference in Atlanta upon the subject of 'The Future of Film Criticism', a future thrown into turmoil by the news that 'the leaky flagship of entertain-ment reporting had recently let go of its senior film and theatre reviewers . . . further thinning the ranks of critics employed by daily and weekly newspapers and magazines of all kinds over the past few years'.

Scott took the 'contrarian, and perhaps also somewhat self-serving position' that criticism still had a future, but upon returning to Chicago, he and Michael Phillips – his co-host on the long-running film review show *At the Movies*, which in its original format had featured Gene Siskel and Roger Ebert – were told by their bosses at Disney that their time on the air was up. According to one Disney lawyer, the programme was 'a dinosaur' in an age where 'the larger viewing public is fractured, fickle and increasingly likely to satisfy its tastes online'. 'Maybe criticism mattered once,' Scott observed of the Internet's role in the demise of the programme, 'but the conventional wisdom insists that it doesn't any more. There used to be James Agee, and now there is Rotten Tomatoes. Rotten movies routinely make huge sums of money in spite of the demurral of critics. Where once reasoned debate and knowledgeable evaluation flourished, there are now social networking and marketing algorithms and a nattering gaggle of bloggers. Or – to turn the picture on its head – a remnant of over-entitled old-media graybeards are fighting a rear-guard action against the democratic forces of the Internet, clinging to thread-bare cultural authority in the face of their own obsolescence. Everyone's a critic! Or maybe no one is.'

A week later, on 7 April 2010, respected writer Ronald Bergan picked up on Scott's theme, filing a blog piece for the *Guardian* online headlined: 'The film critic is dead. Long live the film critic', which opened with the now familiar declaration that 'film reviewing is in crisis. One hears the wailing and gnashing of teeth everywhere in the English-speaking world. Panel after panel discussing "The Future of Film Criticism" has come to the conclusion that there isn't one.' In typically confrontational fashion, Bergan agreed with Scott's assessment that traditional film criticism was on the skids, but pointed out that 'in all the vigils at the bedside of print reviews, rarely has the quality of the professional reviews been questioned. Judging from the many blogs and websites by "amateur" film reviewers, the latter are as good or as bad as most professionals. No wonder readers of film reviews get the impression that "it doesn't take any talent at all" . . .'

Concluding that traditional print and broadcast critics had no one but themselves to blame for their increasingly dodo-like status, Bergan argued that while there were 'excellent reviewers around, some with a devoted following . . . most are indistinguishable from the unpaid ones'. Having previously penned a blog entitled 'What every film critic must know' bemoaning the paucity of knowledge of film theory and history within the profession (a complaint which unsurprisingly drew accusations of elitism), Bergan argued that rather than dumbing down in pursuit of popularity, professional film criticism should be raising its aspirations, distinguishing itself from the babble by which it was now rightly being drowned out. 'Is it asking too much for film reviewers to be as educated about cinema as classical music, literature, or art critics are about their own subjects?' Bergan demanded. 'If professional film reviewing is to survive,' he thundered, 'then critics have to know more than their readers.'

Alas, Bergan's prescription of educated knowledge as an inoculation against the withering of professional film criticism turned out to be itself somewhat ill-educated. On 4 January 2012, that most knowledgeable of film reviewers, Jim Hoberman (of whom journalist and critic Gary Susman wrote that 'aside from Roger Ebert it's hard to imagine a current critic who's been at his post longer, who's had more impact on the indie film world and on other critics, or who's departure would leave a bigger void'), was dropped from the *Village Voice*. After decades blending the best of inter-textual political history and populist movie reportage through both his teaching and his writing (not to mention inspiring several generations of movie-lovers to watch, study and think about films differently), Hoberman found himself cast aside as unceremoniously as all those print journalists whom Bergan had charged with sealing their own fates by being 'starstruck and anecdotal' and lacking 'any analysis – even on a superficial level – of the style or grammar of the film'. 'His layoff', wrote Susman in all-too familiar terms, 'marks the end of an era . . .'

Something far more fundamental than a failure to embrace film history and theory was demonstrably afoot. Writing in *Cinema Scope* about Hoberman's dismissal, Mark Peranson compared the fate of the former *Village Voice* scribe and the subsequent outpouring of grief it pro-voked to the demise of 35mm projection, a subject about which I waxed lyrical in my 2011 book, *The Good, the Bad and the Multiplex*, and which was indeed a central theme of Hoberman's own superior work, *Film after Film*. '[T]he answer to the question "What is Cinema?" is in the process of being reworded,' observed Peranson, wondering – as have many – whether the advent of digital movie-making and exhibition had fundamentally changed the nature of cinema. 'What the Hoberman Affair shows is that we are equally afraid that, with the disappearance of print journalism, film-criticism threatens to become a *Matrix*-like simulation of what criticism once was.' Or in other words, as Internet blogging increasingly eclipses printed journalism, would the very nature of film criticism be altered? '[W]hat can film critics do,' Peranson wondered, 'when the medium's ontological basis is changing in front of their eyes – when their own reality is threatened?'

Asked whether he agreed that his 'privileged position as someone who had a weekly platform to essentially write what they want, how they want, on films they want is going the way of 35mm', Hoberman replied, 'Oh absolutely. I'm not so narcissistic as to identify my losing a paying position to the end of film as we know it, but people did see an historical process at work. In retrospect, I appeared to be like that amiable dinosaur from [Terrence Malick's] *The Tree of Life* . . . cluelessly doomed to extinction. Regardless of what other cinephiles and film journalists may have thought of me or my writing, they understood I had been expelled from Paradise . . .'

Poetic and dramatic as that Miltonian analogy may be, the reasons behind Hoberman's departure from the *Village Voice* were, of course, utterly mundane and largely financial. In the years since Hoberman first started writing for the *Voice*, the paper had gone through several changes of owners and editors, all of whom had variously struggled to 'regulate the anarchic staff' while still maintaining a saleable sheen of critical credibility. Once New Times Media took over in 2005, things became 'immeasurably worse' for Hoberman, with 'periodic bloodbaths' a regular feature.

By the time the *Voice* let Hoberman go, they were 'pretty much out of "high-"salaried writers to lay off – and I'm sure my role as a union activist was an added value.'

Similarly, the loss of Todd McCarthy and Derek Elley from *Variety* turned out to be merely the opening salvo in the collapse of the paper itself. Two years after Tim Gray declared readers wouldn't notice any difference in the paper due to cut-backs, the world-recognized 107-year-old title was unceremoniously sold in what the *Guardian* would disparagingly call a 'fire sale'. The (unconfirmed) price fetched was a mere $25 million, the original asking price having been reportedly dropped by publisher Reed Elsevier from $40 million in their haste to get rid of the title. In what was widely interpreted as a particularly cruel twist of the knife, *Variety* was acquired by the Penske Media Corporation, owners of the website Deadline Hollywood, a thriving part of the brave new digital world to which *Variety* had signally failed to adapt. '*Variety*'s financial decline is a tale of Internet disruption,' wrote the *Guardian*'s Emily Bell, going on to report that Penske's very first move was to dismantle the paywall behind which *Variety* had placed its Internet content in a failed attempt to monetise its dwindling online presence. At the time of acquisition, variety.com had a unique monthly readership of 320,000, in stark contrast to deadline.com's 2.4 million, or the 5.1 million visiting HollywoodReporter.com, a vivid illustration of the fact that 'a venerable brand is no protection' in the emergent digital world. *Variety*, as Bell pointed out, 'is a reminder that paid-for is not a panacea, particularly if you don't have a better answer to keeping the web's reach while safeguarding revenues'.

It was not an isolated incident. As I write, that American institution *Newsweek* magazine is in the process of 'transitioning' awkwardly from print to online distribution, with hard copy going the way of all flesh just as the eightieth-anniversary issues rolled off the press. On 2 August 2010, the Washington Post Company sold *Newsweek* (which had been operating at a loss for years) to Sidney Harman for the token price of one dollar and the assumption of all outstanding financial liabilities. By the end of that year, *Newsweek* was merging with the online publication The Daily Beast; editor Tina Brown took over responsibilities for both titles, and the clumsily named 'Newsweek Daily Beast Company' became jointly owned by Harman and IAC/InterActiveCorps. Predictably, less than two years later, the *New York Times* was reporting that '*Newsweek* [had] buckled under the pressure afflicting the magazine industry in general and weeklies in particular, with their outdated print cycles . . . overtaken by the Internet.' Announcing the cessation of the print publication, Tina Brown informed employees that the transition would include layoffs, and she grew teary eyed when she told employees that she didn't know how many people would be let go.

In this context, *Variety* editor Tim Gray's conclusion in March 2010 that 'it doesn't make economic sense to have full time reviewers' seems to be a savage underestimation of the problem. Rather than being a crisis of criticism, the entire print media industry was imploding in the face of the Internet revolution. Such tales of declining sales and collapsing ad revenues are commonplace, and have caused professional writers everywhere to reassess their career choices. After all, with so many people out there on the

Internet doing it for free, why would any print publication waste good money on a commodity which seems increasingly ubiquitous and, by extension, increasingly worthless?

Just as the advent of digital projection became an excuse for firing the projectionists who were once the heart and soul of cinema, so the rise of online media has been used by many as proof that specialist critics in general, and film critics in particular, are no longer either financially viable or editorially necessary. In the case of cinemas, the culling of professional projectionists was as swift and brutal as it was ultimately self-destructive. In the space of less than three years, all the major cinema chains in the UK went from manned 35 mm projection to largely unmanned digital presentation, with a notable drop in standards being evident to anyone and everyone who paid through the nose to attend an underperforming multiplex where the chances of the right film turning up on the right screen in the right ratio were smaller than Danny DeVito's inside leg measurements. As audiences found out all too quickly, managers who were perfectly good at clicking 'go' on a digital projector had no idea what to do when 'go' turned unexpectedly to 'stop', a situation worsened by their fear of anti-hacking software which would shut the projector down if some untrained person started fiddling with it in the event of a system error. In the words of 'Last Projectionist Standing' Dave Norris, 'Cinema servers are usually user friendly, but it depends how friendly the user is.'

Far from rendering projection skills redundant, the drive to digital actually meant that every cinema now needed someone with the technical know-how of *2001*'s astronaut Dave Bowman on hand to deal with the machines.

In short, we needed a NASA scientist.

What did we get?

Popcorn salesmen.

So, how does all this relate to the fate of the film critic? Am I equating the critical skills of Jim Hoberman or Roger Ebert with those of the people who actually make cinema work – the projectionists? Well, to put it bluntly, yes. And by way of explanation, let me say that along with Roger Ebert calling me 'fair' and 'open-minded', the professional pat-on-the-back of which I am most proud is a certificate from the British Kinematograph, Sound and Television Society 'in recognition of his crusade to improve the standards of Cinema Presentation'. This was presented to me in 2011 at an annual bash organized by the Cinema Technology Committee, a body of technical professionals from across the industry (cinemas, distributors, labs, etc.) who give up their free time to discuss ways of improving the UK film-going experience, and then organize training events to make it so. Circling round the vol-au-vents after the gongs had been dished out, I talked to several projectionists who wondered whether this long-standing awards ceremony would take place at all next year, so catastrophic had been the cull their profession had recently endured. As far as I could tell, many of them felt exactly the same way as all those film critics on both sides of the Atlantic whose livelihoods had collapsed before their very eyes. For some, there was simply no longer a viable future in the projection trade, and the melancholy lurking just behind the bonhomie was palpable. Moving from group to group, all swapping tales of happier times, I was reminded of Mark Herman's wonderful movie *Brassed Off*, in which a virtuoso colliery band battles its way towards a concert at the Albert Hall despite the pit to which it is attached being summarily closed. There was a kindred spirit between the projectionists and those miners, both watching their industries being shut down around them, huge pit wheels grinding to a halt like the dusty spools of a gigantic 35mm projector.

Fast forward a year, however, and contrary to all previous expectations, the BKSTS/CTC awards are still going strong. Moreover, for the first time in their history, the Society has introduced a certificate of excellence for digital presentation, the very first of which was awarded to the team from Saffron Screen, in Saffron Walden. Up in their spankingly clean projection booth (which boasts none of the rank disreputability of similar establishments I had furtively visited back in the celluloid seventies), digital and 35mm projectors stand shoulder to shoulder, facing the same silver screen, handsomely aligned against the forces of darkness. Just as the award-winning projection team had once been tested on their knowledge of the sprockets, pulleys and tensions of celluloid reels, now they were grilled on their understanding of laptops, command codes, and DCPs. Many criteria would remain essentially unchanged: the ability to focus the image correctly on screen, for example, was still a key skill, although now the lens would be moved electronically rather than manually; equally, the strength and quality of the light (measured in good old-fashioned foot lamberts) was of paramount and quantifiable importance. Elsewhere, the test would involve such basics as knowing when and how to change the projector bulb, a knowledge which apparently remains as baffling as black magic to those running dark and dingy multiplexes up and down the country.

And then there are the computerized nuts and bolts of fine tuning the aspect ratio of the picture when the 'fool-proof' automatic settings of the projector fall short of the perfection demanded by even the untrained human eye. I experienced this first-hand at an otherwise excellent film festival with which I was involved when a couple of movies were projected from a hi-definition Blu-ray source which in theory conformed to the specifications of the newly installed digital projector. I say 'in theory' because when the image appeared on the screen it was clear to me (and, I'm sure, to everyone else) that it was almost imperceptibly, but still really annoyingly, out of whack. Although some blowhards insist that only critics and cameramen care about correct screen ratios, it's amazing just how receptive the 'average' audience member is to even the tiniest flaw in visual information. There is a story (perhaps apocryphal) that when Pope Boniface VIII was commissioning paintings for St Peter's, he sent his minions out to track down the best artists in Italy. One arrived at the workshop of Giotto di Bondone, and upon demanding evidence of his talent he was given a single sheet of paper upon which Giotto had drawn a perfect circle, without the use of a compass. The minion was unimpressed, but the artist insisted that the circle was 'more than enough' to demonstrate his talent and sent him away with a flea in his ear. According to legend, the servant then returned to the Vatican where he presented the piece of paper to the Pope, who asked how the circle had been drawn. When he replied that Giotto had simply drawn it right there in front of him, the Pope sent his man scurrying straight back to the artist's studio to assign him the commission forthwith! For the ability to transcribe a perfect circle is very rare indeed; in fact, along with Giotto, the only other people regularly attributed with being able to perform this feat are Leonardo da Vinci and Sir Isaac Newton. But what's most important about this story is that, whilst Giotto has become a figure of artistic legend, no one remembers Pope Boniface VIII as the pontiff who recognized a perfect circle when he saw one. Why? Simple; because everyone can do that.

When checking to see whether the ratio of a projected image is correct, the oldest and simplest trick is to 'look for the circles'. Whether or not we know our Academies from our anamorphics, we can all spot an imperfect circle when we see one. In this particular case, I knew from the moment I saw a slightly irregular clock face on a wall and noticed a couple of wonky wheels on the passing cars that there was something wrong with this picture. My suspicions were confirmed by the arrival on screen of Richard Gere's arse, supremely cinematic in its own way, but not appearing quite as nature intended. Sadly, this detail was lost on the HAL 9000 projection computer running the show; it had failed to notice the irregularity of the actor's much-admired asset, presumably because no one had yet taught it about such things. Remember that moment in the super-squishy eighties remake of *The Fly* in which Seth Brundle sends a piece of raw meat through his new-fangled teleporter before cooking it for his girlfriend, who then spits it out, complaining that it tastes 'synthetic'? In classically Cronenbergian form, Brundle concludes that the problem lies in the fact that the computer has not yet grasped the poetry of the flesh, and he promptly sits down at the keyboard to set about righting that wrong – teaching the computer how to love meat.

If only Brundle had been available to explain to the digital projector about Richard Gere's arse. As it was, it was left to me to complain that his bum did indeed look big in this, and to start fretting about how to rectify the situation in the absence of a BKSTS-approved projectionist. The trouble was that as far as the computer was concerned there was nothing wrong with the picture in general, or Richard's derrière in particular, and thus it was impossible to 'fix' the problem because according to the machines it didn't exist. The projector was simply taking the digital information supplied by the disc and placing it up there on screen in accordance with a series of preset specifications which it had been programmed to follow without regard to the nit-picking tweaks of the unforgiving human eye. You could understand how such a problem could arise; of all the possible ratio presets upon which the projector could draw, this was clearly the closest to being 'correct'. But when it comes to the projected image, close just isn't good enough. Surely there was a way of fine tuning the image, of manually overriding the presets in order to restore the picture to its proper (if perhaps technically irregular) shape?

Some months later, over a pint of Johnny-Knock-Me-Down in a bar in the West End, Cinema Technology Committee mainstay Dave Norris assured me that such an adjustment was indeed possible, as long as you had someone there who knew how to do it. Having recently left his long-time post as head of projection at the Empire Leicester Square to take over in-house duties at Universal, Dave explained that the presets would have been programmed as a general rule of thumb, and nine times out of ten they would be bang on. But if there was something peculiar about the format of the picture information – as seemed to be the case with this disc – a trained projectionist could take control of the exact dimensions of the picture, electronically correcting the image by eye using (amongst other things) the sight of circles – clocks, wheels, etc. – as tells whilst they stretched and squashed the picture accordingly.

'Could they do it from just the sight of Richard Gere's arse?' I asked.

'Hmmm,' replied Dave, pulling thoughtfully on his pint. 'They could if I had trained them . . .'

The bottom line (if you'll excuse the pun) is that, when it comes to the inevitable change from analogue to digital, the medium is not the message – at least, not in its entirety. While digital projection may allow the most incompetent middle-manager to get the odd screening going at the click of a button (something impossible with 35mm projection), it takes skill and training to be able to do this time and time again, with films of varying sizes and formats (and bulbs of constantly changing brightness), and to ensure that each screening is correctly aligned, lit, and balanced, conforming to the high standards expected by even the most undemanding audiences, all of whom have shelled out their hard-earned bucks, and have a positively papal ability to recognize perfect circles (and bums, probably). While digital projection may have allowed monkeys to click 'go', doing so did not make them projectionists. But equally, just because someone is operating a digital projector it doesn't mean they're not a 'real' projectionist. On the contrary, the skill of projection (or lack of it) transcends the medium, and anyone doing the job properly is a craftsman – as the new BKSTS qualification has rightly recognized.

When it comes to film criticism, the parallels are clear; it is once again important to distinguish between the medium and the message. There is no doubt that many old-school film journalists blame the Internet for the apparent demise of their profession, even as they log on to the IMDb, an essential tool we all now take for granted and which began life as a Usenet posting by British computer programmer and movie fan Col Needham. They look down their noses at bloggers, even as sites such as the UK's Den of Geek put their printed reportage to shame. I remember a recent screening of Steven Soderbergh's viral thriller *Contagion* at which the assembled national press critics whooped and cheered at the line 'Blogging isn't writing; it's just graffiti with punctuation', something which clearly struck a chord with everyone in the room – myself included. Scathingly funny as that line may be, it also masks an obstinate laziness on the part of those simply unwilling to see past the end of the printed word. The idea that blogging *en masse* is some sort of coherently disreputable whole is backward-looking baloney, and is no different to the claim (oft repeated on the Internet) that all professional print film critics are snobs. Neither generalization is true (as we know from Chapter One), and both undermine the value of proper film criticism, in all its many forms.

The problem for the blogosphere is that, much like digital projection, its arrival has been linked to a harsh financial imperative which has undervalued the work of paid professionals. Just as the shift from celluloid to digital projection presented an opportunity to save money by firing projectionists, so the publishing world sought to shed writers as it moved inexorably from print to online. In both arenas, the defining factor was money. In the case of cinemas, the market is only now beginning to right itself as patrons start voting with their feet and demanding higher levels of presentation. Thus, when a cinema in Nottingham accidentally showed the opening moments of the 15-rated horror film *Paranormal Activity 4* to a packed auditorium of toddlers eagerly awaiting the arrival of *Madagascar 3*, the resultant audience outcry made national headlines. Having loaded the wrong DCP to one of their many un-manned projectors, overworked staff failed to check the screening until a sea of traumatized four-year-olds were led scream-ing from the auditorium by their parents, with the wrong film still running. Although management claimed that the mistake was 'technical', it perfectly illustrated the need for a human being to stand and watch the first few moments of the film and think: 'Hmmm, this 3D animation about colourful talking animals looks surprisingly like a live action film about possessed maniacs killing people and stealing their babies; maybe there's something wrong.' Clearly, this is not the kind of aesthetic decision a computer can make, and the blame for this debacle ultimately lies at the feet of the multiplex's high command who thought it was a great idea to fire all their projectionists in the first place. (Incidentally, since showing 15-rated material to underage viewers breaches the terms of various licensing laws which should be strictly enforced by the local authority, perhaps

Nottingham Council would care to look at their own role in allowing entertainment establishments to trade with such wanton disregard for the welfare of their patrons. Shouldn't the employment of trained projectionists be part of the Health and Safety regulations laid down by the Cinematograph Act?)

Digital projection can be done properly, and when it comes to film criticism, the same truism applies. The fact that the world is changing and the print medium is in (terminal?) crisis does not mean that film criticism as an art form needs to die out, dumb down, or otherwise disintegrate. But the cost-cutting opportunities offered and demanded by the Internet in a world where no one has yet properly figured out how to monetize online content have caused the bottom to drop out of the film reviewing market, leaving 'professional' film criticism floundering. This is a temporary state of affairs; just as the music business once declared that the Internet would cripple artist royalties and destroy record sales, it now appears that quite the opposite is true. In an article in the *Guardian* dated 5 November 2012, Caspar Llewellyn Smith reported a huge surge in the number of million-selling singles over the past ten years. 'Last year some 178m singles were sold in the UK,' he wrote, 'while the projected figure for this year is 190m. At that rate, this decade will eclipse the 90s as the most successful ever for sales . . . This success is attributed to the advent of digital downloads after sales slumped to 31m in 2003 – the lowest level since the 1950s.' Far from killing music, the Internet (like its bogeyman forerunner 'home taping') has actually revived the fortunes of the music industry – it just took a little bit of time to understand the concept of e-bucks.

As far as publishing is concerned, physical newspapers and magazines may be a thing of the past but the demand for online content is growing by the day. As the number of outlets attempting to service this demand spirals, the only commodity distinguishing one site from another is good old-fashioned quality. Internet users are not stupid – or, to be more precise, they are no more or less stupid than the people who bought a daily newspaper or weekly magazine for the past umpteen years. In fact, many of them are those same people, with the same hopes, dreams, fears and prejudices they always had; the only difference is that they are now online. The challenge to publishers, then, is to find a way of generating e-bucks rather than cover-price revenue. Some believe that online ad revenue is the future, with the success and popularity of free-to-view content being directly linked to the amount of revenue raised thanks to the quantifiability of click-and-score traffic ratings. Others put their faith in the paywall system, which turns site visitors into subscribers and the Internet into a virtual newsagent. The current wisdom seems to be that the most profitable future lies in a combination of free-to-view and paid-for-premium content, particularly for specialist publications with a hardcore readership willing to cough up for top-of-the-line up-to-the-minute information. I, for example, am happy to pay an annual subscription for the IMDb Pro service, even though the 'ordinary' IMDb is free-to-view, because the Pro site suits my working needs better. In the end, the market will prevail and money will continue to be made. If it doesn't, capitalism will collapse and, frankly, we'll all have a lot more to worry about (or rejoice in) than the future of publishing.

As for film criticism, the nature of the (daily) beast may be changing but – like digital projection – the skills required to do it properly remain essentially the same. In the latter paragraphs of his March 2010 piece for the *New York Times*, A. O. Scott noted insightfully that 'As the eulogies for "At the Movies" flow into the larger threnody lamenting the death of criticism, it is worth remembering that the program, now inscribed on the honor roll of the dead, was once implicated in the murders.' Referring back to a piece written twenty years earlier by Richard Corliss in the respected movie magazine *Film Comment* entitled 'All Thumbs, or Is There a Future for Film Criticism?', Scott notes that back in 1990 the success of a TV film review show built upon 'sound bites, video clips and glib quantification' was itself considered to herald the end of movie reviewing – even when that show was co-hosted by the now universally revered Roger Ebert. Astutely recognizing that television's perceived threat to film criticism simply shifted to the Internet, Scott points out that while the 'simple binary code of thumbs-up or thumbs-down voting that Mr Siskel and Mr Ebert trademarked has been supplanted by the crunched numbers of the Metacritic score', the idea that either offers proof of the death and/or dumbing down of film criticism as a whole is both constant and bogus. 'The circumstances in which the art of criticism is practised are always changing,' he wrote, 'but the state of the art is remarkably constant.'

So it was that Roger Ebert, long-time helm of a programme once considered to sound the death knell of film criticism, would eventually be hailed as the last master of the art form. Ebert was a vibrant, intelligent, cineliterate and (crucially) entertainingly popular film critic, not only in America, but also – thanks to the Internet – the wider world. Whilst Ebert's thoughtful, insightful writing used to reach only those living in the catchment area of the *Chicago Sun-Times* and its syndicated papers, the move to online afforded Ebert an international platform, helping to make him the most important and influential film critic in the English language. His global status was massively boosted by his own website, rogerebert.com, and by an army of Twitter followers numbering over 800,000, all of whom were kept up-to-date with links to Ebert's essential articles as and when they went online. In a previous age, the fact that Ebert lost his vocal cords and most of his lower jaw to cancer, making him unable to present TV shows, would have caused his audience to decline, but the Internet allowed his voice to grow stronger than before. Far from heralding the end of film criticism, Ebert demonstrated that the Internet offered a bright new future wherein witty, intelligent, and informative film reviewing could thrive and prosper. He was not only the first film critic to win the Pulitzer Prize, but the first reviewer to have their own star on the Hollywood walk of fame. He was also, significantly, the recipient of several awards honouring his contribution to online culture, having been an early adopter and advocate of the web.

My own experience, although wholly incomparable to Ebert's world-beating reign, is similar inasmuch as the web has proved a boon rather than a bugbear – despite my frequent moans to the contrary. The radio show I present with Simon Mayo has developed a devoted online following, a significant number of whom download the podcast (an Internet innovation) from all four corners of the globe, and with whom we are able to enter into an extremely lively dialogue. Everything I write for the *Observer* is available online the moment it is published in print, and a large section of the readership are alerted to each new column via ever-expanding social media. My books sell almost as many copies through websites as through physical stores. And, of course, were it not for the Kermode Uncut video blog, which exists only on the Internet, I wouldn't now have the satisfaction of being able to say that Roger Ebert not only knew of my work, but also once said something really nice about it on Twitter.

There is, of course, one important caveat to Ebert's extraordinary multi-platform success story. Although Ebert's free-to-view online presence was huge, one must not underestimate the importance of his paid employment at the *Chicago Sun-Times*, his home for many years. Writing in the *New York Times* on 7 April 2013, David Carr described Ebert as a relentless empire builder who 'used all available technologies and platforms to advance both his love of film and his own professional interests'. While Ebert achieved the enviable feat of becoming the most important film commentator on the web, the roots of his continued success lay squarely in the apparently outmoded models of old-fashioned print journalism, believed by so many to have been eclipsed by the Internet.

In December 2011, Sun-Times Media Holdings LLC,

which operates the *Chicago Sun-Times*, announced that it was introducing an Internet paywall for the venerable title – the city's oldest continuously published daily newspaper, dating back to 1844. After twenty free page views in a thirty-day period, online subscribers would be charged $6.99 a month to continue to use the site, while print subscribers could access it for a mere $1.99. 'Publishers across the country are moving in this direction,' said (then) *Sun-Times* CEO Jeremy Halbreich, 'and we see this as the next logical step in our digital business plan. The rationale for moving in this direction is simple. Quality journalism is not free.' Could the same be said for quality film criticism? Having long been the paper's most recognized and celebrated writer, Ebert's reviews were unsurprisingly proving one of the biggest draws to suntimes.com, and the critic was keen for his work to keep its increasingly vast free-to-view audience. Back in 2010, he had blogged that thanks to the Internet his archive of 10,000 reviews was now 'online, being read every day from virtually everyplace on Earth. One in Yemen, one in Pago Pago, it adds up. Daniel from Pago Pago is a valued commenter on the blog. Think how great that makes me feel. If I go behind a paywall, however, and a high school student in Mexico is doing some research, there are lots of other excellent critics on the web, and everybody knows it.' On the day of the announcement of the *Sun-Times* paywall, Ebert told *Time Out Chicago* media blogger Robert Feder, 'As of now I don't know how it will affect rogerebert.com, or, for that matter, my blog.' The answer was: not at all. Clearly sympathetic to Ebert's concerns and (more importantly) acutely aware of his role drawing traffic to the site, publisher John Barron was able to assure the paper's star signing that his content would not be placed behind the paywall, and would continue to be viewable to all-comers from around the world.

Thus it was still possible in November 2012 (when I was in the middle of writing this book) to skip unimpeded over to rogerebert.suntimes.com, where a glowing Chicago-filed review of *Skyfall* ('the best Bond in years') was free to view in my living room in sunny Hampshire via a page that also provided links to all of Ebert's associated writings and click-and-buy links to his library of books. Prominently placed on that same page was a large advert for Ben Affleck's *Argo* – an advert which had clearly identified me as a UK visitor to the site and boasted a very region-specific endorsement of the movie ('Gripping' *Total Film*). If I clicked on the ad, it took me to the film's UK Facebook site, leading me to details of cinemas near me currently showing the movie. So, within less than a minute of visiting Ebert's US-based site, I could be booking a ticket to see the midday screening of *Argo* at the Eastleigh Vue, having been encouraged to do so by a leading UK film magazine. Target marketing doesn't come much more targeted than that. I had visited Ebert's page for free, but his writing came at a cost for which those online ads helped pay. In turn, his reviews attracted more readers to the rest of the editorial content on the *Sun-Times* site. Perhaps my eye would be drawn to a column by someone I'd never heard of before. If I liked their writing enough, maybe I'd come back. Hey, I might even subscribe . . .

The lessons of Ebert's career are clear: quality will out, whether in print, broadcast, or Internet publication; and 'quality journalism is not free' – in the end, someone has to pick up the check. For all the blather on the Internet about the out-of-touch fustiness of boring old 'professional' critics, unpaid amateurism is ultimately unsustainable. Most Internet sites using unpaid film reviewers promise career-enhancing 'reach' as the incentive to write. The pitch for these sites is that getting your copy online will somehow become a badge of merit and thereby lead to paid work: Hey, write for our site for free and someone else will pay you in the future! But where will those promised paid jobs come from in a market in which an endless supply of free copy is available to anybody for whom 'reach' (rather than 'wage') is a legitimate currency?

The hard truth is: writing for free in an arena where someone else is getting paid eventually undermines the possibility of *anyone* being properly remunerated for what they do. This may make me sound like an appalling old Trotskyite – outdated, outmoded, and hanging on to an obsolete model of journalism with no place in the twenty-first century – but if film critics don't think that what they do has worth, then why the hell should anyone else? And if Roger Ebert knew anything, it was the financial value of his work, something which helped make him (in the words of the *New York Times*) one of 'the most famous and well compensated film writers in history'.

Rotten Tomatoes et al. may now include a certain amount of unpaid bloggers in their critical rating tallies, just as *Sight & Sound* opened the doors of its recent top ten polls to a select few whose influence has been achieved without recourse to print. But remove those professional critics from the equation altogether, and where does that leave you? Would those sites flourish if all they did was to tally the random views of those who believe that film criticism should be nothing more than an amateur pastime? Would they attract the same level of traffic if the opinions of professionals were removed from their calculations?

As for Ebert, it may well be the case that his passing marked the end of an era since it's hard to imagine anyone else matching the scope, intelligence and popularity of his film criticism. In terms of the trade, he was a giant – an inspiration to all who read his work, and who were encouraged to think more deeply about what movies really meant to them. But to equate Ebert's death with the demise of film criticism is to do an injustice to his legacy, particularly when that demise is itself linked to the rise of online content. Far from believing that the profession he loved was undergoing some kind of Internet-induced endgame, Ebert saw the web as offering a new dawn for film criticism in which global reach and international dialogue were all part of an ever-widening conversation. By taking the best values of old-school print and broadcast journalism (honesty, accountability, remuneration) and applying them to the new frontiers of the Internet, he managed to secure and enhance his position as a professional film critic at a time when others were falling by the wayside, struggling to find their place in this brave new world. Whilst some of us were wondering what the hell happened to the past, Ebert had his eye on the future. As he had done so often before, he moved with the times, embracing the possibilities of each new medium whilst retaining the immutable qualities that made him the best-loved film critic in the world.

The medium may have changed, but the message remained the same.

God bless you, Mr Ebert. And thanks for the kind words. They may not have been printed, but they meant as much to me as spilled ink ever could.

CHAPTER FOUR

FIRST BUT WRONG

Film criticism is not news – or, more precisely, it's not breaking news.

The idea that there is something of inherent value in the 'first review' of a film, or a play, or a record – whatever – has long held dubious cultural currency. Back in the good old, bad old days, when a killer review could (allegedly) cause a Broadway show to close on its opening night, tradition had it that the producers would retire to Sardi's restaurant where, according to popular folklore, you could order oysters and a main course while the scribes were filing their copy, stuff yourself on dessert as the presses rolled, and then call for either coffee or champagne as the next day's papers arrived on the doorsteps at around 4 a.m., and everyone found out whether they had a hit on their hands or just shit on their shoes.

It's a romantic notion, captured in the films and plays of Woody Allen and Mel Brooks, hard-wired into the self-mythologizing legend of the Big Apple as the entertainment capital of the world. And whilst there are instances where the damning verdict of the so-called Butchers of Broadway all but ended a show's existence, the idea that the morning papers could stop an afternoon matinee is generally a flight of fancy – an embellishment of the altogether more mundane truth that theatres can go dark at almost any time, thanks to the maddening economics of putting on a show.

I argued in my previous book that there is little or no evidence to suggest that critics can actually affect the box office of movies, and if they do, the result is rarely to the film's financial detriment. Whether positive or negative, film reviews appear to serve only as a form of publicity. Think about it – if distributors thought that critics could actually harm their movies, why would they go to the (expensive) trouble of laying on pre-release press screenings for them in the first place? Would that not be financially and politically reckless? In fact, in an age in which social media sites are supposedly making traditional reviews all but redundant, distributors often don't show their movies to the press – the film will do perfectly fine without them, thanks very much. When I first started drafting this chapter, in the autumn of 2012, the computer-game spin-off sequel *Resident Evil: Retribution* in 3D was sliding into the UK box-office top ten, where it joined *The House at the End of the Street* and *That's My Boy*, all of which had been variously withheld from critics, but took plenty of box-office bucks regardless. More recently, the abysmal *Movie 43* made a fleeting appearance in the top ten before dropping like a stone after audiences discovered exactly why the distributors had withheld it from the press; and the Stephenie Meyer body-snatcher fantasy *The Host* opened across the country without ever troubling the inside of a UK preview theatre. In each case, there was no obligation to screen the film to critics in advance. If distributors preview their films for the press, they do so because it suits their primary purpose, which is maximizing the film's potential profit.

Admittedly, not all distributors like to own up to this truth in public, and at some point in their career most long-standing critics will have found themselves banned from certain screenings for saying nasty things about a movie in the press. The great Alexander Walker himself was once struck off a UK film company's lists for filing some now long-forgotten review of an even more forgotten movie. Kim Newman was briefly banned from screenings by the Rank Organisation, after writing a scurrilous piece suggesting the cute robotic reindeer used in *Santa Claus: The Movie* had been made by catching and killing real live reindeer, pulling out their insides, and stuffing them full of Meccano. It was a joke, obviously, but one the powers that be at Rank felt might somehow filter through to the film's target youth audience and have a detrimental effect on the movie's seasonal 'feel good' factor. (I disagree; I felt a lot better about *Santa Claus: The Movie* after laughing myself silly at the idea of Dudley Moore consorting with mechanized animal zombies, dragging freshly culled blood and entrails in their wake.) I was once banned from a UK distributor's press screenings after filing a brief but snotty video review of one of their titles for *Sight & Sound* back in the nineties. The film in question was a drama starring Edward James Olmos, originally titled *Mi Familia* (*My Family*), which had come and gone almost un-noticed in UK cinemas before being renamed *East L.A.* for its video release. Since the distributors had kept understandably quiet about the title change (who wants to flag up a box-office stiff?) I spent a good deal of time attempting to track down a preview copy of *East L.A.* on tape before realizing I'd already seen the damned thing under a different name in the cinema – a waste of time I didn't have: the labour-intensive *Sight & Sound* column usually involved reviewing between twenty and thirty titles a month, many of them unwatchable. It was with a hint of irritation, therefore, that I carelessly penned the lines: 'Having been dumped in UK cinemas, *Mi Familia* suffers a perfunctory title change on video', adding the name of the distributor responsible for the said dumping and altered nomenclature just for good measure. And that was it. The day the magazine hit the news-stands, the distributors were on the phone to *Sight & Sound* and I was banned from all further press screenings.

This was a major problem since, in my then role as resident film critic for Radio 1, I simply couldn't afford to be locked out of key press screenings. Indeed, problems were already arising with the controversial Oliver Stone film *Nixon* which was due out the very next week, and if I didn't get to see and review it then my job at the BBC would clearly be on the line. After all, Radio 1 boss Matthew Bannister had signed me up on the basis that I was young, eager and ready to watch everything – a somewhat untenable position when one has been struck off one of the country's pre-eminent press lists.

The short-term solution to the *Nixon* problem was a trip to France where, for reasons which fail me, the movie was previewing a few days before its official UK release. So, on a miserable Wednesday morning in March 1996, I turned up at Waterloo station and paid a staggering sum of money to Eurostar in order that I might attend a horrible Parisian multiplex and watch Anthony Hopkins pretend to be Tricky Dicky, with French subtitles ('Je have jamais been un *quitter*!') burbling distractingly underneath. It was a thoroughly wretched day, up there with the time I went all the way to Euro Disney to spend four minutes talking to Tim Allen about his abominable new comedy *The Santa Clause* (not to be confused with *Santa Claus: The Movie*), only to discover on my return that the tape recorder had failed and I had nothing but silence for my cross-Channel troubles.

In true Nixonian style, paranoia got the better of me, and I spent most of my time in France expecting to be ambushed by the gendarmerie, who had doubtless cooked up some byzantine extradition treaty with the film distributors of the UK and were even now waiting to deport me back to Blighty, where I would surely face trial for crimes against '*le cinéma*'. By the time I got to the stinking little three-screener which passed for a multiplex in Paris in the nineties, I was sweating bullets, certain of capture. In the event, I was met with only indifference by the cashier at the ticket window; he had little interest in my professional critical crises, and even less engagement with my desire to watch *Nixon* in English.

'Un ticket pour *Nixon* en Angleterre,' I said nervously, waiting for the French elite special forces to pounce.

'Quoi?' came the somewhat bemused response.

'Un ticket pour le film *Nixon*, par Oliver Stone . . . en Angleterre,' I said again, slower and louder, believing (as is the custom in Britain) that the best way to talk to the French is to imagine that they are both hard of hearing and intellectually challenged.

'*Nixon* . . . en Angleterre?' said the cashier, as if he was talking to a very stupid person (which indeed he was).

'Oui!' I replied, proud of my bi-lingual multitasking.

'Monsieur, vous êtes à Paris,' he sneered through a fog of half-exhaled Gitanes.

'Oui, je comprends. Mais, je wish pour voir le film *Nixon* par Oliver Stone en Angleterre.'

'Á bientôt! Allez en Angleterre!'

'Quoi?'

'Allez en Angleterre!'

'Pourquoi?'

'Pour voir *Nixon*.'

'Mais, je want pour voir *Nixon* ici. En Paris. En Angleterre.'

'Monsieur, Paris n'est pas en Angleterre. Paris est en France!'

'Oui. Et je have venir à la France in order pour voir *Nixon* à Paris *en Angleterre*!'

'Mais, Paris est en France!'

Sacré bleu.

'Oui, je comprends that je suis en Paris. J'ai come à Paris pour voir *Nixon* . . . à Paris. Mais, je want pour voir *Nixon* à Paris avec le lingue Angleterre.'

'"Le lingue Angleterre"?'

'Oui, le lingue Angleterre.'

'En Anglais?'

'OUI! Yes! Exactement. En Anglais!'

'Ah!'

'Oui, "Ah"!'

'Je comprends!'

'Vive la France!'

'Ah, bon!'

'La plume de ma tante!'

'Quoi?'

'Never mind, just give me the ticket . . .'

Which he did.

And so I watched a Welshman pretending to be an American, in English, with French subtitles, for what seemed like an eternity (actually two and a half hours), while the local patrons behaved with customary European politeness – talking, smoking and generally carrying on in alarmingly un-British fashion. Afterwards, I trudged back to the Eurostar, got stuck in the Channel tunnel and spent the next eight hours waiting for the 'complimentary coffee' to arrive and ease the burden of our delay. But, like soldiers awaiting re-enforcements from the French Army, it never came.

At the end of this costly international expedition, I concluded that I'd better make amends with the distributors I'd pissed off. I tried ringing their offices, but never got beyond the switchboard; clearly I was properly *persona non grata*. Eventually, Philip Dodd, then editor of *Sight & Sound*, called me to say that he had managed to arrange a meeting with the managing heads of the company in which he and I could attempt to account for our behaviour. It was rather like being called to the headmaster's office; knowing you'd done wrong, but hoping you could wheedle your way out of triple-detention and a hearty caning.

As it turned out, the meeting was something of a revelation. Having been offered the chance to have a lengthy letter published in *Sight & Sound* outlining their grievance about my horribly unfair review (which hadn't been that horrible as far as I could tell), the film company bosses asked for something far more innocuous but altogether more meaningful: a correction. They didn't care whether I had liked their movie or not; after all, I was a critic, and as such was entitled to my opinion. What they objected to was the fact that I had said they 'dumped' a movie. On the contrary, they were able to produce records and charts which showed exactly how much money they'd spent promoting *Mi Familia* in cinemas, and the trouble they'd taken to get their ads for the film in the best possible places. They admitted that the movie had indeed come and gone without much notice in cinemas, but were eager to prove that this was not due to any lack of marketing and distribution oomph on their part. Indeed, the very fact that I'd seen the movie at a press screening where I had been singularly unimpressed by its merits proved that it had been screened for critics in a timely fashion. As regards the title change for video, there was nothing 'perfunctory' about it at all. Having seen the movie sink in cinemas under its original (and un-engaging) title, they had shown both enthusiasm and inventiveness in giving it the best chance of success on video by calling it something more suited to the home-viewing market, a title change arrived at after hours of market research and focus-group work, and with the approval of the film-makers.

And you know what – they were right. When faced with the hard evidence of their efforts I had to admit that they had given *Mi Familia / East L.A.* an entirely laudable push on both film and video. And now, all they wanted from *Sight & Sound* was a small but significant correction to put this on the record. The film itself was still remarkably unremarkable, but they didn't mind about that; as distributors with a lengthy track record they understood that you win some, you lose some. What bothered them was that I had casually called into question their professionalism, and for that they would not stand. They didn't want a long letter moaning about my largely irrelevant opinion of their movie; they just wanted an official recognition that they had done their job properly.

Which they had.

As with my altogether different but nevertheless comparable altercation with Alexander Walker, I learned a very important lesson that day: in the worlds of both film criticism and film distribution, opinions are ephemeral but professional conduct is sacrosanct. Far from leaning on me for being rude about their film, these distributors were (quite rightly) penalizing me for wrongly impugning their professionalism.

And so *Sight & Sound* published a short but sweet correction confirming that the UK release of *Mi Familia* had been 'fully supported', the distributors took me off their shit list, and we have never had a cross word since. Yes, I've slagged off plenty of their movies in the intervening years (and praised many more) but never once have they complained, or objected, or been anything other than thoroughly professional. Occasionally they have released films which they decide (in advance) will not benefit in box-office terms from pre-release reviews (the only point of press screenings) and in these cases they simply don't screen them at all, which is their prerogative. However, they understand that they can't stop people being mean about a movie once they've paid to see it in a cinema, as

I have done many times – purchasing a ticket for a film's first public screening on a Friday morning prior to my regular Friday afternoon BBC broadcasts.

What this illustrates is the symbiotic relationship between film critics and distributors which, contrary to popular belief, has little or nothing to do with opinions, or positive or negative reviews. Despite my reputation for horribly savaging the movies I don't like, the only time I have ever been banned from press screenings was when I overstepped the mark and (wrongly) disparaged a distributor's business practice, a mistake on my part.

When it comes to film reviews, an implicit pact exists between distributors and critics that works to the benefit of both parties. The rules are simple: the distributors show their movies to critics in advance of public release (generally), and in return the critics publish their reviews at the same time the movie plays in cinemas, thereby heightening its public profile – a key to maximizing box-office returns. Despite the endless hooey spouted about the importance of positive reviews and the potential damage of negative notices, anyone who has been in the business for a few years understands that in the long run it's only column inches that count (see *The Good, the Bad and the Multiplex* if you want the full argument). Whilst the age-old adage that 'there is no such thing as bad publicity' may not be quite the whole truth, in terms of film criticism it's alarmingly close.

There is no better proof of this industrial symbiosis between critics and distributors than the much-mocked 'press embargo'. Increasingly familiar in recent years, this usually takes the form of a printed sheet of A4 paper which one is required to sign in order to gain access to a screening. The piece of paper, typically bearing a very official-looking company logo, will state that the film critic in question ('write your name in BLOCK CAPITALS here') has agreed that he/she will not publish any review of the film they are about to watch until a clearly specified date, usually the Monday or Tuesday (but occasionally, and confusingly, the Wednesday) before the film's UK release ('sign HERE'). Sometimes, the embargo date will coincide with the official world premiere, which may be happening elsewhere, but the sanctity of which may be threatened by the international reach of the Internet. Sometimes the embargo will apply to online reviews only (with Twitter being a particular point of contention). But, in general, it will serve primarily to stop reviews appearing until the film is about to open in cinemas, so the reviews – good or bad – will help boost the film's media profile over the all-important opening weekend.

One peculiar side-effect of the rising tide of press embargoes is that they require a certain degree of *Memento*-like mental acrobatics, which can give journalists the (false) impression that they're being gagged. For example, Simon Mayo and I saw *The Bourne Legacy* in advance of its UK opening, so that Simon could record an interview with one of its stars, Ed Norton. Reviews of the film, which peculiarly opened on a Monday, were embargoed until a few days before its release, but for scheduling reasons Simon's interview with Norton was both recorded and broadcast a couple of weeks before the embargo ended – with the film company's agreement. This led to a strange situation in which Simon effectively signed an embargo agreeing not to talk about a movie about which he was then compelled to talk (in contravention of said embargo) in order to fulfil the duties of an interview set up by the same people who had made him sign the embargo in the first place. As for me, I just had to keep schtum, because while Simon was clearly conducting an 'interview' (which was not, it transpired, subject to the embargo), the minute I opened my big mouth about *The Bourne Legacy* we would be within the realms of 'review', and I had specifically signed a form agreeing not to do that until a later date. This was made doubly weird by the fact that I'd already recorded my own review of the film for a Kermode Uncut blog, not to be put up online until the film opened, at which point I would be on holiday in Cornwall. So, when anyone asked me whether I had seen *The Bourne Legacy* yet, my standard response became: 'I don't know – what day is it?'

Such head-scrambling shenanigans give embargoes a bad name, as did the ridiculous restrictions placed in May 2013 upon UK reviews of Baz Luhrmann's *The Great Gatsby*, which were banned until after its Cannes festival premier despite the fact that the film had already opened in America (in the age of global media, regional embargoes are essentially unenforceable once a film is playing to the public anywhere in the world). Some film distribution companies, aware of the potential hostility and confusion which official restrictions can engender, adopt a more softly-softly approach, resorting to embargoes only as a last resort, and relying more generally on a form of gentleman's agreement with the critics to whom they preview their wares. This was the case with an early press show of Nick Love's big-screen reboot of *The Sweeney*, screened way ahead of its opening date in order to ensure that magazines with long lead times (some of the glossier titles 'go to bed' months before hitting the news-stands) were able to cover the film. Shortly after the screening, a daily newspaper ran a lengthy one-star review and gave the movie what Carter and Regan would doubtless have termed 'a right good kicking'. This prompted the distributors to send an irate email to critics *en masse* outlining their displeasure at the pre-emptive review, and pointing out that this was exactly the sort of behaviour forcing distributors to resort to heavily policed embargoes.

Significantly, the email did not complain about the tenor or critical judgement of the review (in my opinion, unfairly negative; one-star kickings should be reserved for vile filth like the aforementioned *That's My Boy*, a movie which finds hilarity in statutory rape and incest, and which had its press screenings cancelled at the last moment on the apparent instruction of Adam Sandler himself). Their complaint was entirely about the date of the review, its existence having been facilitated by the distributors being good enough to show the movie to the press in the first place, and without resort to cumbersome embargoes. In short (they claimed), they had gone to some trouble to enable journalists to do their job properly, in timely fashion, and in return one high-profile publication had responded improperly, in a distinctly untimely manner.

On a simple pragmatic level, they were right. For better or worse, the paper had broken an unwritten agreement which in future would now very likely be written. And to what end? Simply to get the jump on everyone else with 'The First Review' of a movie not scheduled for release for months. Ah yes, I hear you say, but weren't the distributors just kicking up a fuss because the review was such a stinker? Would they have complained if the paper had given *The Sweeney* a glowing five-star endorsement praising its reinvention of a moribund TV franchise and eagerly recommending that readers make a date to pre-book cinema tickets at their earliest possible convenience? Would they have sent out a complaining letter if that pre-emptive review had given them a luscious quote to plaster all over their posters? After all, when the movie finally did open, it arrived with several such glowing endorsements ('The Best British Action Movie in Years' XFM; 'Utterly Brilliant' HeyUGuys) splashed across its various publicity outlets, despite director Nick Love's oft-repeated claim that he didn't 'give a fuck' what critics thought of his film. (Like so many directors on the wrong end of bad reviews, Love rolls out this mantra with entertaining regularity, nowhere more so than on the DVD commentary for his abysmal 2007 shooters-and-slags-fest *Outlaw*, in which he and leading man Dick van Dire assess the critical response to their latest magnum opus. '*Taxi Driver* came out,' opines Love in what sounds like a state of advanced refreshment, 'and got *cu**ed*!')

There's no doubt that the distributors would have been a lot less irate if they'd been able to use that pre-emptive review to their own advantage, a self-evident truth which has emboldened several writers of five-star reviews to break written embargoes in the past, confident that their transgression would be viewed as collateral damage in the greater war to win the hearts and minds of potential audiences. But the fact remains that in order to preserve the right to say whatever one likes about a film whilst still enjoying the privilege of being shown the movie ahead of its release (and, as Kevin Smith keeps pointing out, seeing it for free), it behoves the critic to observe the rules of engagement allowing this time-honoured tradition to flourish. If distributors are put in the position of picking and choosing to whom they show their product, aren't they likely to conclude that the price of access is a good review? Isn't it better to admit that, when it comes to the box office, there's no such thing as a 'bad' review, only an ill-timed one? Shouldn't the price of complete editorial independence be concomitant temporal responsibility?

Wouldn't you rather be embargoed than bullied or banned?

Having worked as a professional film critic for over a quarter of a century, I'd say the answer to this question is a resounding 'Yes'. I'm quite happy to sit on my review of a film until the day (or week) that it's released if doing so enables the distributors to show it to me in advance. And I'd much prefer it if they spent their time worrying about when someone said something about their film rather than what they said because, to be honest, all I care about is being able to write what I like rather than when I like it. If a deal has to be struck on the publication date of a review, then so be it, as long as a similar agreement is reached on the subject of total editorial independence. In my experience that has been the case; behave professionally towards the distributors and, by and large, they will behave professionally towards you. Opinions don't come into it.

The problem is that temporality is not only impossible to police, but it is also increasingly becoming the most valuable commodity in town. To understand why a daily paper ran a review of *The Sweeney* so early, you have only to look at the abundance of social media sites and blogs which beat them to the punch. These days it is not only possible but commonplace to tweet scene-by-scene reviews of a movie whilst it is still playing, so the need for print media to bust a gut to keep up has become ever more pressing. The thumb-to-screen speed of transmission has effectively brought the turn-around time of reviews down to zero, so there really is no time to waste. From a newspaper's point of view, there's nothing more troublesome than a reader-ship who can get their stuff 'published' quicker than you can. In this brave new world, do you still 'hold the front page'? Or just scrap it altogether?

The question, of course, is why you would want to be 'first' in the first place. Unlike news, there is nothing inher-ently valid about a 'rapid response' in film criticism, and the idea that immediacy is somehow a badge of authenticity is baloney which has probably done more to damage the art of reviewing than anything else in an entire century of cinema. In fact, there is an argument which says that no movie can be properly judged or evaluated until after it has had its day in the sun and has dropped beneath the horizon of first-run distribution, during which everyone's opinions are clouded by marketing hype, box-office figures, audience expectations and other extraneous factors. Foremost among my many objections to the horror of the Cannes film festi-val is my firm belief that everyone's critical faculties are screwed by the end of the first day, meaning that the reviews filed (even by seasoned critics) from the madness of that filmy bun-fight are inherently suspect. Watching five films back-to-back in a single day, then filing reviews (which, thanks to the miracle of the Internet, are online before the chimes of midnight), and then going out and doing it all again the next day is not conducive to thoughtful critical analysis. As a result, most working critics find they need to watch films they saw at Cannes a second time before reviewing them in their week of UK release, not simply to refresh their memory of the movie in question, but also to find out whether their initial response had been affected by the fog of festival war.

Nor are the problems of pre-emptive judgement confined to the festival circuit. The history of film criticism is littered with examples of critics 'getting it wrong' in their rush to be the first to review a film. In December 1962, the *New York Times* called David Lean's *Lawrence of Arabia* 'just a huge, thundering camel-opera that tends to run down rather badly as it rolls on into its third hour', while in December 1974 the same paper remarked of *The Godfather: Part II* (now widely hailed as the best of the trilogy) that 'The only remarkable thing [is] the insistent manner in which it recalls how much better [the] original film was', with the esteemed Vincent Canby going on to claim that it was 'not a sequel in any engaging way'. Both these judgements, published at the time of the respective (and respected) films' releases, have since passed into legend as evidence that in weekly film journalism everyone screws up at some point and then lives to regret it. But perhaps the most telling example is of Joe Morgenstern who, in August 1967, dismissed *Bonnie and Clyde* in the pages of *Newsweek* as a 'squalid shoot-'em-up for the moron trade' and then recanted his sternly expressed opinion the very next week.

Morgenstern was not alone in initially hating *Bonnie and Clyde* – even the people who backed it thought it was a piece of garbage until audiences told them otherwise. Studio head Jack Warner, who used to judge the merit of a film by how many times he had to get up and go to the loo, famously branded it a 'three-piss picture', while Warner's head of advertising and publicity Dick Lederer later admitted that '*Bonnie and Clyde* was a watershed film, but no one knew it', adding that, 'Through the years, many producers and directors have claimed that their films were mishandled but in this case they're right.'

Morgenstern first saw *Bonnie and Clyde* the week before it opened, in the Warner Bros offices on New York's Fifth Avenue, where he sat next to Warren Beatty. 'I don't know if it made me nervous or not,' Morgenstern told *LA Times* reporter Patrick Goldstein thirty years later as he reassessed his first reaction to the movie. 'But it was certainly unusual, especially since Warren spent the whole time trying to read my notes.' According to Goldstein's piece, which thoughtfully picked through the wreckage of the now-classic movie's divisive opening, Morgenstern began to realize that he may have got it 'first but wrong' during the movie's opening weekend. 'I think I subconsciously sensed that I'd missed something,' he candidly told Goldstein. 'When we went out on Saturday and my wife asked what movie I wanted to see, I said, "*Bonnie and Clyde*". The audience just went wild, and the cold sweat started forming on my neck. I knew I'd blown it.' Presumably fearing for his reputation, Morgenstern went back into the *Newsweek* offices on Monday morning and wrote a lengthy reassessment of *Bonnie and Clyde* which 'began with a description of the previous review, and then said, "I am sorry to say I consider that review grossly unfair and regrettably inaccurate. I am sorrier to say I wrote it".'

'Can you picture it?' Beatty asked Roger Ebert back in 1967. 'Morgenstern is honest enough to admit he changed his mind. So he goes in to the editors, and they say, Good Lord, you can't change your mind. You're a critic, you're infallible. But Morgenstern stands his ground so they let him have his way. I bet some doors slammed at *Newsweek*.'

A cynic might conclude that Morgenstern, only in the second year of his residence, was simply trying to cover his backside and protect his job, and that his editors would have been more than happy for him to change his mind. After all, Bosley Crowther, whom Ebert described as having ratcheted up 'twenty-nine years as the dean of U.S. movie critics', suddenly found himself stepping down from his position at the *New York Times* after repeatedly blasting *Bonnie and Clyde* in the paper's pages. Having first complained that the movie was nothing more than 'a cheap piece of bald-faced slapstick comedy that treats the hideous depredations of that sleazy, moronic pair as though they were as full of fun and frolic as the jazz-age cutups in *Thoroughly Modern Millie*', Crowther went on to lambast this 'strangely antique, sentimental claptrap' in two further articles, as well as in spirited responses to readers' correspondence, leading several commentators to conclude that he had been 'retired' for 'slamming the film and campaigning against its brutality'. Even *Time* magazine, which (according to Ebert) had 'never changed its mind about anything', reneged on its own first-run slagging of the film. 'In a dramatic about-face,' wrote Ebert, '*Time* put *Bonnie and Clyde* on its cover and assigned Cinema Writer Stefan Kanfer (its new critic, replacing the guy who didn't like the movie) to write the story. This time, *Time* found the movie a brilliant achievement.'

In this kind of hire-and-fire economy, it's not surprising that Morgenstern may have felt the need to retract an opinion which seemed woefully out of step with popular public taste. Yet there's a sincerity about his account that will ring true with any critic who has ever misjudged a movie on first viewing and then experienced the peculiar stomach-tingling weirdness of watching the film for the second time and realizing that 'you really blew it' (as Pauline Kael, who championed *Bonnie and Clyde* from the outset, told a chastened Morgenstern shortly after his first review hit the news-stands). There's not a critic worth their salt who hasn't journeyed through that particular lake of fire, arising the morrow morn both sadder and wiser, the albatross of a hastily turned and thoroughly wrongheaded review hanging mournfully around their neck, a constant reminder that speed really isn't everything. My own Damascene conversion came after storming out of a screening of David Lynch's *Blue Velvet* in the eighties and penning a stinky review for *City Life* magazine. That review earned me a punch in the bar of Manchester's Cornerhouse (see *It's Only a Movie*), the pain of which was nothing compared to the white-hot embarrassment of watching what appeared to be a completely different film the second time around. Like those American writers whose critical radars were kicked out of whack by the strange inchoate rage provoked by *Bonnie and Clyde* (Crowther's anger is palpably blinding as he rails against a film which is 'as pointless as it is lacking in taste'), I shared Morgenstern's feeling that 'I'd missed something' even while writing my first utterly misguided review. The difference is that it took me several months – perhaps even years – to recant on my initial mauling of *Blue Velvet* (which I now consider a fearsome masterpiece), while Morgenstern went from nay to yay on *Bonnie and Clyde* over the space of a single weekend.

Amazing how the threat of losing one's job really focuses the mind.

As a result of my own chastening experience, I became intensely aware of the need to allow a film time to settle in the mind before reviewing it, a process which has occasionally been met with incredulity by those who can't understand how it's possible to watch a movie and not know immediately whether you liked it or not. To illustrate the nature of such 'settling', I occasionally use my BBC Kermode Uncut blog to film an 'initial response' to a movie: I walk out of a screening and immediately deliver a straight-to-camera (and often incoherent) reaction. What's significant about these rapid-response blogs is that they are not reviews; they are the unformed, un-analysed burblings of someone who has just stumbled out of (for example) Gaspar Noé's *Enter the Void* or Darren Aronofsky's *Black Swan* and is still struggling to come to terms with what they have seen. The reviews come later, sometimes a few days, often a few weeks, but ideally several months after those first screenings, and on many occasions they will appear to contradict what I said on the blog.

Personally, I see no problem with such contradictions – the point of the blogs is to demonstrate how one's opinion of a film can change with time, and in my experience the more powerful the film, the greater that change is likely to be. I have a particularly strong memory of filing a flummoxed 'initial response' blog immediately after a screening of William Friedkin's jet-black gothic neo-noir *Killer Joe* which had left me utterly sideswiped and not a little anxious. Boasting a raw intensity notably lacking from his more mainstream late-period movies such as *Rules of Engagement*, *Killer Joe* had something of the controversial whiff of *Cruising*, Friedkin's 1980s psycho thriller which provoked outraged pickets both during and after production. In the case of *Killer Joe*, I was torn between my admiration for the crackling vitality of the drama and my anger at the jaded 'virgin/whore' motif which ran through the play-turned-screenplay from writer Tracy Letts. Most problematically, the now infamous scene where Gina Gershon's bedraggled character is forced at length to fellate a piece of fried chicken (believe me, it looks worse on screen than on the page) seemed to me to have been played for misogynist laughs and had set several politically correct alarm bells ringing. While I had loved Friedkin's previous collaboration with Letts (the still massively underrated *Bug*), this was altogether harder to stomach. Thus it was with a mixture of admiration and annoyance that I announced my utter befuddlement about *Killer Joe*, causing one commentator on the blog to wonder 'How can you not know whether you like a film or not?!' To which I can only reply that the longer I do this job, the more I wonder how you can ever know what you actually think of a film, so influential are the circumstances under which you first saw it, and the subsequent opportunities you may or may not have to re-evaluate your first response. (In the case of *Killer Joe*,

I concluded ultimately that I liked the film but with reservations; the chicken-bone scene had been misjudged – at least in my opinion. When I interviewed Friedkin about the movie for the *Culture Show*, I told him to his face that I found the scene repugnant, a response in which he took typical delight.)

In a perfect world, film criticism would not be a series of rapid responses fixed for ever in tablets of stone, but would rather be a slowly evolving debate in which nothing is certain and everything is up for grabs. The problem with this ideal (which is largely the privilege of more academic 'film studies') is that it is completely impractical when it comes to the nuts-and-bolts reality of the weekly film critic's working life, and is also undesirable from the reader's/viewer's/listener's point of view. Quick responses may not be definitive, but they can be both informative and (more importantly) entertaining, providing an informed snapshot of a movie about which the reviewer's opinions remain entirely personal and wholly subjective. There are some critics who, over the years, develop a particular talent for turning out a well-reasoned verdict in a matter of moments. Kim Newman, for example, has an uncanny ability to walk straight out of a screening and straight to a typewriter where he will reel off a thoughtful, funny, and typically pithy review, more than likely to stand the test of time – a talent of which I am in awe. But Kim is an exception, and there are very few critics who can do what he can do – and as fast as he can do it. For this reason, he has remained at the top of his game for three decades, and he stands as a reminder to the rest of us just how much of a skill film criticism can be when practised by a master craftsman.

Yet such craftsmanship should not be mistaken for mere hasty hackery, nor should a talent for turning things round quickly (rather than properly) be lauded in and of itself. Whatever benefits the Internet has brought, clearly it has also played a significant role in the headlong rush towards instant reaction over considered response. Today the fetishization of the 'first review' has more clout in the critical marketplace than ever before, elevating the importance of speed above and beyond the value of merit, thanks in part to the arrival of the information super-highway. Why worry about getting something right when the only real imperative is being wrong before everyone else?

For better or worse, the blogosphere operates in a universe in which time is money, and in this new economy traditional print and broadcast outlets have become the poor relations. The consequences for news journalism are huge and unfathomable, but in the main largely positive. Whereas once it was possible for repressive regimes to suppress and control the flow of information about the ground-level realities of their tyrannical rules, today anyone with a mobile phone can send frontline footage from even the most inaccessible areas to be broadcast around the world to revolutionary effect. Would the so-called 'Arab Spring' have dawned so quickly without the unparalleled accessibility of the Internet? Would Aung San Suu Kyi still be under house arrest were her supporters not able to take to their blogs to raise international awareness of her heroic struggles when the established media failed to do so?

In the midst of such epochal upheavals, the changing nature of film criticism is clearly pathetically irrelevant. But just as Charlotte Gainsbourg rushed to huddle her son into a shelter made of sticks as worlds collided in *Melancholia*, so the professional film critic with an eye on the future is duty bound to worry about the safety and continuation of their irrelevant trade, even as publishing collapses and reforms about them, ushering in a brave new world where nothing is forbidden and everything is possible – as long as it's possible right now.

For the film industry, the arrival of the Internet has been both a blessing and a curse. On the upside, the whirlwind of fan websites proliferating in the early twenty-first century has provided a near-infinite number of outlets through which movies can be promoted at little or no cost to distributors. Whereas traditional forms of advertising (posters, trailers, TV spots) are costly, time-consuming and cumbersome, the web offers the forward-looking film-maker a boundless all-but-free space in which to promote. Conclusive proof of the web's ability to conjure a box-office hit from thin air came as far back as 1999 when Haxan films found their way into the *Guinness Book of Records* for generating the 'top box-office-to-budget ratio' of any feature film with *The Blair Witch Project*; it cost $22,000 to make and took $240.5 million (that's $10,931 of ticket sales for every dollar spent). Drawing on the 'found footage' motif first popularized by *Cannibal Holocaust*, *The Blair Witch Project*'s central conceit (three film students disappear and this video is all that's left behind) was fresh and convincing enough to convince many viewers that what they were watching was real. (Incredible in this age of *Para-snoremal Activity 4* to think of a time when the 'found footage' gimmick seemed new and inventive!) This air of credibility was cannily boosted by a viral Internet campaign providing bogus back-story news pages on the 'history' of the so-called Burkittsville Wood disappearances for anyone attempting to separate fact from fiction via the use of Google. The web pages were a stroke of genius and they turned word-of-mouth into click-of-mouse, pushing *Blair Witch* onto the world's news pages where it was variously reported on as both a screen and marketing sensation.

A few years earlier, Austin-based film-fan and movie-memorabilia geek Harry Knowles had started making a name for himself as the founder of the Ain't It Cool News (AICN) website, which he set up in a room in his dad's house whilst recovering from a debilitating accident. Having previously trawled movie newsgroups, sharing opinions and gossip about upcoming films, Knowles put AICN on the map by drawing upon a series of anonymous industry insider sources who appeared only too keen to give him the skinny on what was really going on in movie land. Secretaries, production assistants, set dressers, writers, producers – all were apparently contributing to AICN's increasingly indispensable pool of knowledge which rapidly became the go-to Internet site for (often unprintable) breaking movie news.

Although reviews were not AICN's primary purpose (Knowles has said that he started the site as a memorabilia swap-meet), they swiftly became a significant part of its online menu, with writers working under super-hero-inflected pseudonyms (Robogeek, Capone, Moriarty, Monty Cristo, etc.), all vying to file the most up-to-date info on films no one else had seen yet. If traditional media outlets respected such industrial niceties as review embargoes (as we know now, mutually beneficial to critics and distributors), AICN revelled in a punky irreverence, saying what they wanted when they wanted, answerable to no one but themselves – something which scared film-makers no end.

Things came to a head in 1997 when AICN ran a series of negative pieces on Joel Schumacher's forthcoming comic-book adaptation *Batman & Robin* and the studio blamed the movie's disappointing box-office performance on pre-release Internet scuttle in general, and AICN in particular. This was clearly damage limitation – *Batman & Robin* was a stinker from the outset and everyone involved knew it, not least leading man George Clooney, who remarked only half-jokingly that he had played a significant part in killing the franchise stone dead. When reviews from traditional media outlets echoed AICN's pre-emptive knocks, the site's credibility rose, and established magazines such as *People* and *Newsweek* (the latter of whom had got their fingers burned over their early review of *Bonnie and Clyde* all those years ago) came circling, eager not to be left out of this emergent new world.

In hindsight, *Batman &Robin* was something of an easy target. Anyone who had caught even the briefest glimpse of its campy pantomime schtick would have known in an instant that the movie had major problems, and the only really baffling thing was how on earth Warners allowed Schumacher to wreak this havoc upon what had until then been a veritable fruit-machine franchise. I should also say for the record that, in typically contrary fashion, I was one of the very few journalists who had a good word to say about *Batman &Robin*, at which I laughed like a drain from beginning to end. I remember very clearly trotting along to Leicester Square with Fergus Dudley from Radio 1 (where I was working at the time) to see the National Press Show on the Monday before it opened, the two of us screaming like barn-owls at the sheer draggy silliness of it all, our enjoyment made all the more ripe by the stony-faced silence of everyone else in the cinema. Like my experience of watching the equally badly received *Hudson Hawk*, in which the more everyone else hated it the funnier it got, *Batman & Robin* appealed to the infantile part of me that took great delight in seeing big movie stars make utter fools of themselves at gargantuan expense, and I'd be lying if I didn't admit that thinking of it still warms the cockles of my heart – and, as Woody Allen said, what's better than hot cockles? (Incidentally, Allen reportedly delivered one of the most damning verdicts on *Batman & Robin* when Schumacher, who had worked with Woody on great films like *Love and Death*, called him to bemoan the awful reviews. 'They're saying I've made the worst film ever,' cried Joel, to which Allen sympathetically responded, 'Making the worst film ever would actually be an achievement – you haven't even done that.' Who says critics are mean?)

Having made headlines with *Batman & Robin*, Knowles cemented his reputation as the Internet's premier movie geek, and was soon being fêted as one of the most important movers and shakers in the business; not bad for a guy who just wanted to sell some stuff on the web. At first the movie industry was terrified of Harry, largely because he didn't play by the rules, making him an unmanageable commodity in terms of publicity. As we observed, it's the early reviews and 'leaks' that put distributors in a tizzy because they have no upside in terms of attendance: tell someone a movie stinks when it's playing at their local cinema and chances are they'll go and see for themselves whether you're full of crap; tell them it stinks months before it's released, and all anyone can do is nod sagely and bow to your superior judgement because, hey, you must have some special inside track on the movie.

Personally, I have little time for the faux elitism of the 'first review'. If you're judging the credibility of criticism on nothing more than its sell-by date, then you're going to wind up prioritizing premature ejaculations over considered assessments every time. And if you honestly think that Harry Knowles's take on a movie is more important than that of Philip French just because Harry got there first, then stop reading NOW.

What's interesting is that my own stuffy reservations about first-past-the-post film journalism have long been shared by others, including those who have made their home on the web. In 2000, a very public spat blew up between AICN and rival site Film Threat, following the pre-emptive publication of what Knowles believed to be a major scoop; an inside track on the forthcoming Academy Awards nominations. Although the exact details of the story's origins are unclear, Film Threat charged AICN with failing properly to investigate its sources in its rush to publish, thereby lending newspapers (many of whom were already deeply suspicious of online media) a stick with which to beat Internet journalism. 'The old press tends to be lazy and a little nearsighted when it comes to making distinctions between groups other than themselves,' wrote

Film Threat's Ron Wells in a controversial series of articles entitled 'Deconstructing Harry' which attempted to draw clear distinctions between their own modus operandi and those of AICN. 'Bottom line: Harry screws up, we all get blamed.'

To counter this perceived homogeneity, Film Threat (which began life as a fanzine and magazine before migrating to the web) attempted to construct an 'Acceptable Code of Behavior' which ran contrary to the AICN model and demonstrated just how disparate net culture had actually been since its inception. Their suggestions, which matched and perhaps even superseded the best codes of conduct observed by the traditional media, included: a rejection of sock-puppet anonymity ('one of the most important lessons you learn as an adult is being able to question the bias or motivation behind the information presented to you'); a promise not to accept studio freebies or hospitality which essentially turned the writer into 'a marketing expense' ('no more paid set visits unless you're willing to be somebody's bitch'); and, most significantly, a pledge not to review unfinished films. This last was of particular importance, since it recognized a fundamental rule of proper film criticism which some other websites had chosen not merely to ignore, but to flout. As is the case with most valuable lessons, Film Threat had learned from its own mistakes. Writing with disarming candour, Ron Wells recounted that 'In 1991, Chris [Gore] and former editor Dave Williams attended an early test screening of George Romero's *The Dark Half* as guests of the special effects people. After writing about story problems in *Film Threat* magazine, the producers and Romero were pissed.

The effects guys were nearly fired and Gore's friendship with them was destroyed.' As a result of this chastening experience, Film Threat concluded that reviewing work prints was 'not fair to the filmmakers who should have the time to work out the problems', whilst also adding on an equally cautionary note, 'Don't judge a film so much by a test screening. It can actually get much worse . . .'

Anyone who has served time in the trenches of film journalism knows the accuracy of this assessment; no movie can be judged before it is finished and to do so is not only foolish but also detrimental to the craft of film-making and the experience of the audience. This is not to say that forensic after-the-fact dissections of a movie's path to the screen might not be insightful and informative, particularly when DVD and Blu-ray have made alternative versions (Director's Cuts, Extended Editions) more obligatory than optional, with no film ever 'finished' any more, at least not in the traditional sense. But until a film takes its first public bow (whether at a festival, press screening, or in a public cinema), passing judgement upon it is both pointless and foolhardy, and does little to help anyone other than those outlets dedicated to picking up more hits by virtue of being first but wrong.

All of which brings us to the strange case of Ridley Scott's *Prometheus*, one of the most eagerly awaited movies of recent years and a textbook example of how muddle-headed marketing and rush-to-publish pre-emptive film criticism can become a massive headache for everyone: film-makers, film distributors, film critics, and (most importantly) film-goers. In the months leading up to the release of *Prometheus* in June 2012, a mixture of secrecy, speculation and rampant expectation combined to make it the most talked-about, argued-about subject on the net. Was it, as early reports had suggested, a prequel to *Alien*? Would the narrative tie up directly with the fates of Ripley and the crew of the *Nostromo*? Would the unanswered questions about the evolution of the epochal xenomorph finally be answered? And what exactly did that enigmatic title mean?

Interestingly, all these questions were being asked by fans who didn't actually want to be told the answers prior to finding out for themselves on their own viewing of the finished film. More than any other genre, sci-fi fantasy attracts diehard devotees who relish the prospect of experiencing strange new worlds without the mediating influence of anyone else – press, publicity, or even other punters. Like a child pleading to be told what delights await them in the enticingly wrapped packages lurking beneath the tree on Christmas Eve, the true fan understands that knowing would just spoil the magic of the big day itself. Whether the present turns out to be a doozy or a duffer, they want to experience the thrill of unwrapping it themselves; of tearing away the shiny paper of secrecy as the lights go down in the auditorium and the cinema screen begins to shimmer anew.

Prior to the release of *Prometheus*, I received hundreds of emails, texts and tweets from eager, anxious cinema-goers imploring (nay, commanding) me not to 'spoil' the movie for them by revealing any salient secrets or pertinent plot details in advance. I understood exactly how they felt. As a fan myself, I shared that same sense of sublimely adolescent excitement about watching *Prometheus* for the first time, and I'd spent the last couple of months desperately trying to avoid the welter of spoilerific trailers, adverts, puff pieces and preview clips which had become as unwelcomely omnipresent as the acid rain in *Blade Runner*. I'd binned a copy of *Empire* magazine when it arrived in the post brandishing a whopping 'exclusive set report!', replete with pictures and interviews; I'd stayed away from the numerous tweets and Internet links promising to 'spill the beans on the year's most eagerly awaited movie!'; I'd stopped watching television for fear of stumbling upon yet another 'exclusive' extract in the middle of a show only tangentially related to movies; I'd even run out of a cinema when, as I was waiting to watch another movie altogether, the marketing wags attempted to take advantage of the fact that I was already wearing their stupid stereoscopic goggles by playing a thundering *Prometheus* trailer which came leaping off the screen at me in 3D. There was nowhere to hide! Everywhere I turned it seemed that Fox were determined to show me as much of the movie as possible without actually showing me the thing itself. Never have I had to work so hard to avoid seeing the whole film in bits before getting the chance to watch it *in toto*.

The situation was hugely frustrating, and there is evidence that Ridley Scott was as fed up about it as the rest of us. During a conversation with Scott Free (Ridley's production company) prior to a BBC Radio 5 live interview, it became apparent that the director had been dismayed by Fox's decision to include in their publicity a number of giveaway images (a giant head, a crashing spaceship) which blew a substantial part of the movie's cover prior to its release, in stark contrast with the publicity for *Alien* which had been terrifyingly oblique (an image of an egg over a patchwork of ropes?) and stunningly successful. I remain convinced that the negative word of mouth that greeted *Prometheus* when it finally opened (*Empire* later dubbed it 'the most disappointing film of 2012') was in large part a reaction to the carpet-bombing publicity campaign heralding its arrival. Yes, I'm sure it stoked 'audience awareness', but only while simultaneously laying the groundwork for a huge fan backlash. It's notable that many of those who were most keen to see the film in the first place were also the most vehement in trashing it when it finally arrived, with *Prometheus* going from being the most eagerly anticipated film of the year to the worst film of the year in the space of its opening weekend. Never mind how much money it took (around $404 million worldwide at the time of writing), there was no getting round the sense of let-down, the inevitable fall-out of all that hype.

Personally, I rather liked *Prometheus*, and was particularly proud about seeing it (on the Tuesday before it opened) without having read a single article in advance. Painfully aware of the responsibility to let the fans share that same pristine experience, I went out of my way to avoid spoilers in my review; on the day of the film's opening I attempted (probably cackhandedly, but hey) to assess the merits of the movie without describing in detail what actually happens on screen. The one time I talked about the movie on Twitter, it was in a manner so cryptic I figured no one could accuse me of giving anything away. (My tweet read: '2012/2093, >15, 2.35 x 127.36 (124.35 x 1.44/1.78) @24 x 1/60, 2 >3d, +/- ¿223/426? (> -1) =7.25/10.' Decoded, this meant that the 15-rated film, which I had enjoyed but not loved, was set in 2093, had different running times on celluloid and digital, was better in 2D than 3D, and wasn't set on the planet LV426, therefore was not a direct *Alien* prequel. I was quite proud of how oblique I'd managed to make myself, but the minute that tweet went up I got a tweet back saying, 'Oi! Stop it with the plot spoilers!' No kidding.

Now, call me arrogant (everyone does), but for all its faults I think that the approach I took to reviewing *Prometheus* was the correct one; honest about my responses and analytical about the movie whilst still being respectful of the fans, without whom the film would never have existed in the first place. Things were very different over at AICN where they predictably opted to take the opposite tack, treating readers to a barrage of reports and rumours, and ensuring that Harry would be the first to review the movie, whatever it took.

As it turned out, 'whatever it took' meant reviewing the film before it was finished, only this time it wasn't from test screenings or preview tapes but on the basis of a pirated copy of the script which had somehow fallen into Knowles's overly eager hands. 'This was Damon Lindelof's 2nd Draft', wrote Knowles in his boisterous AICN feature, when it appeared in early April 2012 (a full two months before the film's release), going on to outline the action taking place on the planet Zeus in typically Knowlesian geek-speak. The article was an international sensation and (as with the Oscar story twelve years earlier) drew lots of traffic and attention to the AICN website. Unfortunately, it also turned out to be wrong.

'Hate to break it to you,' tweeted Lindelof after reading Knowles's apparently insider story, 'but there's no "Planet Zeus" in my draft.' And, as anyone who has seen *Prometheus* (which Knowles hadn't at that point) knows, he's right –

there isn't. The planet on which most of the action takes place is LV223 (as per my own cryptic review), and nowhere in the movie does anyone ever mention 'Planet Zeus'. Clearly there was only one explanation for this massive discrepancy. As Lindelof himself put it: 'I think you've been duped.'

So where did Knowles's bogus *Prometheus* script come from? Who knows? Some think it was knocked together by a rival geek working from information gleaned entirely from the vast ocean of pre-release publicity which included viral Internet shorts shot by film-makers such as Scott's son Luke to bolster the 'reality' of *Prometheus*'s future-world in a manner first explored by the makers of *The Blair Witch Project*. Others insist that its heritage was authentic even though what was in the script bore little resemblance to what finally ended up on screen. When I asked Lindelof to clarify what he knew of the debacle, the writer reassured me that 'the script which Harry reviewed was a total hoax – a fan-written script (though I don't know who wrote it) that I had seen floating around on the web during the production of the movie. I didn't debunk it publicly because I like having misinformation out there. But once AICN posted the review, I felt the need to email Harry directly and tell him he had been duped.' When I asked if the review had caused him any upset or concern, Lindelof affectionately replied, 'It didn't bother me . . . I just felt bad for Harry.'

Yet there was no need to feel bad for Harry – none at all. Having reviewed a 'total hoax' script set on a planet a world away from Scott's finished movie, AICN's status as the world's premier independent movie website merely increased. For in an age in which it has become entirely respectable to be 'first but wrong', Harry announced proudly that he had 'no shame' whatsoever about publishing something that turned out to be a hoax because 'AICN has always been about reporting news & rumors and that is what this was.'

So is this what the future of film journalism looks like? Reviewing a bogus script for an unfinished film under the catch-all cloak of completist fandom? Back in the sixties, high-profile critics feared for their jobs and beat themselves up in public for the crime of reviewing a movie they had watched from start to finish but perhaps misjudged in their haste to file copy. Now they stand proudly by reviews of films they haven't even seen – because they haven't been made yet – and everyone stands back and applauds. Bosley Crowther may have lost his job at the *New York Times* for calling it wrong on *Bonnie and Clyde* in the sixties, but in the twenty-first century you can call it anyway you like, just as long as you call it first.

And what of the fans? Lindelof felt sympathy for Harry having been duped (for all his errors, Knowles is widely liked among the film geek community and seen as something of a role model in the online revolution), but wasn't it the fans who had frequently expressed their desire to judge *Prometheus* for themselves, who had the most to lose from the publication of anything and everything pertaining to the movie at the earliest possible opportunity? More importantly, how did the AICN story – a potent cocktail of the premature, the over-eager, and the plain old incorrect – add to either the movie-going experience or any sensible debate about the state of modern film culture? In what way did it contribute to the pool of knowledge about what was actually going on behind the scenes in movie land?

In short, what good did it do? And for whom did it do it?

A few days after *Prometheus* opened in the UK, I was walking down Oxford Street in Central London when a young man in his twenties stopped me to ask a question about the movie. He'd seen it over the opening weekend and been baffled about the exact location of the planet upon which it was located. Like many, he'd presumed it was all taking place on the same planet featured in *Alien* – LV426 – and was trying to figure out why the position of the 'space jockey' (the giant dead extraterrestrial from the opening act of *Alien*) didn't match up with what he assumed was the 'next' movie. I pointed out that in fact *Prometheus* took place on LV223, that this was a different space jockey to the one discovered in *Alien*, and that Ridley Scott had said in his 5 live interview that the story of *Prometheus* was 'at least two movies' away from being a direct prequel to *Alien*.

'It's all there in the podcast,' I told him. 'Haven't you listened to it yet?'

'Oh no,' he replied assertively. 'I never listen till after I've seen the film.'

This was something I'd heard many times before; several of our more devoted listeners habitually make a point of watching the films before hearing what Simon Mayo and I have to say about them, and many more have commented that their favourite part of the show is the UK top ten rundown because that's where we talk about films about which they have already formed their own opinion. For them, the real pleasure of film criticism is being part of a conversation to which they can contribute, and that means discussing movies which have been out in cinemas for a few weeks.

This may seem horribly obvious to you, but the realization that movie reviews do not have to precede the first public viewing of a film and can in fact benefit from following a movie's opening, will come as a shock to many in my trade. It certainly surprised the heck out of me when I was made aware of it by correspondence from the 5 live listeners, from whom I clearly have much to learn. (Perhaps that's the difference between 'reviews' and 'criticism' – the former comes first, the latter comes later?) But the idea that anything which has opened in cinemas is old news is entirely alien to film-goers, and this temporal misalignment can cause reviewers to become disengaged from punters, adding to the idea that they are snobby, aloof, and out of touch with popular opinion. Hence, as we noted in Chapter One, loving movies becomes synonymous with hating critics.

For all the eagerness to review films first, if a quarter of a century of film criticism has taught me anything at all, it's that readers and listeners would much rather they did it last.

Last, but right.

CHAPTER FIVE

WEREWOLVES OF LONDON

Monday morning. Alarm. Up. Wash. Let the dog out. Dog doesn't want to go out. Insist dog goes out. Dog not going out. Dog goes and lies on the sofa. Tell dog she is not allowed on the sofa. Dog looks unimpressed, as if to say, 'You're not in charge.' Which I am not. Trudge back upstairs. Start to shave.

Noise from downstairs. Dog yowling to be let out. Consider leaving dog to suffer, but realize she will only scratch the paintwork on the door. Plus, she will poop indoors and I will have to clear it up afterwards. Trudge back downstairs. Look sternly at dog. Dog still not impressed. Open door. Dog goes out. Cold air comes in. Stand there in a T-shirt feeling miserable. Call the dog to come in. Dog doesn't come in. Call again. Still nothing. Bugger it; shut the door and trudge back upstairs. Immediately, dog starts yowling to be let back in. Consider leaving her to suffer but realize she will only scratch the paint on the outside. Trudge back downstairs. Open door. Look sternly at dog. Dog looks unimpressed and goes back to lie on the sofa.

Kitchen. Coffee, coffee, coffee.

School run.

Park the car in the station's overpriced car-park. Buy coffee and the *Guardian* from Mike at the platform kiosk. Train. Full and standing. Trolley. More coffee. Find a seat after Winchester. Sit down. Realize the person sitting next to me has the loudest headphones in the world. Stand up again.

Suffer in silence all the way to . . .

Waterloo. If it's raining, Bakerloo Line to Piccadilly or Northern Line to Leicester Square. If it's sunny, walk across Waterloo Bridge and be momentarily struck by how beautiful the city can look at this time of day – the vista down the Thames towards the Gherkin, the Shard and St Paul's. Feed the birds, tuppence a bag. The BFI Southbank, the National, the London Eye. Hugh Grant being told that he is 'no longer my brother'. Terry meeting Julie, crossing over the bridge where they feel safe and sound.

Snap out of it as you hit the Embankment, play *Death Race 2000* with the cabbies on the Strand, up past St Martin's, round the edge of theatre land and into the thick of Movieville.

When I first started doing this job back in the eighties, all the major film companies were located within a square mile of each other. 20th Century Fox were in Soho Square, just across the street from the British Board of Film Classification (formerly Censors), while Columbia and Guild were across Oxford Street, in the environs of Wells Street where CFC (the Computer Film Company) now make their home. With time, the film businesses would expand and migrate to nearby Golden Square, once the domain of UIP and Paramount, and now the centre of operations for Sony Pictures UK. Today, Universal are situated in what appears to be a very large brightly coloured Lego Block, just around the corner from Forbidden Planet on Shaftesbury Avenue. As for Warners, they're located way out on Theobalds Road, beyond Holborn, a full fifteen-minute walk from their original (and natural) home slap bang in the middle of Wardour Street, the very epicentre of the film universe.

Back in the eighties, the group of film journos with whom I habitually hung out (Nigel Floyd, Alan Jones, Kim Newman, etc.) referred to ourselves self-mockingly as the Dogs of Wardour Street, prowling in packs from one screening room to another, stopping occasionally for a swift half in the Nellie Dean (by coincidence home to the nastiest, yappiest, most aggressive ankle-biting cross-breed in town). The part of Soho around Wardour Street and Dean Street was awash with screening rooms, large and small, stinky and extremely stinky. Of the more 'intimate' venues there were the Crown and the Coronet (which I would constantly confuse for obvious linguistic reasons) and the aptly named Bijou, a place so pokey that, if you took a couple of chairs out and turned on the lights, it would have looked just like somebody's living room, albeit somebody with very shabby personal habits and the lingering whiff of Norman Bates, or Mark Lewis. It was here that I first saw *The Crying Game* in the early nineties, at a time when its release seemed less than certain (Palace Pictures were in the process of expiring) and its 'big reveal' was still a secret unshared. Thanks to the uniquely compact layout of the Bijou, I viewed Neil Jordan's surprise hit with a proximity to the screen which meant that Jaye Davidson could very well have taken someone's eye out with that. To this day, I feel you haven't really enjoyed the full impact of that movie unless you've had it unexpectedly thrust upon you at 10 o'clock on a Thursday morning with your face all but pressed up against the projected image in a manner which proved once and for all that you don't need stupid glasses to experience full-effect 3D, thank you very much.

It was also here that I saw a number of movies for which the term 'straight to video' was not a criticism but an aspiration – movies so poisonous and unreleasable that the only reason the distributors were showing them was to see if they actually contravened health regulations and made people physically ill. From the jobbing journo's point of view, this was something of a problem, because if a movie didn't get released you'd never have the chance to get paid for writing about it. Yet companies like Medusa and Colourbox, who specialized in such uncertain fare, understood that the way to a journalist's heart was through their stomach, so lavish sandwiches would be laid on, providing the necessary carrot to lure in the critics before beating them over the head with the stick of a very bad movie indeed.

Anyone familiar with *Private Eye*'s Lunchtime O'Booze column will know that journalism has long been considered to be awash with alcoholics, but for some reason film critics have always been more interested in food – something to do with the uncertainty of the profession, perhaps; not knowing where your next meal is coming from. While the crisis discussed in the previous chapters has made everyone hyper-aware of the fragility of their careers, being a film critic has never been a particularly stable trade. Whenever

I'm asked what qualification one needs to become a movie reviewer, I always reply that a tolerance for watching *Fred: The Movie* without screaming is best, because the surest way to find employment is to review the films no one else wants to watch. Perhaps this is why so many film critics complete their apprenticeship of good sandwiches and terrible films with a finely honed ability to be nasty about movies but almost no experience of how to say anything nice. After all, what's there to be nice about?

The writer Raymond Chandler once said of the much-loathed New York critics that 'it is wrong to be harsh with [them] unless one admits in the same breath that it is a condition of their existence that they should write entertainingly about something which is rarely worth writing about at all'. The same claim could be made of anyone professionally required to find something witty and interesting to say about movies as soul crushing as *The Holiday* ('desperately wants to be *Love Actually* but is Toilet, Actually'), *Babel* ('art with a capital F'), *New Year's Eve* ('so bad even stupid people will hate it') and *Elizabethtown* ('things got so bad I half expected oxygen masks to drop down from the ceiling while red and white lights guided us all to the nearest exit'). Like the Internet (best thing, everyone has access to it; worst thing, everyone has access to it), the triumph and tragedy of being a film critic is that you get to see everything that gets released, along with a whole bunch of things that never even made it that far. Statistically speaking, if you happen to see a couple of good films in any given week, you're doing pretty well, and considering that I've been averaging ten to twelve films a week for the past twenty-five years, that means I've waded through an awful lot of crap to get to the good stuff. Or, to use a now popular movie colloquialism, there's been a lot of Shawshank before the Redemption.

Occasionally, swimming in the river of effluence that is the week's new film releases can make you wonder exactly why you're doing this, a question to which even the very finest sandwiches known to humanity cannot provide a satisfactory answer. It doesn't help, of course, that many of the people whom you most admire don't see much point in what you're doing either. If you think critics can be mean about artists, you should see what those artists have to say about critics – personally and professionally. However cruel we may have been, traditionally the creative fraternity have given as good as they've got. 'What decent person would want to spend a life picking and cavilling?' asked the sainted Stephen Fry, dismissing the entire canon of criticism in biblical terms. 'Picture this scene. A critic arrives at the gates of heaven. "And what did you do?" asks Saint Peter. "Well," says the dead soul, "I criticized things." "I beg your pardon?" "You know, other people wrote things, performed things, painted things, and I said stuff like 'thin and unconvincing', 'turgid and uninspired', 'competent and serviceable' . . . you know."' On which basis, after a lifetime of enduring movies like *Club Dread*, *Good Luck Chuck*, *Transformers 1*, *2* and *3*, *Die Hard 4*, *Scary Movie 5*, *The Phantom Menace*, *The Da Vinci Code*, *The Devil's Rejects*, *Revolver*, *Bride Wars*, *W.E.*, *Sex Lives of the Potato Men*, *Zack and Miri Make a Porno*, *Run for Your Wife*, etc., I am clearly going to be turned away from the gates of Elysium and sent to spend all eternity in the other place. To which I can only say that, however hellish the torments of eternal damnation may be, they can't be any worse than paying to watch *Piranha 3-Double-D* at the Cineworld Trocadero first thing on a Friday morning because the distributors didn't press-screen the wretched thing. To borrow the tagline from *The Devils*, when it comes to film critics being cast into the fiery pit, at least 'Hell holds no surprises for them'.

Meanwhile, the understandable contempt for criticism from those within the movie business continues. 'Don't pay any attention to the critics,' Samuel Goldwyn famously declared, 'don't even ignore them.' Walt Disney lived and died (professionally at least) by the maxim that: 'We are not trying to entertain the critics. I'll take my chances with the public.' Artist and director Man Ray was rather more direct when he declared that: 'All critics should be assassinated', his choice of verb both specific and intriguing – apparently just plain old 'killed' wasn't personal enough. Even when the critics are positive, the reactions are no better. 'Having the critics praise you,' said Eli Wallach, 'is like having the hangman say you've got a pretty neck' (or, in more modern parlance, like having the woodsman tell you you've got a purdy mouth). Dustin Hoffman used a similar metaphor when he declared that: 'A good review from the critics is just another stay of execution.' As for British actor and comedian Robert Webb, he recently told a national newspaper that the thumbs up I gave to one of his movies 'relieves us from the burden of ever having to take Mark Kermode seriously again'. There really is no pleasing some people.

There is, of course, a long and glorious tradition of artists (not just film-makers) badmouthing critics with exactly the kind of piercing one-liners in which the reviewing profession specializes, and which we sampled in the Prologue: 'There has never been set up a statue in honour of a critic,' said Jean Sibelius famously, while anarchic dramatist Edward Albee held that: 'The difference between critics and audiences is that one is a group of humans and one is not.' Fellow playwright John Osborne concurred when he snarked that 'asking a working writer what he thinks about critics is like asking a lamp post what it feels about dogs'. The daddy of all critical put-downs belongs, in my opinion, to Brendan Behan, who set the bar high with his savagely comical, 'Critics are like eunuchs in a harem; they know how it's done, they've seen it done every day, but they're unable to do it themselves.'

In terms of film, however, Fellini probably nailed it best when he said, 'No critic writing about a film could say more than the film itself, although they do their best to make us think the opposite', an observation which has long haunted most of us in the profession. What if he's right? What if nothing we say or write contributes anything to movie culture at all? No wonder so many critics become more bitter and twisted as the years wither away whatever love of film and optimism about the industry may once have thrived in their now darkened hearts. After all, if it really is impossible (as Fellini suggests) for a critic to add to the experience of watching a film, then they might as well go hell for leather and just concentrate on taking something away.

All of which brings me to one of my favourite literary characters, with whose personality I identify more than any other. I've admitted elsewhere that my worldview has always been more Arthur Dent than Jay Gatsby, but when it comes to *The Hitchhiker's Guide to the Galaxy*, I find myself increasingly at one with the rigorously offensive Bowerick Wowbagger, better known (to Douglas Adams fans, at least) as Wowbagger the Infinitely Prolonged. Born mortal, Wowbagger had immortality rudely thrust upon him following an accident with 'an irrational particle accelerator, a liquid lunch, and a pair of rubber bands'. Lacking the inbred eternal calm of his fellow immortals (whom he considers a bunch of 'serene bastards'), Wowbagger is exhausted by life, and wracked with anger at the endless void of his existence. To keep himself busy and give vent to his spleen, he decides to set himself a task: he will insult every single living being in the universe, and (here's the kicker) he'll do it in alphabetical order. When told that such a task is impossible, not least due to the fact that the universe itself is not alphabetical, Wowbagger responds, 'A man can dream, can't he?'

I was dreaming of Wowbagger one Tuesday afternoon, walking the streets of Soho alone, separated from the pack – the Dogs of Wardour Street no longer the proud kings of these once-happy sandwich-hunting grounds. As anyone with experience of the canine world will know, dogs in packs can be scary but it's the rabid strays you have to watch out for – the ones who've gone a bit mad, and been left to drool on their own. In this particular case the crushing weight of the week's rotten movies had turned me into something beastly, like David Naughton in *An American Werewolf in London*, only without Jenny Agutter to make it all better. Don't get me wrong, being a film critic is brilliant, but despite the fact that watching movies for a living is an insanely privileged existence, you can still occasionally lose your sense of perspective and wind up wondering what the hell is the point of it all? So, having been pushed over the edge by one lousy sequel too many, I did what all flea-bitten sickly mutts do – I stopped licking my own wounds and decided to bite someone else. In a moment of mangy madness (and still smarting from that encounter with Bert Schnick in the BFI), I decided to make it my mission in life to track down every film-maker whose work I had ever found lacking and do them the (dis)service of telling them so, to their face, and ideally in alphabetical order.

Right, I thought, let's start with the As. Who have I slagged off whose name begins with 'A'. Adam Ant? No, he's a pop star (*was* a pop star), so that doesn't count, although I was passingly rude about his appearances in a string of straight-to-video titles (*Spellcaster*, *Sunset Heat*, *Love Bites*) that I wound up reviewing for *Sight & Sound* back in the early nineties. What is it about former British pop stars (particularly those of a 'new romantic' bent) that means they end up serving time in the kind of schlocker fare which, in happier times, would have been accompanied by top-of-the-range sandwiches? Only the other week I'd suffered the humourless horror of *Strippers vs Werewolves* (imagine *Lesbian Vampire Killers*, but even less funny), beginning with a scene in which former Spandau Ballet bassist Martin Kemp sprouts hairy ears and pointy teeth whilst writhing in quasi-orgasmic ecstasy beneath the gyrating backside of a scantily clad lap-dancer. Is it written into their contracts at the beginning of their rise to superstardom? 'You will make three gold albums and tour the world wearing a kilt with a tea-towel over your shoulder before succumbing to plastic appendages in the pursuit of cheap screen entertainment'? Whatever, Martin Kemp is a 'K' (and was actually pretty good in *The Krays*), so I'm getting ahead of myself. Where was I? On the As. Adam Sandler? Nope, he's an 'S', although I'd happily change the rules if it meant getting the chance to say something terrible to Adam Sandler sooner rather than later. I already know what I would say to him: 'Mr Sandler, you starred in one of my favourite movies of all time, *Punch-Drunk Love*, a beautiful black comedy about the inherent psychosis of love. You proved that you know what really great film-making looks like. So what the Sam Hill do you think you're doing making me sit through *Jack and Jill*? How could you possibly live with *That's My Boy*? Aren't you ashamed of *Grown Ups*? It's one thing for people who don't know any better to make movies that bad, but you do know better, and somehow that just makes your multiple crimes against cinema even worse.'

Sounds pretty damning, huh? Sadly, Adam Sandler isn't around to hear it. Best revert to the old plan. On to the Bs . . .

Michael Bay? Lives in L.A.

Uwe Boll? Too punchy.

John Boorman! An acclaimed maestro with more right than anyone to take issue with my arsey reviews. Right, I need to track down John Boorman and tell him just what I think is wrong with his films, to his face. Shouldn't be difficult; I once almost bumped into him in this very part of London. It was weird, I was walking out of a screening at Mr Young's (actually the 'Soho Screening Rooms', but the old name still sticks) on D'Arblay Street, just off Wardour Street, and as I pelted to the next screening over at Fox in Soho Square I saw someone I recognized coming across the road towards me. I did that instinctive thing of slowing down because it would be rude not to say hello, or at least nod in friendly acknowledgement. As I slowed, he looked up momentarily, and our eyes met very briefly. It was only at this point that I suddenly realized it was John Boorman, about whose films I have been extremely – and frankly unfairly – rude, often for cheap comic effect. If I was John Boorman and I saw me running towards me (here playing the role of John Boorman) with a cheese-eating grin on my fat, unlovely face, I would have slapped me. But Boorman did nothing of the sort, merely returning the fleeting acknowledgement with a polite micro-smile and walking on by, getting on with his day, unbothered by the chance encounter with someone he almost certainly didn't recognize as a parasite who had taken his good name in vain, in public, on several occasions. After all, why the hell should he recognize me? The man has an extraordinary body of films under his belt, has worked with some of the finest screen actors of all time, and is widely regarded by those in the know (from film critic Michel Ciment to film-maker Neil Jordan) to be an inspirational visionary genius. Indeed, it is precisely because Boorman has been so widely and magnificently fêted as a bona-fide artist, and has enjoyed such popular and critical success, that I felt it was perfectly OK to be snotty about his movies. Being rude about film-makers at the bottom of the evolutionary pile lacks dignity, not to mention comedy. But Boorman has a back catalogue so vast and unassailable that it could surely withstand the insignificant sarcastic swipes of some annoying twerp on the nation's leading medium-wave sports and news network.

Ironically, my problem with John Boorman's films is that they've always seemed a testament to the potentially damaging power of overwhelmingly positive reviews. Film-makers bleat on all the time about how awful critics are who slag off their work, but no one ever addresses the character-building power of surviving a full-on critical tsunami, or the equally corrosive effect of basking too long in the radioactive sunlight of universal praise. I've always felt, for example, that nothing has done Quentin Tarantino more harm than being surrounded by people who tell him how brilliant he is all the time, rather than people who are willing to call him a self-indulgent arse when the need arises. Yet ever since Harvey Weinstein called Miramax 'the house that Quentin built', Tarantino's unruly talent has suffered from being sorely unmatched by an equally powerful controlling force, preferably a strong producer standing over him in the editing room with a very big stick reminding him of Roger Corman's maxim that few films would not benefit from shedding a third of their running time.

As for John Boorman, he started out as a talented and tenacious young film-maker who learned his trade in documentaries and television, grafting long and hard to turn in solid work with limited resource, over which he did not have complete control. Good reviews of his first feature, the sub-Beatles Dave Clark Five romp *Catch Us If You Can*, led to Boorman landing the job helming *Point Blank*, a big(ger) budget Hollywood thriller (from the 'Richard

Stark' novel *The Hunter*) with an A-list star, Lee Marvin, who stood behind his director during the inevitable fights with the producers. Boorman had high artistic aspirations for the project, stills from which are now regularly used as textbook examples of groundbreaking framing and composition on film-studies courses. The studio wanted a nuts-and-bolts thriller, but having ceded script and casting approval to Marvin, who promptly passed on those privileges to Boorman, they wound up with an avant-garde existential classic. It did poorly at the box office, but wowed the critics, and is now regularly cited as one of the 100 Best Movies of all time. As I write this in 2013, *Point Blank* is enjoying a revival in the UK, touring cinemas and headlining a major retrospective of the director's work at the BFI Southbank. I saw it again the other week, in a spanking new print; it really is very good (and very strange), and still looks edgily modern even after the passing of all these years.

After *Point Blank*, Boorman re-teamed with Marvin for *Hell in the Pacific*, which got good notices but lost money, and then worked with Fellini regular Marcello Mastroianni on *Leo the Last*, which bagged him a prestigious Best Director award at Cannes. Clearly, Boorman was something of a hit with the critics, if not necessarily the public. All that was to change with *Deliverance*. Adapted from a somewhat pulpy novel by James Dickey (who cameos as a befuddled officer of the law, and with whom Boorman battled constantly over the script), the movie was a breathtaking controversial gem. Brilliantly negotiating the divide between European art house invention and American grindhouse exploitation, it now stands as one of the touchstone texts of the so-called American New Wave (even though its director is British). A tale of city folk finding themselves way out of their depth whilst canoeing in the rivers of the Appalachian mountains, *Deliverance* can be variously read as a savage ecological tract upon the destruction of natural terrain; a class-war expose of the ongoing battle between the privileged rich and the disenfranchised poor; an examination of the ancient town/country, North/South cultural divide which continues to haunt modern-day America; a metaphorical tale of the evils of imperialism, with dark overtones of the fall-out from the war in Vietnam; or (most popularly) a brilliant dissection of a broiling contemporary crisis in masculinity which performs a genre reversal on cinema's traditional rape-revenge narrative to leg-crossing effect. Or just a bloody good horror thriller in which a group of likeable but foolhardy dorks are terrorized by inbred banjo-playing rednecks with one eye and not an opposable thumb between them, set against spectacularly eye-catching scenery. Whichever way you slice it, *Deliverance* is a masterpiece, the work of a film-maker at the very height of his creative capabilities, forging a silk-purse of sheer cinematic brilliance from the potential sow's ear of the source novel, and providing Burt Reynolds with a vehicle for the greatest performance of his otherwise occasionally cheesy career.

Unlike Boorman's previous works, *Deliverance* was a hit, taking over $22 million in US theatrical rentals (having cost only $2 million), and earning Oscar nominations for Best Editing, Best Director, and Best Picture. Boorman was clearly a genius, and everyone told him so. And that, it seems to me, is where the problems really began. Long admired by film critics and now basking in the glory of an unexpected box-office hit, Boorman was effectively told,

'You are not just a great film-maker, an artist who has managed to make his mark in an industry frequently known for crushing the spark of individuality; you, good sir, are an "auteur".'

'Auteur' is a term coined by critics to identify a defining vision amidst the myriad warring forces and influences (artistic, financial, personal) combined in creating a finished movie. According to so-called 'auteur theory', the very best works of cinema are guided by a singular voice, not that of the writer (although many have argued that it could/ should be) but more usually that of the director. An 'auteur', therefore, is someone whose personal vision is so strong that it informs and inflects every aspect of the movie, meaning that no matter how many people contributed to the final film, they alone are effectively its 'author'.

Auteur theory has its roots in *Cahiers du Cinéma*, the influential French publication for which Truffaut wrote in the 1950s before accomplishing his ultimate goal of becoming a film-maker (thus presumably making him OK in Kevin Smith's book – which must be a great relief). In the sixties, American critic Andrew Sarris picked up Truffaut's French baton, applying it to directors working within the Hollywood studio system, arguing that film-makers such as John Ford and Alfred Hitchcock had a personal style which transcended the demands of studio production and was evident from film to film, thus somehow unifying their body of work. In the seventies, with the American New Wave in full flow, every director working in the US was tipping their hat towards the French *nouvelle vague* and being proclaimed an 'auteur' by the popular press – Friedkin, Coppola, Scorsese, Bogdanovich, and, of course, John Boorman. Then, in 1980, that over-praised American auteur *par excellence*, Michael Cimino, torched an entire studio with the catastrophic *Heaven's Gate*, over which he was granted total control by producers in awe of his 'great man genius' reputation. So, by the time everyone was quoting Barthes and pronouncing the 'death of the author' in literary circles, Hollywood was following suit and pronouncing the 'death of the star director', thanks largely to the work of ball-busting producers like Don Simpson who, along with his partner Jerry Bruckheimer, developed a string of moneymaking hits (*Flashdance*, *Top Gun*, *Beverly Hills Cop*) on which they called the shots. Simpson, incidentally, was a prodigious consumer of drugs with a fondness for firearms whose worst nightmare was 'a screenwriter with a gun'. Today, we have Simpson and Bruckheimer's legacy to thank for the career of Michael Bay.

Thanks for that.

Many people, particularly those who work within the industry, often alongside those labelled 'auteurs', think that the idea of the single defining vision is a load of old bunkum, an excuse for pretentious critics who understand nothing of the essentially collaborative nature of all film-making to heap praise upon a cherry-picked canon of star directors while effectively ignoring the work of those who really made the movies: the writers, producers, performers, technicians and (perhaps most crucially) editors. I have some sympathy with this position, as would anyone who has ever been on a film set and witnessed first-hand the

organized 'co-operative' chaos involved in getting a movie
– any movie – made. You only have to look at the army
of people swarming across even the cheapest, lowliest film
production to realize how daft it is to suggest that any one
person can be held responsible for all this madness.

But I also sympathize with the enthusiasm of anyone
who sees film-making primarily as an art-form (rather than
a commercial process) to elevate the importance of personal
inspiration above the mundanity of mere industrial intrigue. Take, for example, the splendidly boisterous Bertrand
Tavernier, who, in his seventies, continues to make vibrant
movies like *The Princess of Montpensier*, a wonderfully vig-
orous costume drama with a rich and somewhat radical
political and religious underpinning which the director
can rightly claim to be uniquely and distinctly his own.
Back in the nineties, when Tavernier was a mere stripling
of a thing, the film-maker treated me to a magnificently
outraged lecture on the evils of those American money-
men who were attempting (as he saw it) to redefine the
term auteur to incorporate studios and production heads.
'So . . .' he spluttered, barely able to contain the fury of
his boiling Gallic blood, 'Warner Brothers is the auteur
of *Unforgiven*!?' His eyes boggled at the very thought,
while his handsomely jowly face scrunched itself up into a
mask of revulsion and despair. 'It's stupid!' he said, waving
his hand in the air, as if to swat the notion out of his
field of vision, or to waft the stench of idiocy away from
his face. 'It's stupid,' he repeated, 'and . . . *it's a crime!*'

Nor did he appear to be joking. As far as I could tell, he
would have happily seen those cultural vandals threatening
the founding principles of auteurism taken to the Tower

and disposed of in the manner of the bewigged aristos rounded up whilst others were storming the Bastille. When he used the word 'crime' he meant it literally rather than metaphorically. And jovial as he had been throughout the rest of our conversation, his tone turned to steely resolve when he solemnly told me of the GATT (General Agreement on Tariffs and Trade) battles of the early nineties, during which the French stamped their feet about protecting their indigenous film industry (to the annoyance of the Americans) and fought to define the word auteur as 'a living, breathing human being', as opposed to some creative corporate cabal. Clearly this was something about which Bertrand was not alone in being profoundly exercised, and a quasi-legal ruling was considered not merely efficacious but absolutely necessary.

When it comes to auteurs, the French can be very serious.

Back to John Boorman. Having made the achingly visceral *Deliverance*, he found his name promptly added to that growing circle of visionary young men (and make no mistake, they were all men) who, according to the world's press, were redefining modern cinema with their boldly auteurish ways. (The notes to the recent Boorman BFI retrospective, penned by Michel Ciment, proudly open with the phrase 'Definitely an auteur . . .') And having been told that he was an auteur, a singular genius with a unique overarching talent, it seems to me that Boorman made the mistake of believing his own press, and promptly went off the rails.

You want proof?

Zardoz.

You want more proof?

Exorcist 2: The Heretic.

Staggering as it may seem, the man who made *Deliver-ance* – one of the outstanding works of seventies cinema – followed it up with the worst science-fiction movie ever made, and then followed that up with the worst movie ever made. As falls from grace go, that is surely one of the most spectacular.

So what went wrong?

In the case of *Zardoz*, the answer is simple: total control. 'The movie is an exercise in self-indulgence', wrote Roger Ebert with typical insight, 'by Boorman who more or less had carte blanche to do a personal project after his immensely successful *Deliverance*' – which is a rather more elegant way of saying that success went to his head. Having previously excelled at making movies where creative fights were commonplace, Boorman lost the plot (as did Cimino) when allowed to do exactly what he wanted, promptly producing a turkey of intergalactic proportions – a film which manages to be staggeringly boring despite basically being about the contents of Sean Connery's jockstrap. Oh, there's a whole lot of other balderdash in there about the kind of serene immortals whom Wowbagger would have stabbed in the eye with a pencil, wandering around in purple velvet pantaloons and generally refusing to die until Connery turns up from the barbaric outlands and scares them all with his untamed willy, bringing death (and there-fore ironically life) to their sterile existence as he gets an erection which reasserts the natural order, blah blah blah. I'm *not* making this up; the film actually involves the flying head of a false god vomiting guns onto a beach whilst declaring, 'The penis is evil! The penis shoots seeds!' If you think this sounds poor, you should have been there when the film first opened in 1974; according to a retrospective article in *Starlog* magazine, patrons emerging from a matinee screening of *Zardoz* looked so nonplussed by what they had just endured that the crowds queueing for the next performance dispersed forthwith. The word of mouth wasn't bad – it was terrible.

As for *The Heretic*, it is (by Boorman's own admission) the work of someone making a sequel to a movie they don't like in a genre they don't understand. And if there's one thing worse than a really bad horror movie, it's a really bad horror movie made by someone who thinks that they are somehow above horror movies. Having reportedly turned down the chance to direct *The Exorcist* back in 1972 (Boorman disliked the script so much that he told Warners 'not only do I not want to make this, I don't want anyone else to make it either'), the director signed on to helm the sequel on the basis that doing so could somehow heal the wounds inflicted upon the world by the original. 'Every film has to struggle to find a connection with its audience,' he declared. 'Here, I saw the chance to make an extremely ambitious film without having to spend the time developing this connection. I could make assumptions and then take the audience on a very adventurous cinematic journey.' In other words, he could take all the hard work which William Friedkin and William Peter Blatty had put into making a movie he found 'repulsive' and then hijack it to his own 'metaphysical' ends without having to bother with all that tedious nonsense of actually getting the audience to care about or invest in your characters or their stories. In effect, *The Exorcist* had warmed the audience up; now *The Heretic* could jump in and give them all a collective spiritual orgasm.

When *The Heretic* first opened in New York, audiences laughed. Boorman panicked and re-cut the movie. They laughed even more. Someone told Warners they should re-cut it again, but then *they* laughed – albeit mirthlessly. When *Exorcist* author Blatty sneaked into a public screening, he and everyone around him laughed so much that 'you would have thought we were watching *The Producers*'. Friedkin described *The Heretic* as 'the product of a demented mind'. Leonard Maltin called the film 'preposterous'. Danny Peary dismissed it as 'absurd'. In the *Golden Turkey Awards*, counting down the fifty worst movies of all time, *The Heretic* came in at Number 2, losing out on the top spot to Ed Wood's *Plan 9 From Outer Space*. Frankly, it was robbed – *Plan 9* is a much better movie than *The Heretic*: shorter, cheaper, and altogether less stupid. And it doesn't involve people taking flying lessons on the back of a locust.

'It had one of the most disastrous openings ever,' Boorman admitted candidly. 'There were riots! And we re-cut the actual prints in theatres, about six a day, but it didn't help, of course, and I couldn't bear to talk about it, or look at it, for years.' Today it has become fashionable for people to attempt to reclaim *The Heretic* as some kind of misunderstood gem, a flawed masterpiece in the manner of *Heaven's Gate*. On its release, the ever-contrary Pauline Kael had been a lone voice in its defence, insisting that Boorman's film had 'more visual invention than a dozen movies', an admirably outlandish claim. In his book on Boorman's career, Michel Ciment actually argues for a third version to add to the first two, and then starts waxing lyrical about how much he admires a movie that doesn't exist anywhere except in his own head – so much for Fellini's claim that critics can't add anything to cinema.

My own disdain for *The Heretic* is fairly well rehearsed and there's really no need to go through it all again here. What there is a need to do is to look at what Boorman did next, and to ask whether there was any justification for my flippantly calling him 'the worst film-maker of all time' just because he made the worst movie of all time.

The short answer is no.

The long answer is . . .

In the wake of *The Heretic*, Boorman made a whole bunch of movies, none of which I particularly like, but several of which are quite rightly revered and respected by people whose opinions I revere and respect. Movies such as *Excalibur*, a glitteringly modern revisiting of the old Arthurian legend considered by many to be Boorman's masterpiece, a symphony of shining armour, lusty passion, bloody battles, and ripe misty-moored cinematography. Or *Hope and Glory*, a very personal evocation of childhood in wartime, which many rank alongside *Chariots of Fire* as a genuinely great and classically British movie. Or how about *The General*, a black-and-white crime movie (inspired by real events) with standout central performances from Brendan Gleeson and Jon Voight, the latter finding the kind of form he seemed to have lost after his heyday in the seventies when directors like Boorman helped him give his very best.

None of these are movies I feel strongly about, but they all have their champions, as does *The Emerald Forest*, an eco-friendly adventure in which the director cast his young son Charley in a starring role.

Of course, there were still some flat-out failures, most notably *Beyond Rangoon*, in which Patricia Arquette ventures intrepidly through Burma (no, I didn't believe it either) where Aung San Suu Kyi is facing house arrest and democracy is almost as scant as audience interest. When former-art-house-enfant-terrible-turned-arsey-exploitation-hack Luc Besson revisited the story of Aung San Suu Kyi nearly two decades later in *The Lady*, he did so in a manner altogether more exciting and intriguing than Boorman's movie. And believe me, when Luc Besson is making movies that seem more intriguing than yours, the time may have come to throw in the towel.

But of course, Boorman did not throw in the towel, despite my outrageously arrogant suggestion on BBC Radio 1 (the biggest and most-listened-to radio station in the UK at the time) that he should do just that. Casting my mind back to those heady poptastic days when I was the upstart 'voice of film' for '1FM' (as it was futuristically known in those pre-DAB-and-download dark ages), I remember using *Beyond Rangoon* as a blunt instrument with which to batter proponents of the auteur theory in general and John Boorman in particular. And, working on the dual principles that a) there's no such thing as a cheap laugh and b) if a joke's worth telling once, it's worth telling a hundred times, I slipped into the habit of being flatulently dismissive of his movies wherever and whenever the mood took me.

This was nothing more than stupid laziness on my part, and the more I think about it the more I realize that rather than tracking John Boorman down in order to harangue him (in alphabetical order) I should in fact seek him out in order to apologize, to grovel, to eat humble pie and to say 'sorry'. In the pursuit of an easy jibe and a smart-Alec dismissal, I'd taken two movies from an otherwise extraordinary career and used them as an excuse to be small-minded, mean-spirited and thoroughly wrong-headed about Boorman's often brilliant work. Understanding, as I said in the Prologue, that the quickest way to make a name for yourself in this profession is to be nasty, I did just that. It is easier to laugh than to laud; it's also shameful, dumb and embarrassing, and if Wowbagger were faced with the same situation I'm pretty sure he'd have given up the ghost and started being nice to people instead.

What makes it worse is that I don't think the good reviews Boorman has earned served him much better – certainly not in terms of their effect upon his work. Perhaps he doesn't read reviews at all – many claim not to, and it's easy to see why; there's plenty of evidence to suggest that film-makers really are better off without critics, protected from both their lavish praise and baying boos. I haven't been kind to Boorman over the years, but were the people encouraging him to make *Zardoz* really doing him any favours? Wouldn't it have been better if he'd just been allowed to get on with the business of making movies, answerable to no one but the ticket-buying public and the budget-conscious studios? I'm not saying that the reviews of those who supported and encouraged Boorman were anything like as inane and unforgiveable as mine, but in terms of what they 'added' to his body of work, were they really any more valid?

Has calling someone an auteur even done them any good?

Isn't all criticism – good or bad – just white noise; waffle; static hiss; a distraction from the real business of making films?

What, in brief, is the bloody point?

Sunday afternoon. Around 2.55. I am sitting at home, staring at a newspaper I'm never going to read, brooding upon the emptiness of my professional existence, facing the Long Dark Teatime of the Soul.

The dog sits on the sofa.

The dog is not allowed on the sofa.

I look at the dog sternly.

The dog gets off the sofa. A first!

The dog slinks out of the room, towards the kitchen.

Then, a noise.

The dog is scratching at the kitchen door.

I ignore it.

The dog scratches at the door some more.

I'm not falling for this again.

The dog starts to yelp, to scratch, to howl. The dog actually comes all the way from kitchen to get me from the living room. She looks at me as if to say, 'No, really, this time it's serious . . .'

This must be serious.

I put down the paper and trudge all the way from the warmth of the living room, through the cold of the kitchen, to the back door which passes for a front door in our oddly misshapen house. The dog is back at the door, glaring, growling, even making a strange mooing sound.

I look out into our pokey little garden and see a peculiar man, draped in golden robes with an ostentatious collar, wafting serenely across the lawn. He is tall – unusually tall. And green. His skin has a lustrous grey sheen which makes it look as though he's actually glowing. His head is strangely flattened. He is carrying a clipboard.

He looks at me through the windows of the door and knocks.

The dog is now cowering – not barking, but whimpering.

I open the door.

'Yes, hello?'

'Kermode?' says the grey-green tall flat-headed man, looking at his clipboard. 'Mark James Kermode?'

He looks at me with strange little alien eyes.

'Er, yes? Can I help?'

He stands up straight, even taller now.

'You are a jerk,' he says smartly. 'A complete asshole.'

He looks down at his clipboard, ticks his list, turns, walks back towards the spaceship parked behind my knackered Ford Capri, and disappears off into the stars.

CHAPTER SIX

THE ANTI-SOCIAL NETWORK

Once upon a time, way back in the late eighteenth century, an extraordinary machine dazzled, baffled and entranced all who laid eyes on it. Known as the Mechanical Turk, this life-sized chess-playing automaton, powered by whirring cogs and watch-like springs, took on all-comers from Europe and America in a game which had become an index of intelligence itself – and won. Emperors, queens, presidents – all were eager to discover if a machine really was a match for a man, or a woman. Some were terrified, believing the enigmatic figure – with its black beard, grey eyes, turban and robes – was powered by witchcraft, possessed of a demon, or perhaps inhabited by the spirit of a dead person. How else, they demanded, could a machine outwit a human being, if not driven by some infernal force? According to one reporter, the Turk was dressed 'in the traditional costume of an oriental sorcerer', something that added to the eerie air of mystery, as did the exotically long pipe the automaton would hold in its left hand as its face seemed to move and grimace in a strange imitation of life. No wonder

Edgar Allan Poe, the leading author of the uncanny and the grandfather of modern horror, became obsessed with the Turk – famously reporting on it for the *Southern Literary Messenger* in his April 1836 essay 'Maelzel's Chess Player'. Certain no machine could perform the amazing feats that came so (un)naturally to this strange creation, Poe (who asserted that 'the Turk never lost a match') concluded that the automaton must be operated by 'a mind' – although exactly how remained a mystery.

Poe's essay caused something of a sensation and its reverberations are still felt today; it is cited, for example, in Shawn James Rosenheim's scholarly 1996 publication *The Cryptographic Imagination* as prefiguring the key motifs of early science fiction, and refining the analytic thought processes for which Poe's detective fiction became world renowned. As for the Turk itself, it entered modern mythology, offering a crystal-ball gaze into a future in which mankind was superseded by machines that had become 'more human than human'.

Fast forward to the present day: we all rely upon machines few of us understand (computers, mobile phones, Blu-ray players, etc.) and the anxieties raised by the Turk over two hundred years ago still lurk in our common unconscious. There's a reason we keep making science-fiction movies (*2001: A Space Odyssey*, *Blade Runner*, *The Terminator*, *Alien*) in which robots smarter than us become a danger to our continued existence. And if the robots start becoming creative – playing chess, painting works of art, writing novels, composing music and poetry, having opinions of their own – isn't that really the end of the line for humanity?

Personally, I think a little of that sci-fi fear is gnawing away at the generation of journalists (myself included) who started their careers in the distant pre-digital age – people who filed copy written on typewriters which was then physically handed over to human editors and sub-editors through whose skilled hands it would have to pass before magically appearing on the printed page. This was how things worked when I first started writing for *Time Out* back in the late eighties, with every Tuesday morning spent taking the train from East Finchley to Covent Garden in order to hand in my reviews at the *TO* office on the fifth floor of their creaky old tower block on Southampton Street. Once there, I never wanted to leave. I remember loitering in reception watching film editors Geoff Andrew and Brian Case reading something I had written, making strange occult-like markings with a red biro, drawing lines through certain words and phrases, then handing it over to the subs who would perform yet more bizarre crypto-graphic rituals upon my copy before laboriously retyping it by hand into what then seemed like extremely futuristic 'typesetting machines'. Each of these people was a skilled operator, an artist in their field, and watching them work was like watching someone play the violin. Like all good editors, what they were doing was more than technical – it was intuitive, and it involved a combination of strictly defined skills and utterly indefinable inspiration. They knew a good turn of phrase when they read it, they understood the power of a pithy one-liner, and if they didn't laugh at a joke it was because it wasn't funny. Brian once sat silently reading a lengthy piece I had written about fifties sci-fi remakes, after which he stood up and theatrically tore the piece in two, putting one half in the bin, and presenting me with the other, saying, 'Make it this long. And better.'

I loved being in that office. It was so seductive, so exciting, so full of . . . people.

All that changed with the arrival of the fax machine, a new-fangled invention for which I had saved up for six months after hearing other journalists tell me that the device had 'transformed their lives'. The machine had been designed to save time, to remove the need for someone (or something) to make a physical journey, to leave their house and interact with the real world. And so it was that one Tuesday morning, rather than skipping off to the train station, I got up, made a cup of coffee, took my copy out of the typewriter, slipped it into the fax machine, dialled the number for *Time Out*, and waited.

There followed a brief pause as the phone rang twice and made a couple of gurgling noises, then suddenly my room was transformed into the set of a sci-fi movie as two robots separated by a distance of some ten or fifteen miles started talking to one another in incomprehensible bleeps and whirrs. The fax machine flashed a few lights, ground a few gears, and started to eat my film review. The whole operation took a few minutes, and then with a flurry of noise it was over.

I was stunned.

I rang *Time Out*.

'Hello,' I said, still somewhat shocked. 'I just . . . "faxed" over some copy. Is that the right word, "faxed"? Is that what I did? Faxed it? Have you got it? The fax? That I faxed? Just now.'

'Yup, thanks.'

'You have?'

'Yup.'

'You've got it all?'

'Let me check. Yeah, looks like it's all here.'

'All here? All *there* . . . in Covent Garden.'

'Seems so.'

'What I just "faxed" from here in East Finchley, is now *there* . . .'

'Yes.'

'Wow.'

'Is there anything else?'

'What? No. Not if it's "all here". Or "there". The fax. That I just "faxed".'

'Righto, bye, then.'

They hung up the phone.

I had sent a fax. I was a 'faxer'.

I looked at the clock. It was 9.05 a.m.

What the hell was I going to do with the rest of the morning?

I'll have a bath.

I had a bath, languished in the warm waters of free time and day-dreamed of the space-age world of information into which I had just been inducted; a world free from wearying responsibility, where fantastical machines could perform the boringly menial tasks on which we'd wasted so much of our lives, leaving us free to think, and write, dream, create . . .

Utopia.

But as is the way of such things, as the water grew colder so the dream turned darker, and I found myself wondering how long it would be before the machine that just delivered my copy in an instant began to think the copy wasn't up to scratch, wasn't worth teleporting. How long before the machine figured out how to edit as it faxed, or indeed to write the copy itself? I began to worry that anything capable of zapping a perfect facsimile of something through space like Scotty in *Star Trek* was probably well on the way towards making informed value judgements. How long did I have before *Time Out* didn't need film critics any more because the computers had developed opinions of their own – smarter, funnier, faster and cheaper opinions than those of their human counterparts?

How long would it be before I was out of a job? Redundant?

I was filled with a vision of myself in the late-eighteenth century, sitting across a table from the grand Mechanical Turk, his robes glittering with magical power, his face full of automatic meanness, the air thick with the smoke from his pipe and ringing with the cackling laughter of princes and paupers, all watching as the machine unblinkingly beat me into humiliating submission.

As the laughter grew, the Turk moved his hand across the table, sweeping the pieces from the board in a gesture of defiance, his beady inanimate eyes fixing me with their shark-like stare, his artificial voice box repeating its triumphant one word refrain:

'*Échec! Échec! Échec!*'

Checkmate.

In March 2012, *Radio Times* film editor Andrew Collins – an excellent writer of long-standing service – drew his readers' attention to an interesting phenomenon. Browsing through his local paper, Collins had noted that the current edition carried an advert for the movie *The Best Exotic Marigold Hotel* duly splattered with delighted reviews ('the must-see film of the year!'; 'a truly wonderful experience') attributed not to Peter Bradshaw of the *Guardian* or Derek Malcolm of the London *Evening Standard* but to 'Sheena, 55, Pudsey, West Yorkshire' and 'Richard, 51, London'. A few pages further on in the same paper, Collins would find similarly ringing endorsements for the teen video-camera comedy *Project X*, this time citing the source of the rave reviews ('One of the best movies ever, everyone should watch it') as Twitter, the social networking site without which no self-respecting teenager can function in the modern world (nor indeed any self-respecting fifty-year-old journalist).

On the surface, these movie endorsements seem disarmingly candid and (more importantly) demographically specific. In both cases we have the appearance of an audience member talking directly to their peer group, reassuring those cut from a similar social cloth and age range that the film in question has been road-tested by one of their own and found to be rollickingly fit for purpose. Never mind what the snot-nosed critics think – here are people like you who have seen and enjoyed these movies, and who know from shared experience that you will do the same.

In fact, although *Project X* got a pretty rigorous kicking from much of the critical establishment (I was off the week it came out, and confess that I can muster little enthusiasm to fill that particular gap in my knowledge), *The Best Exotic*

Marigold Hotel was generally well-received by a wide range of scribes, many of whom thought it far less twee than the title and poster suggested. I really liked the movie, and stressed in my BBC Radio 5 live review that although its success would depend on the same older crowd who had made *The King's Speech* such an unexpected hit, it nonetheless had plenty to offer anyone still of reproductive age. The critics were enthusiastic, but clearly, as far as the marketeers were concerned, nothing I or any of my fellow reviewers said could match the personal endorsements of the film's target audience, who seemed to be represented on that advert in abundance.

Or were they?

In the case of *The Best Exotic Marigold Hotel*, it was impossible to verify whether the opinions of Sheena from Pudsey or Richard from London were bona fide, although Collins conceded (entirely fairly) that 'if I'd stood outside my local cinema after seeing it and harvested quotes from my fellow patrons, I'm sure I could have filled two adverts with raves', noting that it was 'at the end of the day, a people's film'. What worried him more were the quotes pimping *Project X* and so, ever the proper journalist, he decided to check the Twitter accounts to which those quotes were attributed. The results: one belonged to someone with 119 followers whose account featured 'no other biographical information' except for a name and an 'avatar of a sunbathing woman whose head is cropped off'; the other belonged to 'a London band "using music to spread the message of Islam"' whose 'quote is nonetheless being used to spread the message of *Project X*'. They had thirty-seven followers.

'Two questions arise,' wrote Collins. 'One: are ads in which the reviews and quotes come from members of the public poised to oust the once-regal film critics from their ivory towers? . . . Two: why should we trust these quotes?' Despite tiptoeing very carefully around any accusations of fraudulence ('I'm sure the two quotes used by *Project X* are 100% independent and genuine . . .'), Collins could not help but conclude that, 'Anybody could start an account on the social networking site, give themselves a stupid name, and write a great review of *Project X*. Who's to know?'

Exactly. Who's to know?

Ten months later, in January 2013, with the phenomenon of Twitter movie quotes now not so much a novelty as a firmly entrenched reality (see how quickly that happened?), the concerns about their veracity and their impact upon film criticism were gathering momentum. Writing a blog for the *Independent* under the headline: 'Is social media beginning to undermine film criticism', Kieran Turner-Dave noted that the distributors of *Argo* and *The Impossible* (both potential awards contenders with strong critical support) had 'chosen to adorn their posters with a selection of favourable opinions from random Twitter users'. In the opinion of Turner-Dave, this tactic was 'incredibly misleading, as not only does the opinion on the poster have no basis in expertise whatsoever, but a quote from a Twitter user can be easily influenced, cherry-picked, or just plain fabricated without any legal difficulty.' While conceding that the 'growth of social media has greatly widened the scope for the discussion of cinema and allowed for film writers and distributors to more successfully meet their target audience', Turner-Dave nevertheless implored his readers to 'consider a variety of erudite and reasoned opinions before seeing a movie – but not those of a carefully selected, and potentially untrustworthy, stranger'.

Meanwhile, over at the *Daily Telegraph*, chief film critic Robbie Collin could be found raising the same questions about advertisements for *The Impossible*, becoming the latest in a long line of professionals to ask rhetorically, 'Who needs film critics?' Quoting some of the 'real opinions from real people' such as 'Katie M Kelly', who wrote that the film 'makes you look at what is important in life', Collin mockingly continued that, 'judging by her own Twitter feed, this includes heavy lunches ("the best thing about Sundays is the roast dinner!! #favourite meals")' before pointing out astutely that 'the power of social media lies in the fact that you are only connected to people whose opinions you value, so the opinion of someone with whom you have no connection is worth absolutely nothing'. Somewhat less guarded than his *Radio Times* predecessor, Collin perceived 'a more insidious, long-term agenda at work' in the use of such apparently unprompted virtual word-of-mouth, suggesting that 'if an online recommendation could be plucked from the ether and propelled to national stardom, both the volume and gusto of such recommendations might well increase'. Discreetly sidestepping the fact that established national critics are not above including gushing phrases in their reviews simply to get their names on a poster, Collin reminds us that 'on social media, you can find enthusiastic support for any opinion, no matter how deranged', citing as typical examples: 'Keith Lemon The Film is so funny ahahahaha omfg' and 'Will there be a new Keith Lemon the film? LOVE TO SEE A SEQUAL!!!! <3' 'Much as advertisers might hope to convince us otherwise,' Collin concludes, 'a critic's word carries more weight than an offhand blog or tweet'; a statement with which his readership seemed wholeheartedly to agree. Asked to answer the question: 'Whose verdict on a film do you value the most?' those visiting the *Telegraph* online voted in favour of professional critics first (47 per cent), with 'friends or family members' a close second (46 per cent) and 'random tweeters' bringing up the rear with a measly 7 per cent. The article was promptly posted on the front page of the Film Critics' Circle website, where you could almost hear the collective sigh of relief reverberating across the Internet.

Safe, at least for now. Take that, Twitter!

Over in the world of book reviewing, however, a somewhat different picture was emerging. Like movie critics, some professional book reviewers were starting to wonder whether their jobs were potentially under threat from the largely anonymous amateurs whose opinions were increasingly gaining prominence thanks to the customer feedback functions of online marketing websites. Things really started to heat up on 16 May 2012, when the *Guardian* ran an eye-catching feature provocatively headlined: 'Amazon consumer book reviews as reliable as media experts' which reported on the findings of a study conducted by the Harvard Business School into the veracity (or otherwise) of contributions posted on what had become the world's largest non-professional online review website. According to the article, Professor Michael Luca and his co-authors had set about comparing the verdicts of established critics and 'ordinary' consumers regarding a varied selection of books in order to ascertain once and for all whether the professionals really knew any better than the amateurs when it came to giving the critical thumbs up, or thumbs down. To this end, they had analysed the top hundred non-fiction reviews from forty media outlets, including the *New York Times*, the *Washington Post*, metacritic.com and Amazon, ranking reviews culled from both print and Internet sources in terms of positive and negative responses. Their conclusion, greeted with a mixture of alarm, dismay and dismissal from the more entrenched sections of the established critical community, was that 'experts and consumers agreed in aggregate about the quality of a book'. Worse (or better) still, it transpired that in certain areas the amateurs were actually more skilled at predicting popular hits than their highly paid professional counterparts. 'One drawback of expert reviews,' said the study, 'is that they may be slower to learn about new and unknown books', meaning that Amazon customer reviewers were 'more likely to give a favourable review to a debut author' – thus apparently putting them ahead of the sloth-like critical establishment.

In effect, the survey suggested that the public at large (or rather 'online') were not only just as likely as the critical establishment to make the correct call (positive or negative) on a book, but were also likely to do it quicker – first, but right! And while the readers of the *Telegraph* may have reassured Robbie Collin that they would always trust the views of a professional over the random responses of an Internet amateur, the Harvard survey seemed to demonstrate that, when it came to books, the latter may have the upper hand.

Although the survey (and subsequent *Guardian* report)

centred on a different media, their conclusions struck a chord with anxious film critics eagerly fighting a rearguard action against the rise of random Twitter reviews which were supposedly undermining film criticism. If the general public were every bit as good as professional book reviewers at doing their job, couldn't the same be true of movie-goers? Weren't the film companies who laid on the screenings and sandwiches for an elite cadre of film critics soon going to realize that in the age of social media there was no need to waste any more time and money on such arcane niceties? Moreover, at a time when home-viewing sales were merrily outstripping cinema attendance figures, weren't reviews of the DVDs and Blu-rays for which Amazon had now become the prime supplier more important than those of the theatrically released movies, the cinema life of which was ultimately ephemeral, an overture to the main act of viewing in one's front room?

This is a key paradigm shift. Film critics, as we know from Chapter Four, generally file their reviews to run in tandem with a movie opening in cinemas, but it is widely understood that many of their readers, listeners and viewers will only see that movie when it comes out on disc or download, meaning that reviews tied to the home-viewing market are arguably more relevant and influential than those associated with theatrical release. Indeed, in an ironic twist of fate, the home-viewing market is increasingly becoming the only place where some movies can be viewed intact. Using the model recently adopted by *Taken 2* and *Die Hard 5* (aka *A Good Day to Die Hard*) it has now become common practice to cut action movies for a 12 certificate in cinemas before releasing them uncut on 15-rated

DVD and Blu-ray. In effect, anyone wanting to watch the whole film has to wait till it comes out on disc or download – although in the case of both of these two cynical stinkers, watching just *some* of the movie was more than enough. As for the job of DVD reviewers, having begun my career writing for *Video Trade Weekly* back in the late eighties and early nineties, I am well aware of the 'second-string' status traditionally afforded to critics who cover home viewing. Yet my experience of writing a DVD column for the *Observer* has been that it prompts as much social media response as any of my 'film reviews', suggesting that if movie criticism is going to mean anything in the twenty-first century, it must take at least as much account of the home-viewing as the theatrical marketplace.

In such an economy, websites like Amazon have become hugely important; they provide the world's largest market-place for film products, eclipsing more traditional outlets. When the home entertainment giant Blockbuster Video went into administration in January 2013, it was widely accepted that it had been effectively laid low by online competition, of which Amazon was an integral part. Today, not only does Amazon own the Internet Movie Database (the largest movie information resource in the world) and Love-Film.com (the pre-eminent movie rental/streaming site), but it has also spawned 'Amazon Studios', through which it now develops its own movies and television shows. Combine this with Amazon's already vast customer feedback resource (a database of un-matched international reach) and we see a model emerging in which the production, distribution, and reviewing of movies are brought together under one single roof. (When Amazon recently purchased

GoodReads.com, the acquisition provoked howls of outrage about monopolistic practices in the book trade.) All of which means that anyone interested in the future of film criticism needs to understand how Amazon's increasingly influential customer feedback works.

As we observed earlier, the problem with many social media reviews is that they carry no weight because the people who write them have no track record, and therefore have nothing of value invested in their accuracy or honesty. This is in stark contrast to the milieu of the established press which, for all its many faults (highlighted by the 'Hacked Off' campaign), still involves a healthy level of risk for both the writer and the publisher of any given review. Most importantly, in the world of newspapers and magazines, reviews must pass through the filter of an editorial system which engages, checks, and ultimately endorses the critic and their opinions – even when they are being contrary. If a critic is found wanting (if, for example, they review a product they haven't read or watched, or badmouth something for reasons of undisclosed personal rivalry), then their editors are answerable to their readers, and the reputation of the publication is at stake. Thus reviewers may be held accountable for their words, and editors are both expected and required to protect the good name and circulation of their publications by guarding against the sort of malpractice that reduces reviewing to mere personal axe-grinding. This does not mean professional reviewers can't be mean, bitchy, callous, spiteful, irrational, unreasonable, or just plain wrong-headed in their expressed opinions. But it does mean that their wrong-headedness is placed within the context of their work, past and present; and of their publisher's reputation for even-handedness or otherwise. Crucially, both writer and publisher have something to lose (their commission, their readership) and this element of risk lends these reviews whatever validity they may possess.

To illustrate: imagine if I was to use my review column in the *Observer* to praise or slag off a film everyone else in the sentient world had either hated or loved respectively – something that has happened on more than one occasion. In the event of such a scenario, readers would know that the opinion in question came from someone who thinks *The Exorcist* is a masterpiece and is on record as saying that skiffle is 'the greatest musical genre', upon which basis they could judge my review accordingly. More importantly, they would know that the review had been approved by an editorial body with a respect for the rules of good journalism, and to whom they can complain if they genuinely think the review is unworthy of publication. It would then be for the editors to make a judgement call and decide whether the complaint had merit.

Now let's imagine that someone claimed that I hadn't actually seen the film I had loved/hated, or (worse still) had some unrevealed involvement in it, or in a rival production, or some hidden personal grudge against its makers. That would be a very grave matter. Indeed, were my editors at the *Observer* to conclude that my reviews were either unsubstantiated or covertly prejudiced (as opposed to just plain old wrong-headed and dumb), then I would lose my commission forthwith, and rightly so. Same with my work for the BBC, or for *Sight & Sound*, or any of the organizations for whom I have had the privilege to write or broadcast, all of whom boast editorial staff of the very highest calibre, and for whose input I am eternally grateful. (Like all journalists, my critical backside has been saved on several occasions by an editor asking, 'Are you sure this is right . . . ?')

Compare this to the Amazon customer book reviews used by that Harvard study, and deemed no less 'reliable' than their professional counterparts. That same report acknowledged that Amazon reviews came with 'virtually no quality assurance' and could be ' "gamed" by publishers or competitors submitting false reviews'. As it happens, in the months following the publication of the Harvard report, the extent of such online 'gaming' became clear. High-profile spats involving professional writers Johann Hari and Orlando Figes using fake identities to launch anonymous Internet attacks upon their named rivals prefigured the embarrassing spectacle of crime-writer Stephen Leather admitting to using 'sock puppets' to 'build buzz' about his own works from behind the cover of online *noms de non plume*'. Then, in a real-life detective story which made international headlines, thriller writer Jeremy Duns tracked down and outed best-seller R. J. Ellory as the author of a string of aliased Amazon reviews that not only puffed his own work ("a modern masterpiece . . . magnificent", etc.) but also slagged off the work of his competitors, such as Mark Billingham, whose new book – according to Ellory's sock-puppet review – 'just didn't work on any level'. Caught red-handed, the review-rigging writer was forced to issue a mea culpa regretting his uncharacteristic 'lapse of judgement'. The statement did little to quieten the chorus of outrage.

On 4 September 2012, in the wake of the Ellory–

Amazon scandal, a number of high-profile authors (Lee Child, Jeremy Duns, Helen FitzGerald, Joanne Harris, Charlie Higson, Val McDermid, Tony Parsons, Ian Rankin and thirty-nine others) put their names to an open letter published in the *Telegraph* to 'condemn this behaviour and commit never to use such tactics' while simultaneously praising the 'exciting ecosystem' of Internet book sales. Online reviews and recommendations were hailed as an intrinsic part of a 'free and honest conversation among readers', a conversation now being threatened by 'writers . . . misusing these channels in ways that are fraudulent and damaging to publishing at large'. Aware that the anonymity of the Internet made the policing of such dirty tricks all but impossible, the letter concluded with a rousing call to arms, a plea for the masses to man the virtual barricades. '[T]he only lasting solution is for readers to take possession of the process. The Internet belongs to us all. Honest and heartfelt reviews, good or bad, enthusiastic or disapproving, can drown out the phoney voices, and underhand tactics will be marginalized to the point of irrelevancy. No single author, however devious, can compete with the whole community.' Stirring stuff – to which let me add that, as the author of several books, I have never written a single review, positive or negative, of any product on Amazon, either under my own name or a pseudonym, nor added a comment – not one word. So I suppose you can sign me up to that letter too.

What's interesting about this case is that Amazon had recognized the problems of bogus reviews long before this story broke, and had already taken highly publicized steps to address the issue, imposing an element of editorial control in the form of a complex automated filter system. The fact that they did so (doubtless at great cost) is significant because it tells us how much Amazon value the independence and reliability of their customer feedback, and the degree to which that reliability has become part of their sales pitch. As a marketplace whose main purpose is to sell as much product as possible to the maximum amount of people, Amazon has neither a mandate nor a duty to ensure the integrity of their customer reviews. Yet such integrity is in itself a saleable product, a form of virtual window dressing which draws customers into their online shop, making it an attractive and interesting place to browse, peruse, and generally loiter. In terms of commerce, a significant function of what has now become 'the largest single source of Internet consumer reviews' is presumably to draw and hold Internet traffic, and the more 'reliable' the reviews, the more attention they will attract. Thus, Amazon have created a series of intricate computer algorithms and response evaluation procedures (the precise workings of which remain a closely guarded secret) which act as automated online editors, safeguarding and monitoring the ongoing impartiality, honesty and reliability of comments published on their website. Trip switches set to detect 'campaign voting', for example, automatically identify the feedback of customers whose responses indicate hidden agendas. Moreover, in order to help customers distinguish between the chaotic babble of 'unmediated' voices and root out the 'real' reviews from the 'fake' puff pieces, those editing algorithms cleverly order the millions of submissions of their customer reviewers, electronically sifting the wheat from the chaff.

Picture the scene. You've decided (for reasons obvious to me, maybe less so to you – bear with me) to purchase a copy of the 1968 Charlton Heston simian sci-fi charmer *Planet of the Apes* on brand spanking new Blu-ray. And (as Barry Norman apparently never actually said) why not? It's a great movie, even if the disc cover does feature a massive plot spoiler. As you search for the title, Amazon's auto-mated system analyses your browsing habits, divines your interest in ape-related fantasy frolics, compares them to the interests of others who have made similar searches and *voilà* – suggests you may also be interested in buying Rupert Wyatt's 2011 series reboot *Rise of the Planet of the Apes*. No great logical leap, but a helpful and efficient prompt nonetheless. Your eyes glance at the link for *ROTPOTA* (as it became known amongst fans – yes, really) and you notice immediately that it has four-and-a-bit out of a potential five stars, an aggregate drawn from over 190 reviews, a pretty good recommendation. Duly intrigued, you click on the link; it directs you to a page where Amazon tells you that *ROTPOTA* (which was previously listed as being 'by James Franco' – the lead actor, rather than the writer or director) has well over one hundred five-star ratings, and over thirty four-star approvals, hugely outweighing the relatively few one- and two-star critiques. Clearly, the overwhelming majority of people really liked the movie, while a far smaller number found it rotten to the core. This all sounds good, but you'd like to know a little more before shelling out £10 plus postage and packing because you previously got your fingers burned paying a similar amount for Tim Burton's 2001 *Planet of the Apes* remake, which turned out to be dull as ditchwater and you don't want to get caught out twice.

There are eighteen pages of reviews, and to read and assess all of them would take as long as watching the movie. But fear not because Amazon's electronic editors have automatically sorted through all of those reviews and arranged them for you in order – starting with the 'most helpful' reviews, and working downwards from there.

So how do those editing machines, which perform a function as complex as that of the Mechanical Turk, decide which of these reviews are 'most helpful'? 'We rank customer reviewers based on the opinions of customers like you,' Amazon's Review Guidelines page explains. 'Each time you indicate that a customer review was helpful or not, we use that vote, along with votes from other customers, to determine how helpful a review is. A reviewer's rank is determined by the overall helpfulness of all their reviews, factoring in the number of reviews they have written.' Thus, a vote for or against a review will define its prominence on the product page, whilst the reviewer themselves will accordingly move up and down within Amazon's overarching 'Top Reviewers' ranking, with those consistently proving most 'helpful' working their way towards a coveted Amazon endorsement as a 'Top 1000 Reviewer', 'Top 500 Reviewer', or, better still, 'Top 10 Reviewer'. 'We want our top reviewer rankings to reflect the best of our growing body of customer reviewers,' say Amazon, '[and] review helpfulness plays an important part in determining rank.' Since any clearly scurrilous shill or vindictive attack will doubtless be noted as such by Amazon's millions of customers, it will naturally attract negative votes, causing the editing algorithms to drop it to the bottom of the review pile. The net effect is to allow customers to see at a glance how helpful their consumer peers have found a particular review – and a particular reviewer – and decide for themselves whether a judgement has been made in good faith by a reliable party rather than puffed by a publicist or attacked by someone with an axe to grind. Unlike those random Twitter quotes dismissed so easily, these movie reviews come with the verification of solid and wide-ranging audience feedback. It's a very commendable system, and one which the boffins at Amazon have clearly taken a lot of time and energy to get right. Perhaps this really could be the dawn of 'reliable' consumer reviewing, a new way of sourcing criticism boasting the immediacy of social media, the back-up of democratic verification, and the efficiency of automatic editing.

It all sounds very impressive. So how does it work in practice?

Well, in the case of *Rise of the Planet of the Apes*, had you clicked on the product on 20 May 2013 (as I did), the algorithmic editor would have fore-grounded two reviews: 'the most helpful favourable review' and 'most helpful critical review', placed side-by-side with a 'Vs.' symbol in-between to indicate a healthy battle of opinions. In the left corner we have a glowing, but not wholly uncritical endorsement by 'Top 1000 Reviewer' Rob Payne. Headlined 'A fantastic action film, with brains', Payne's review has been approved by '52 of 55 people'. And no wonder; an intelligently written piece, it could happily hold its own against the published work of many professional critics, myself included. Following all the rules of good criticism, Payne describes the film accurately, identifies its key creative components correctly, places it within historical context, highlights its successes and failures, offers a personal response, and does all of the above in a manner both pithy and entertaining. Crucially, whilst broadly praising the movie (he calls it 'a thoughtful, intelligent and stirring piece [which] has a stab at doing what Tim Burton spectacularly failed to do in 2001'), he also argues that 'sadly the performances of the human contingent are less spectacular' than their CGI simian counterparts, a flaw he admits is 'partly due to the fact that they have increasingly little to do as the film progresses'. Whilst Payne's views don't entirely chime with my own (I disagree with him about the humans, particularly James Franco), I admire his writing and his arguments, as do other Amazon customers. 'What an excellent review,' comments N. Haynes, to which Morgan Pugh adds, 'Superb review which I agree with completely.' Clearly this is the Amazon review system at its best, with the site's automated systems helpfully prioritizing an intelligent assessment which has garnered widespread approval from other Amazon customers. In this particular case, to quote Lincoln Steffens: 'I have seen the future, and it works.'

As for the 'most helpful critical review', it's a two-star panning entitled 'Weak, poorly scripted' from another 'Top 1000' reviewer which, despite its contrary stance (no problem there, diversity of opinion is always a plus), boasts a 100 per cent approval rating, albeit with a mere '1 of 1' score. There are plenty of other critical reviews which have gained many more 'helpful' ratings from customers. But, without exception, these have also acquired a few negative votes (a common complaint is that negative Amazon reviews are automatically voted down by fans of any given product) and thus they have been pushed aside by the editing algorithms in favour of something which has only one 'helpful' vote, but *no* 'unhelpful' ratings at all.

Or has it?

In fact, that 'Weak, poorly scripted' review has received several negative votes from Amazon customers since it was first published in 2011, more than enough to push it to the very bottom of the 'most helpful' pile. So how come it now has a 100 per cent approval rating? And what happened to all those 'unhelpful' votes? The answer is, they've been 'vote washed', conjured away through a loophole in the automated system which has become popular amongst reviewers whose critiques do not find favour with other customers, but who nevertheless wish to exploit the cache of Amazon's increasingly valued reviewer endorsements.

How does it work? To explain, let us turn to the UK Amazon Customer Forum, where 'Janet (Cornwall)' asked on 4 September 2011, 'Can you explain to me about vote washing?' 'Sure,' comes the reply from a fellow forum contributor, 'it's just a term given to a way of getting rid of unfair negative votes. You simply delete and repost your review . . . For instance, I have a review of the film *Up* – I only gave it two stars so it always seems to pick up dozens of negative votes. So each time it reaches around the 30 mark, I'll delete and repost it. It's a bit like pressing reset.' The reply goes on to admit that 'some people frown on the practice' and 'claim it to be a cheating way to climb rankings' but nevertheless concludes that 'I would never stop. . . [and] the process takes seconds, so it's no effort'.

As of May 2013, this particular respondent (who posts under an Oracle-like pseudonym) had achieved both 'Top

100' and 'Vine Voice' status, the latter bringing 'free products that have been submitted to the programme by participating vendors'. According to their official explanation of the trademarked Vine programme, 'Amazon invites customers to become Vine Voices based on their reviewer rank, which is a reflection of the quality and helpfulness of their reviews as judged by other Amazon customers' – which (at the risk of stating the obvious) means that there is a tangible material benefit to be gained from increasing one's position in the reviewer ranking scheme. And if vote washing can increase your reviewer ranking, then why not use it? It makes clear market sense, about which this forum contributor is disarmingly unabashed.

Of course, there are plenty of other Amazon reviewers who feel very differently about this practice, which not only deletes the votes but also censors the comments of other customers. 'Washing votes by deleting and reposting is unethical,' wrote long-time Amazon forum contributor Peter Durward Harris on 18 April 2013, adding pointedly that 'reviewers who value their credibility do NOT delete and repost'. Meanwhile, 'Hummingbirder' states that 'I don't like vote washing . . . The fact is, those people are falsifying their ranking.' Clearly, those who have most to lose from such sharp practices are the vast majority of honest Amazon reviewers whose own votes, comments, reviews and rankings are negatively affected by others playing the numbers – a problem inherent in any system which attempts to edit through automation. Yet despite being widely discussed on the Amazon forums, 'washing' remains largely undetectable to the casual observer. Thus most customers reading that two-star assessment of *ROTPOTA* would have been entirely unaware that its 100 per cent approval rating had been achieved by repeatedly posting, deleting, and reposting the same review – often changing the headline, always expunging negative feedback. (Prior to its current incarnation, that review had variously drawn scores of '0 of 2'; '0 of 1'; '1 of 4'; '0 of 4'; '1 of 3'; '2 of 4', and so on . . .) I only found out about these multiple repostings after several years trying to figure out why this same customer's enraged reviews of my books (something I mention in the interest of full disclosure) were always top of the pile, outranking several other more coherently argued put-downs. I don't mind one-star reviews (I've had plenty, and will get more) but the habitual censoring of *other* Amazon customers' comments and votes (on one occasion, 119 'negs' were deleted at a single stroke) sets my free-speech alarm bells ringing. Perhaps by the time you read this, Amazon will have finally closed this evident glitch in their ever-evolving editorial system. But the more influential their customer reviews become, the more incentive there will be for the unscrupulous to try to uncover and exploit any areas of vulnerability. As soon as this chink in the virtual armour is fixed, they'll be looking for the next one, and the next one, and the next one . . .

The bottom line is that no matter how well constructed they may be, automated systems will always be gamed, and whilst a good (human) editor can spot someone artificially rigging their rankings in an instant, an algorithm cannot ultimately make a judgement call on the integrity of a review any more than those automated rail platform announcements can be 'sorry' that your train is going to be late. How can they? They're just computers. I once spent a mind-buggering ninety minutes at Southampton Airport Parkway listening to a machine telling an increasingly packed platform just how sorry it was that their various services had been disrupted, with the level of apologetic unhappiness automatically adjusted to the varying degrees of lateness. So, for trains that were up to twenty minutes late, the computer said 'I am sorry for the delay to your service', an impossibility since there was no 'I' to *be* sorry, only an automated voice-box. For trains delayed by more than twenty minutes, the computer said 'I am *very* sorry for the delay to your service', a surreal sentence suggesting that a machine incapable of being sorry in the first place was now even more not sorry than it wasn't ten minutes ago. And for trains over forty minutes late, the machine proclaimed itself to be 'very sorry for the *severe* delay to your service' – an improvement inasmuch as the adjectival addition was at least correct, even if the machine still wasn't 'sorry' in the slightest . . .

Apologies can be automated, but being 'sorry' (like being a good editor) requires the human touch, and it troubles me that no one has yet been strung up for programming the tannoy to spout such sci-fi balderdash. Although *Blade Runner*'s enigmatic android Roy Batty may have 'seen things you people wouldn't believe' whilst traversing the galaxy in search of 'more life, fucker!' (or 'father', depending on which version you're watching), the automated announcement service on Platform 2 of Southampton Airport Parkway has never seen anything more spectacular than the inside of an electronic railway timetable, and frankly there's little chance that Rutger Hauer will be signing on to play it any time soon. (Imagine that. 'I am sorry to announce that the 2.35 service from Weymouth has been delayed by tears in rain, and also attack ships on fire off the shoulder of Orion. But frankly, since I have watched C-Beams glitter in the dark by the Tannhauser Gate, it's hard for me to be sorry about the disruption caused to your puny human journeys. Time to die . . .')

The truth is that the independence of reviews which by their nature are predicated upon that most human commodity, 'personal opinion', cannot be policed by machines alone. Only commerce works that way. There is a crucial difference between an editor (the heart of good journalism) and an abacus (the soul of a marketing machine) and if science fiction movies have taught us anything it's that placing important decisions in the hands of robots always ends with someone getting shut out of the airlock without a helmet. All of which brings us back to the eighteenth-century chess-playing automaton, the so-called Mechanical Turk. Designed by Wolfgang von Kempelen to impress Empress Maria Theresa, the Turk proved itself able to outwit grand masters near and far, and even as a party piece to perform the so-called 'knight's tour', requiring the player to move their knight through an extremely complicated series of manoeuvres to land on each of the board's sixty-four squares – only *once*. Amongst those with whom the machine did battle on its tours of Europe and America were none other than Napoleon Bonaparte and Benjamin Franklin, increasing the machine's fame and notoriety to that of visiting royalty. For decades, the Turk puzzled and delighted spectators and players, all of whom were bewitched by the subtlety of its understanding, the quick-wittedness of its responses, the astonishing intuition of its game plans. How on earth could a mere machine think so fast that it could outwit a human?

The answer, of course, was that it couldn't; the Mechanical Turk – the wonder of the modern age – was nothing of the sort. It was an elaborate magician's box, hiding a living, breathing, all-too-human chess master inside, curled up at the mannequin's feet, playing the game from behind a veil of secrecy, like the Wizard of Oz behind his velvet curtain. It may have looked like a super computer, but in fact it was just people – an impressive array of chess players all playing Debbie Magee to an arcane Paul Daniels.

Despite its fairly simple deception, the Turk became a much-debated icon of popular culture. In 1940, the great writer and philosopher Walter Benjamin referred to the Turk in his 'Theses on the Philosophy of History', using its 'little hunchback' as an analogy for the process of historical materialism which can 'easily be a match for anyone if it enlists the services of theology, which today, as we know, is wizened, and has to keep out of sight'. In cinema, too, the ghost of the Turk is everywhere visible. The 1927 French silent film *Le Joueur d'Échecs/The Chess Player* features a character named 'Baron von Kempelen' who helps to save a handsome Polish man from occupying Russian forces by hiding him inside a chess-playing automaton. In a bizarre twist of fate, von Kempelen is ordered to St Petersburg to present the machine (replete with its Polish stowaway) to the Empress Catherine II, who promptly attempts to beat it by cheating. In an echo of a real-life event widely attributed to the Turk's encounter with Napoleon, the chess player moves his arm across the board to sweep the figures from the table in disgust at Catherine's illegal move – the symbolism would not have been lost on the movie-going audience.

Since then, the legend of the Turk has inspired everything from the French TV programme *Histoires extraordinaires: Le joueur d'échecs de Maelzel*, adapted from Poe in 1981 by Buñuel's son Juan Luis, to episodes of *Doctor Who* (Steven Moffat's 'The Girl in the Fireplace' drew on it as an inspiration for the eerie clockwork mannequins; and there's a Cyberman version of the Turk, complete with Warwick Davies inside, in 'Nightmare in Silver', by Neil Gaiman). Time and again, film-makers have returned to the spectre of the mysterious automaton which was tied up with the invention of cinema itself. Stanley Kubrick's interest in the Turk fed into his ongoing obsession with *A.I. Artificial Intelligence* – his unfilmed movie about a robot child, abandoned after he spent several years attempting and failing to build a real robot boy to star in the movie. The project would ultimately be brought to the screen by Steven Spielberg who, in an echo of von Kempelen's original deception, concluded that it was easier just to use a 'real boy' whose humanity could be hidden behind the smoke and mirrors of special effects – and brilliant acting. The scene in which the body of David, played by an unblinking Haley Joel Osment, is dismantled by doctors while his head carries on talking is pure magical theatre, drawing on traditions dating back to von Kempelen's cabinet: Philip Thicknesse, in his book *The Speaking Figure and the Automaton Chess Player: Exposed and Detected*, described it as 'a complicated piece of clock-work' hiding a child 'to misguide and delude the observers'. (Coincidentally, Kubrick's other passion was an unrealized biopic of Napoleon, which may well have included the ruler's legendary encounter with the Turk.) Similarly, in Martin Scorsese's semi-historical *Hugo*, the real-life figure of Georges Méliès, the father of cinema, is tracked down by a boy who has spent his young life attempting to un-lock the key to his past by reassembling an automaton, a clear distant cousin of the Turk. Méliès was fascinated by automata, and Scorsese draws parallels between his work with clockwork toys and the invention and perfection of the projector, a machine capable of conjuring spectral ap-paritions from thin air, mimicking the appearance of life, even resurrecting the dead from the grave. For Scorsese, the mechanics of projection are the logical extension of the automata craze, making the mysterious Turk the great grandfather of cinema itself.

Today, the ghost of the Mechanical Turk has moved into the ether. In 2005 a crowd-sourcing website known as 'MTurk' was established to allow computer programmers ('Requesters') to farm out 'Human Intelligence Tasks' too complex or expensive for machines. The tasks themselves were not especially taxing, but they required specifically human skills which 'Providers', or 'Turkers', could per-form easily, often for a pittance. Playfully characterized by its creator as pioneering 'artificial artificial intelligence', MTurk is described on its Wikipedia page as providing a web service that 'allows humans to help the machines of today perform tasks for which they are not suited' – an entry sounding for all the world as if it were written by a robot with a tin ear for the strangely threatening undertones of its sentence construction.

The MTurk website was a groundbreaking idea; unsurprisingly, it proved extremely popular. By January 2011, there were a reported 500,000 'Turkers' performing tasks in over 190 countries, an international workforce fired into action by the miracle of the worldwide web. And inevitably, in a world in which automated 'likes' have become the currency of the future, it wasn't long before the workers started being targeted by those wishing to increase their online approval ratings in a range of Internet forums. In 2010 Panos Ipeirotis and his students at the Stern School of Business in New York analysed the activities of MTurk and concluded that 40.92 per cent of its tasks were spam, including generating 'a fake rating, vote, review, comment, or "like" on Facebook, YouTube, DIGG, etc.' 'In other words,' wrote Professor Rita Gunther McGrath of Columbia Business School in New York, 'what the workers are being asked to do is "fake" social interactions, social media, or interest in whatever the poster is flogging . . . And the insidious thing is that these are real people doing these things, so a lot of the automated spam preventers . . . won't pick up the spammy nature of their activities. Very creative, if a tad creepy'.

Of course, what's most creepy for a die-hard technophobe like me is a vision of a future in which what was once an expression of human opinion (to 'like' or 'dislike' something – the real function of a critic) has become nothing more than an automated action, a mechanical process in which people have no more creative role to play than the human batteries which fuelled *The Matrix*. Having learned so many important lessons from editors over the years, I cannot help but worry about anything which attempts to replace their crucial creative input with algorithmic equations, which claims to be able make value judgements on the basis on gameable binary codes, or which blurs the boundaries between the human and the robotic – the creative and the mechanical. Like its eighteenth-century namesake, the Internet version of the MTurk performs a magic trick in which machines imitate people and people imitate machines, each pretending to be the other ('artificial artificial intelligence') to baffling and bemusing effect. For some this is the shape of things to come, the future of global interaction; commercial, recreational, critical. And of course, in the increasingly monopolistic world of the Internet, MTurk is owned (like IMDb, GoodReads, Love-Film, Audible.com et al.) by Amazon.

So, how do you 'like' that? Did you find it helpful or unhelpful? Would you recommend it to other customers?

Click here to vote.

On 5 July 1854, the original Mechanical Turk was destroyed in a fire at the Chinese Museum of Charles Willson Peale in Philadelphia. It had been donated by Poe's personal physician Dr John Kearsley Mitchell, who acquired and restored it after the death of Maelzel. Although there was no operator hidden within its secret recesses, Mitchell swore that he heard 'struggling through

the flames . . . the last words of our departed friend, the
sternly whispered, oft-repeated syllables . . .
 "*Échec! Échec!!*" '
Checkmate.

CHAPTER SEVEN

ASK THE AUDIENCE

I got my heart broken quite a lot as a child, but never by girls. Only by movies.

Two films stand out as being of defining importance in my adolescence, both shot through with a profound sense of melancholia that still haunts me to this day. The first was the science-fiction film *Silent Running*: a touchstone of my earliest pop-culture obsessions, it tells of a solitary astronaut cast adrift in the vast abyss of the galaxy with only a couple of walking dustbins for company. There's a room in our house with wooden beams upon which stand incredibly detailed cardboard models of those silent 'drones', a gift from a friend who understood just how much this oft-ridiculed genre movie meant to me. The film's harshest critics accuse it of making no sense ('How could the Earth survive without any trees? Where would the oxygen come from? How could a botanist forget about photosynthesis? How the hell can you take any of this seriously?'), but for me its power has always been emotional rather than rational. It's not a film about the destruction of the Earth's forests (although it does somewhat foolishly touch upon that subject); it's a film about separation and loss, about dreams and disappointment – about loneliness. At the end, when Bruce Dern's broken astronaut Freeman Lowell leaves a single drone to tend his extraterrestrial garden alone in space for ever, I still find myself reduced to tears, engulfed in paroxysms of weeping more befitting a child than a fifty-something old fart.

After I first saw *Silent Running*, at the age of eleven, I came home and dreamed lucid visions of the film's final moments, wakening from sleep, calling out the poor lost drone's name ('Dewey! Dewey!'), my cheeks and pillow wet with tears. There was no question it had upset me, but at the first possible opportunity I went straight back to the cinema to see it again, desperate to rekindle the emotional connection. Very quickly, *Silent Running* became my favourite film ever, and I started to collect any memorabilia (magazines, posters, stills, models, soundtrack albums) relating to its tender magic. When it finally came out on video in the mid-eighties, I was first down to the store to grab a copy – astonished finally to own the strange object of desire I had been duly stalking through rep cinemas for over a decade, travelling stupid distances at anti-social hours to catch a screening whenever *Silent Running* showed up on the late-night picture-show circuit. Today I have umpteen copies, on VHS, Laserdisc, DVD and Blu-ray – the latter in a collectible 'steel tin' edition I haven't ever opened because I want to keep a pristine copy just in case nuclear war breaks out or the world gets hit by an asteroid and the sole preservation of this modern masterpiece is left to its biggest fan . . .

My obsession with *Silent Running* is well documented, and in terms of repeat viewings it comes a close second behind *The Exorcist* as the most watched movie of my admittedly peculiar life. This is to be expected. What's more surprising is that the other film from this period which had an equally earth-shattering effect is a movie I had watched only once – that is until December 2012.

In *It's Only a Movie*, I wrote about seeing the early seventies teen romance *Jeremy* as a supporting feature to the boring Charles Bronson Western *Breakheart Pass*, and described the experience as being like getting my heart broken for the very first time. Having never had a girlfriend (nor would I for several years), the effect of watching the titular gawky teenager fall for, win, and then suddenly lose the girl of his dreams – all in the space of ninety minutes – was simply overwhelming. Honestly, words fail me – something I realize is pathetic coming from someone whose chosen profession is to talk about movies. But just as surgeons aren't allowed to operate upon loved ones, or policeman aren't allowed to investigate cases with which they have a personal connection, so *Jeremy* frankly falls outside the remit of my supposed critical faculties. Try as I might, I just can't be dispassionate about that movie. All I can think of is the all-too-final sequence where Jeremy says goodbye to Susan in the terminal of a godforsaken airport and then wanders out, stunned, into the miserable New York daylight, his anorak hunched around his shoulders, his glasses smudged with salt water, his face a long-lens picture of despair. After seeing *Jeremy* as a kid, I walked home from the Hendon Odeon to my parents' house in Finchley, three or four miles of cold lonely pavement, traversing the vast

North Circular Road and crossing Dollis Brook, downhill to the four-lane intersection on my way to St Mary's Avenue and Cyprus Gardens. As I got to the Brook, bewildered and disorientated, I decided to turn left, following the footpath along the river to the playground where we used to ride our bikes; where my brother Jonny got his hand caught under the roundabout and my sister Annie hit some passing bully with a stick; where Paolo from next door had once attempted the superhuman feat of jumping the river on his Chopper, with spectacular – if unsuccessful – results. All this now seemed very distant, like the implanted memories Rachael comes to realize are not her own as the awful truth of her origin is callously revealed in *Blade Runner*. The world had been irrevocably changed, knocked clean off its axis by the awful power of love, left spinning aimlessly in the empty void of space, like Dewey with his watering can, looking up at the stars while Joan Baez's voice warbled beautifully on the soundtrack – alone again, naturally.

Even as a child I was a pretentious pain in the arse.

After its brief B-feature engagement at the Hendon Odeon, *Jeremy* simply disappeared from my radar, and though I would search for it from time to time in the rep cinema listings, it never showed up. Why would it? No one else had even heard of it. With the advent of video I had an inkling that *Jeremy* would resurface, particularly since it seemed for a while that every seventies release, no matter how neglected (whether deservedly or not), was now getting a second lease of life on Betamax and VHS, distributors and dealers clearly desperate for product, with little thought of quality control. But somehow it never broke cover, never showed up on videotape, nor later on laserdisc or DVD – at least not here in the UK. When I wrote so passionately about *Jeremy* in *It's Only a Movie*, I was writing entirely from a very distant memory. Yet I felt as though I knew the film as intimately and precisely as any of the die-hard favourites I'd viewed and re-viewed so obsessively, over and over, time and time again. I could remember scenes, characters, dialogue, textures, camera angles, even edits as clearly as if they were being played out before me on a Moviola. And although I have a habit of completely misremembering movies, I think I knew that the version of *Jeremy* still playing in my head after all these years, all these decades, was pretty close to the original. The film had burned itself onto my brain, a perfectly exposed memory ready to be processed and re-projected at will. In that cinema, on a Sunday afternoon in 1975, I had become a movie camera and *Jeremy* was the light pouring into me.

Then, in the winter of 2012, I finally came face to face with my first true love again. The reunion came about thanks to the efforts of the Cinemagic Festival in Belfast, a terrific event with a focus on young viewers at which I'd been presenting movies on an annual basis for several years. Starting with an introductory talk and audience Q&A hosted by the vivacious Brian Henry Martin, we'd screened *Mary Poppins*, *Local Hero*, *The Buddy Holly Story*, *Dougal and the Blue Cat* and, of course, *Silent Running*, all films I hold dear, and all appropriate for a 'family' audience – whatever that actually means. As the deadline for choosing 2012's selection approached, I mentioned in passing that there was a film from the early seventies that must have been certificated as suitable for children (because they'd let me in to watch it unaccompanied at the age of 12), a film I remembered being exceptionally powerful in a bittersweet way, but which never seemed to get screened anywhere. I gave them the title and thought no more about it.

A couple of weeks later, the organizers of Cinemagic called to tell me they had tracked down not one but two 35mm prints of *Jeremy*: one looked like it had certainly done the rounds, the other was pristine. Exactly where this new print had come from was something of a mystery; the technician who examined it said he was pretty sure it had never been through a projector, so perfect was its condition. Whatever the answer, we now had the opportunity to show one of my favourite movies on celluloid – a film I had only seen once before, but had dreamed about a thousand times or more.

I immediately started to feel nauseous. As the weekend of the festival approached, my symptoms grew worse. Aware that I had seen *Jeremy* at a very impressionable age, and conscious that it could no more live up to my idealized memory than Daisy's perishable breath could ever match Gatsby's 'unutterable vision', I started to panic about what was going to happen when the film finally unspooled itself in front of a packed and expectant audience. Would it be any good? Would it be horribly inappropriate? Would people walk out in laughter, disappointment, or worse? Would I get out of this alive? I became deranged with anxiety, wracked with self-doubt, consumed by a desire to pull the plug on the whole damned show and just screen *Mary Poppins* again instead. I began to fantasize about ways to get out of this horrible mess, imagining phone calls from the projection box at the Queen's Film Theatre to tell me that 'unfortunately when we opened the cans the entire film spontaneously combusted – you know how it is with old movie prints'.

When the day of the event finally arrived, my pre-screening talk was less of an introduction and more of a pre-emptive apology, an attempt to explain the strange set of circumstances responsible for luring this audience in to see a film that might turn out to be utterly terrible – an appalling mistake on my part for which I craved their indulgence and forgiveness. *Jeremy*, I explained, had looked really good to me forty years ago – but then, so had The Rubettes, Alvin Stardust, and *John Craven's Newsround*. I made some feeble plea for the magic of celluloid, hoping that even if the film itself stank, nostalgia for the format would carry the day. Then I scuttled up the aisle to the very back row of the cinema and hunkered down into the aisle seat nearest the exit, ready to make a run for the door when the crowd turned nasty. All the time, all I could think was – 'you've remembered it wrong, you've remembered it wrong, you've remembered it wrong . . .'

But I hadn't.

As the lights went down and the curtains went back, the United Artists logo appeared on the screen and the film's plaintive 'Blue Balloon' theme came crackling out of the speakers ('I have a blue balloon, a happy tune, dreams enough to last me all through the afternoon . . .') and suddenly I was right back there at the Hendon Odeon in 1975, cast like a wandering spirit into the body of my weedy, lonely twelve-year-old self, staring up at the silver screen, ready to be amazed, unprepared to be devastated. Everything was just as I remembered it; the close-up shots of the chess pieces, the horse-racing posters on the wall of Jeremy's room, the zoom-lens views from out of his bedroom window, the tuning keys on the head of the cello – all of it came flooding back in a Proustian rush that ranks amongst my most profound cinematic experiences. It was overwhelming – so much so that I briefly stopped breathing. At Jeremy's first meeting with Susan, the girl who becomes his first love, I found myself mouthing whole swathes of his stumbling dialogue; stored up somewhere in my subconscious it came pouring out like the words to a song I'd forgotten I knew. Their courtship was electrifying, their gentleness extraordinary, their intimacy utterly believable. And then, just as everything fell beautifully into place, so it all had to end, as I knew it must. Susan's father announced they were moving to Detroit ('Don't you understand, Jeremy, I'm not coming back . . .') and a few cruel moments later we were at the airport, love tearing us apart, again.

'Promise you won't forget me . . .'

'I won't. I promise.'

It's a promise I kept for forty years.

As the all-too-abrupt end credits rolled (this was from the golden age when credits lasted minutes rather than hours), the house lights went up and the audience (almost all of whom had stayed) started to make their way up the aisle towards the exit. Most were quiet, many seemed moved, some were wiping away a tear.

I was inconsolable. I honestly don't think I've wept that much in years, and it was all I could do to bury my face in my hands to hide the extent of my sobbing. I took off my glasses and went through a pantomime of cleaning the lenses, rubbing my eyes and squinting as if to say, 'Hey,

I'm fine but these varifocals are really giving me eyestrain.' For a fleeting moment I wished the movie had been in 3D because, as we all learned from *Toy Story 3*, those stupid dark glasses do at least give you the opportunity to cry in private. As it was, I just had to sit there like a blubbering fool as, one after another, members of the audience attempted to engage me in conversation, to reassure me that they had liked the movie and that I had no need to apologize for it after all. Their reaction was lovely and kind, but at that moment I wanted to be anywhere but there – I wanted to be alone with my grief, walking the lonely road from Hendon to Finchley, with no one to whom to talk or explain myself. Just like Jeremy.

Nor was the moment passing. It followed me out into the foyer, where several of Cinemagic's wonderfully cine-literate patrons gathered round for photos and a chat, all with something intelligent and encouraging to say – the perfect audience for a film festival. I have no idea exactly what happened in the foyer; all I know is that a bunch of people in Belfast now have photographs on their iPhones of an ageing film critic pathetically smiling through the tears, struggling to maintain a semblance of dignity, and failing spectacularly in this endeavour.

The tears continued in the cab and all the way back to the home of my great friends Paul and Janice, with whom my family was staying, and who met me at the front door with food, wine and good cheer. They continued through the night, haunting my broken sleep, resurfacing again in the beautiful light of a Belfast morning. They followed me on the plane back to London, on the train to Southampton, clinging to me as tenaciously as they had when I saw the movie all those decades ago. I know it sounds like I'm exaggerating but I swear to you by all things unholy, I spent the best part of a week in some form of melancholic rapture, utterly unable to wrest myself from the movie's eerie spell, as unable to forget its final stanza as any heartbroken kid attempting to get over the pain of being chucked for the very first time.

It was awful. And at the same time wonderful.

But still bloody awful because, as with *Silent Running*, the movie didn't end the way I wanted it to. In both cases, I had made a huge connection with, and emotional investment in, the central characters and their predicament. Stylistically the films couldn't have been more different, but I believed in them equally, gave myself over to them wholeheartedly, and wished with all my being that both had ended better; that Lowell had gone on for ever as an interstellar gardener, and that Jeremy had realized Detroit wasn't so far away after all and he could spend a year or so seeing Susan on weekends before they were old enough to leave home, get married, and live happily ever after . . .

That latter scenario is one I turned over in my mind obsessively, desperately trying to find a way to give *Jeremy* the happy ending for which I longed. I'd imagine a coda where Jeremy returned to his parents' apartment, the phone would ring and it would be Susan saying the flight took no time at all and he should come and visit her . . . next Saturday! Then the film would end with him getting off the plane in Detroit, rushing into her arms as she waited at the security gate, shouting, 'I love you, I love you, I love you . . .'

It's a rubbish ending, I know, but that's what I wanted

– something, *anything*, other than the terrible finality of their on-screen parting.

So here's my question: what if I had been part of some focus group to whom either *Silent Running* or *Jeremy* had been screened in advance of their respective releases in order to gauge the movie's potential success with its target audience? What if I had been one of the people on whom the producers decided to road-test their product to see if there was anything they really wanted to change? What if the film-makers had asked for my opinion?

Such groups are part of the day-to-day furniture of the modern movie business, and the influence they can have on the finished product is enormous. By the time any of us (critics and paying punters alike) get to watch a movie – any movie – the chances are it will have been intensively tested against a series of very specific focus groups made up entirely of what the studios like to call 'real people'. Unlike critics, these 'real people' will be given the chance not only to evaluate but also to reshape the movies they watch. Preview audiences have the ability to take control of a story, redirecting its focus, its mood, its tenor, even its outcome. While the myth of directorial final cut continues to pervade perceptions of mainstream film-making, the sobering truth is that the most powerful people in a town like Hollywood are often the preview screening audiences whose main – nay sole – qualification for the job is that they match a certain age and gender demographic and have no professional interest whatsoever in movie making, reviewing, or distribution. These are people for whom the lack of qualifications is in itself a qualification. And they wield the ability to bend a movie right out of shape and ensure that it makes no sense whatsoever – as long as it does what they want it to do. Or what they *think* they want it to do.

Back in 1987, director Adrian Lyne was completing work on his zeitgeisty erotic thriller *Fatal Attraction*. Michael Douglas plays family man Dan Gallagher, who has a fling with Glenn Close's seemingly independent businesswoman Alex Forrest, and is then shocked when she turns into the phrase-coining 'bunny boiler' who sets about destroying his cosy home as vengeance for being rebuffed. Inspired by *Diversion*, a little-seen short film by writer-director James Dearden (almost all copies of which were purchased and destroyed by Paramount to protect their own product), *Fatal Attraction* started life as a screenplay entitled *Affairs of the Heart* which contained a killer sting in its tail based upon a recurrent *Madama Butterfly* motif buried deep within the structure of the movie's increasingly operatic narrative. Having been rejected by Dan once too often, the increasingly unhinged *femme fatale* succumbs to the tragedy of Puccini's opera, the subject of a deep and meaningful conversation with her putative paramour, for which she has bought a miserably unused pair of tickets. Alone in her apartment, Alex commits suicide by slicing her neck with a carving knife – the same knife Dan had wrestled from her grip earlier in the drama, and which now *carries his fingerprints*! In the original version of the script, the cops arrive and arrest Dan for Alex's murder, a terrifically twisted and completely coherent conclusion in which, in the words of Lyne, 'she got him from beyond the grave'. Brilliant! But grim – perhaps too grim for the mainstream. So, in an attempt to second-guess the responses of the preview audiences through whom the movie would have to pass before making it into theatres, Lyne and Dearden came up with a slightly softened finale. In this version, Dan is still arrested, but his long-suffering wife Beth (played by Anne Archer) then conveniently finds a cassette tape recorded *before* Alex's death in which she says she's so crazy she's going to kill herself, and Beth realizes immediately that this crucial piece of evidence will prove her husband's innocence and allow their nuclear family to live happily ever after.

This was the ending filmed by Lyne and co., and duly presented by Paramount to preview audiences made up of 'real people' (rather than snot-nosed film critics), who were then asked to tell the film-makers exactly what they thought.

Here's what they thought: they loved the movie, but they hated the ending.

I know what you're thinking, you hated the ending too, right? All that nonsense about cassette tapes and recorded confessions and cosy happy endings, blah blah blah. And you're right; it's nonsense. But that's not what the preview audiences hated. No-sirree, Bob. They had no problem at all with some half-baked narrative contrivance allowing the good wife to triumph over the wicked slut and reclaim her rightful place in the marital bed. On the contrary, they wanted Alex to get her comeuppance. They wanted her to rot in hell while Dan and Beth rode off into the sunset. What pissed the preview audiences off so much was the fact that Alex the home wrecker had been allowed to commit suicide, to take her own life rather than having it forcefully taken from her. What they famously wanted was for Beth to 'Kill the bitch!'

'Kill the bitch!' That inchoate shriek of rage would inspire a thousand magazine articles (and a couple of books) about an anti-feminist backlash after studio executives bankrolled extensive reshoots to give the audience exactly what they wanted. Under the guise of industry-standard 'pick-up' shots (brief inconsequential inserts used to clarify story and bridge editing gaps), the film-makers and all three stars reconvened for two additional weeks of production and the entire third act of *Fatal Attraction* was rewritten, reshot, and then re-presented to preview audiences in the hope that the film would now duly fire their money-spinning blood-lust. And it did. Like Caesar judging the crowd's mood before giving the thumbs down and sentencing a combatant to be torn apart for the entertainment of a baying mob, *Fatal Attraction* had its ending reconfigured in order to please people too whipped-up to know better and too important to be ignored. No matter that the movie now made no sense whatsoever – that its underpinning operatic motif was nothing more than a bit of inconsequential window dressing. At least it would now make money. Bags of it.

By the time *Fatal Attraction* opened in America in September 1987, Alex had gone from being a suicidal Madame Butterfly to a homicidal Lady Vengeance, a knife-wielding psycho whose grief had turned to rage and hate, and who needed to be dealt with accordingly. Whilst Dearden and Lyne's original ending presented Alex as a tragic figure worthy of at least a degree of sympathy, the revised ending stripped her of any power of self-determination, turning her into a homicidal nut-job who breaks into the Gallagher family home where she is battered, drowned, and then finally shot to death by Anne Archer's gun-wielding soccer mom.

The crowd went bananas.

As did the box office.

Watching the grosses roll in as a movie which had cost a mere $14 million went on to take an estimated $320 million worldwide, the makers of *Fatal Attraction* knew that they had hit a lucrative nerve for which they had the preview audiences to thank. With its revised ending the movie became the prototype 'water-cooler' hit – so called because of the heated discussions it provoked in the workplace. And as with all genuine blockbusters, *Fatal Attraction* broke out of the entertainment ghetto to become a news story; reports of its controversial success provided publicity and promotion far in excess of what could be paid for. For months, you couldn't open a newspaper, browse a magazine, or watch a TV show without coming across some talking-head heatedly discussing the underlying morality/misogyny of a movie single-handedly credited with putting married men off extra-marital affairs for fear that their homes, jobs, lives and pets would be threatened by a shrieking woman scorned for whom hell hath no comparable fury.

Would *Fatal Attraction* have become such a phenomenon were it not for that radically altered ending? Would audiences have embraced it quite so wholeheartedly had Alex been allowed to take her own life? Would it in fact have been better if left unaltered? On an artistic level the answer to that last question is simple – of course it would! For all its flaws, the original cut of *Fatal Attraction* was at least coherent, following the arc of its narrative threads through to an inevitable (if ultimately compromised) conclusion. In its revised form the movie appears to have been put together by a madman with no sense of storytelling and the memory span of a goldfish. How come we linger on the sight of Michael Douglas getting his fingerprints all over that carving knife if there's never going to be any doubt about whether or not he used it later on? Why is Glenn Close's character clearly depicted as self-harming if she's only going to wind up attempting to kill somebody else? And what's with all the over-egged *Madama Butterfly* stuff in the body of the movie that miraculously evaporates into thin air in the final act?

Narratively speaking, who's driving the boat?

Years later, both Adrian Lyne and James Dearden could be found asking those exact questions, fretting about the fact that, despite its huge financial success, *Fatal Attraction* hadn't quite worked out the way either of them intended. While they accepted (rightly? wrongly?) that the reshoots had boosted the film's box-office, both personally admitted to me that they preferred the original ending for all the reasons outlined above. And despite having reaped the benefits of preview screenings on *Fatal Attraction*, both had also suffered the tyranny of having others tell them how to make their movies better in a manner that was anything but helpful. For Lyne, the crunch had come with *9½ Weeks*. It began life as a dark and somewhat dangerous erotic thriller about a sado-masochistic relationship that drives its heroine to attempted suicide (a familiar theme), but wound up as a soft-core romp in which Mickey Rourke throws the contents of his fridge at Kim Basinger after studio executives and preview audiences decided they didn't like the 'dark' stuff. For Dearden, his remake of the 1956 thriller *A Kiss Before Dying* (from Ira Levin's novel) suffered the death of a thousand cuts after test-screeners demanded a 'more dramatic' finale, likened heavy-heartedly by Dearden to the audience reworking of *Fatal Attraction* – the main difference being that, even after complying with the audience's demands, *A Kiss Before Dying* still flopped.

As for *Fatal Attraction*, a clue to the potential success it may have enjoyed in its superior version is offered by the reaction of Japanese audiences, who got to see the original cut after domestic distributors decided they were just too smart for the dumbed-down American bodge. Responding to demands from their overseas bookers, Paramount agreed to allow the 'suicide' version to play in Japanese theatres where it promptly became a whopping box-office hit. This was potentially embarrassing for the US studio as they had spent the preceding months vehemently denying that the version of *Fatal Attraction* playing in American cinemas had been substantially messed around with to appease test-screening audiences – a practice still then shrouded in a degree of secrecy and shame. In a hilarious example of studio double-speak, they explained to *Variety* that while the American version was still the 'proper' version of *Fatal Attraction* (director's cut, intact artistic vision, blah blah blah), the *Madama Butterfly* cut was somehow better suited to the cultural quirks of Eastern viewers with their different 'expectations' of narrative in general and cinema in particular. In other words, they were still right to change the ending of the American version because the only people who'd get the 'original' version were funny foreigners who are a bit weird like that (which is completely different to saying that they had to dumb the movie down for American audiences, but not for their smarter Japanese counterparts).

There is, of course, nothing new about preview screenings prompting changes to movies. As early as the 1920s, Harold Lloyd was relying heavily on test screenings to shape his films, recording the level of audience reaction to individual gags in an attempt to maximize the comic potential of each scene. His 1922 movie *Grandma's Boy* was reworked by Lloyd and director Fred Newmeyer to include additional jokes after test screenings recorded negative reactions to the more serious tone of the original cut; the result was both a critical and commercial hit, now regarded as one of Lloyd's finest films.

In 1925, Buster Keaton noticed that test-screening audiences weren't laughing as much as he'd expected at a scene in *Seven Chances* where his character James Shannon, who is about to inherit a fortune, runs away from an army of would-be brides responding to a newspaper ad. The scene was falling rather flat, but Keaton noted that as James made his escape down a hill, the sight of a few rocks dislodged by his feet apparently chasing the hapless hero provoked unexpected chuckles. As a result, the director/ star went back and reshot the sequence to include a virtual avalanche of papier-mâché rocks, ranging from tiny stones to giant boulders, all of which he attempts to dodge to rollicking effect. In its revised format, that scene has become the celebrated highlight of *Seven Chances* – for proof, just put 'Seven Chances' into the YouTube search engine and see what comes up.

As film distribution expanded and movie-making became more expensive, studios became increasingly interested in using test screenings to assess audience reaction prior to release, under the pretext of efficiently planning their release strategies. When George Gallup's Audience Research Inc. (ARI) were enlisted to road-test new releases, they took a lead from Lloyd's 'Laugh-o-meter' with the invention of their own 'televoting' system; they gave every test audience member a small control panel with a knob which could be turned to register their changing reactions to a movie, ranging from 'Very Dull' or 'Dull' to 'Like'; and 'Like Very Much' – options considered to have 'covered all the bases'. (Just try assessing a Béla Tarr movie using only those categories and see how far you get.)

Although these tests were nominally employed to help studios decide how much money to spend on printing and promoting, inevitably they led to changes being made to the movies themselves. Something of a blunt instrument, preview screenings started to attract a bad reputation amongst many film-makers, who saw them as a tool with which the studios could bludgeon directors into dumbing down their movies.

In 1942, Orson Welles became the industry's most celebrated victim of negative preview screenings after RKO showed an early cut of *The Magnificent Ambersons* to a test audience in Pomona with catastrophic results. According to popularly received (and now hotly contested) wisdom, the movie got a resounding raspberry from the audience:

it was too long, too boring, and (especially) too damned depressing. 'I have never been present in a theatre where the audience acted in such a manner,' RKO head George Schaefer famously wrote to Welles after the Pomona preview. 'They laughed at the wrong places, talked at the picture . . . I don't have to tell you how I suffered, especially in the realization that we have over a million dollars tied up.' Concluding that Welles needed to appease 'the younger element' and make films 'for the box office' from now on, Schaefer decreed that *Ambersons* should gain a new ending and lose a substantial amount of its running time. (Legend has it that Bryan Foy suggested they should 'just throw all the footage up in the air and grab everything but forty minutes'.) With Welles in Brazil, knee-deep in the unfinished *It's All True*, the job of re-cutting *The Magnificent Ambersons* fell to a young Robert Wise, under the command of manager Jack Moss. Welles had a direct phone line installed from his hotel room in Rio to an office in Hollywood, but it soon became clear that RKO were fed up with Orson's input: the phone was left to ring unanswered, telegrams found their way straight into the bin. Meanwhile, Wise set about replacing Welles's closing tour of the decaying Ambersons' mansion, and lopping out whole sequences from the body of the film – causing Welles to complain that the re-cut movie looked like it had been 'edited by a lawnmower'. The excised footage was promptly destroyed by RKO, who insisted that they needed the storage space, although the fact that Welles wouldn't be able to reverse any of their changes was clearly an added bonus. Outraged, composer Bernard Herrmann disowned the movie, as did

Welles who blamed Wise (and, for a while, leading man Joseph Cotton) for co-operating with RKO in the destruction of a film he believed could have been 'better than *Kane*' before the preview audiences got hold of it.

In the end, the re-cutting process turned out to be a ruinous waste of time and money – despite all the dicking around, *Ambersons* bombed in theatres, losing RKO over half a million dollars (a huge sum at that time) and shuffling its wounded way across America as the lowly second feature on a double bill with *Mexican Spitfire Sees a Ghost* (nope, me neither), the latest instalment of an ongoing comedy franchise alongside which Welles's movie must have looked particularly unloved.

One of the reasons now regularly given for the less-than-ecstatic test screening responses was the Pomona preview's proximity to the Japanese bombing of Pearl Harbor. Convulsed with grief and now steeling themselves for war, the only people to see *Ambersons* the way Welles had intended proved to be in entirely the wrong frame of mind for its complex tone and downbeat desolate conclusion. (Nor did it help that the film was preview screened on a double bill with a Dorothy Lamour musical at the express instruction of RKO executive Charles Koerner, who had already seen Welles's film, had decided it was too long, and was looking for a loop-hole to override Welles's contractual right to edit the picture to his taste – a loop-hole provided by the 'negative' results.) We observed in Chapter Four the first-response problems that can befall even those professionally battle-hardened critics who have taught themselves to take into account their mood on any given day and perhaps to adjust their reviews accordingly. Yet preview audiences are encouraged to do the opposite – to let the studio know how they feel about a movie right now without any time for reflection or reassessment, or consideration of the specific circumstances of the screening. In his excellent book *Despite the System: Orson Welles versus The Hollywood Studios*, Clinton Heylin notes that 'the preview system itself was based upon a very skewed form of faith in the innate wisdom of the paying public' and notes that an audience enjoying Dorothy Lamour was probably not best placed to assess and evaluate *The Magnificent Ambersons*, regardless of the specific historical context. He goes on to quote David Selznick writing about the possibility of previewing Hitchcock's *Rebecca* in December 1939, and concluding that 'I don't want to take the chance of finally editing it according to the instructions of an audience that has come to see a Marx Brothers picture'. (The ending of the novel had of course already been altered for the screen to appease the censors.) Selznick is clear that the problem is not a Marx Brothers audience per se, but the circumstances under which that audience would then be asked to judge *Rebecca*. OK, so you've just finished laughing your head off – now look at this 'very tricky picture, with very peculiar moods and a very strange sort of construction and playing' and tell us how we can make it better.

Right here.

Right NOW.

Go!

The same was true of *The Magnificent Ambersons*, a film requiring time for reflection and re-evaluation, which even the most devout cineaste would have difficulty digesting and appreciating at a single sitting. Even with the right audience, the very fact of demanding an immediate response to provocative material is fraught with peril and misconception. The people who inadvertently helped RKO turn *Ambersons* into irreparably damaged goods weren't stupid – rather, they were shocked and depressed by recent life-changing news stories, wrong-footed by the double-bill pairing with an upbeat musical, and given no time to consider or process their reactions to a movie accepted by its greatest fans to be 'challenging', even in its bowdlerized form. Instead, they were effectively harangued into being 'first but wrong', told to make reductively immediate yes/no judgements by a studio which had long lost faith in its star director and was looking for an excuse to get busy with the scissors. Blaming the test audiences for getting it wrong is a classic case of shooting the messenger – they did what they were asked to do under very specific (and very biased) circumstances. In fact, in his book *Movie Wars*, Jonathan Rosenbaum argues that the Pomona 'comment cards' were far from universally negative, and that 'declaring the preview "a disaster" on the basis of those cards is a highly subjective matter'. Nevertheless, the negative responses soon became the only responses and Welles's film was found to be wanting and in need of 'correction' – in the same way that the twins from *The Shining* were 'corrected' with the aid of an axe . . .

Often (if not always) audiences don't actually know what they want, or what's 'good' for them, or what would be 'better' if they were allowed to change it. Why should they? It is not the job of an audience to tell the film-maker how to make their movie – it's their job to watch. And before you get all uppity about me, the poncey critic, looking down on lowly audiences, let me state again that being a film critic is nothing more or less than being a devoted member of the audience, someone who watches movies for a living. After all you've read in this book, you may well think it's not much of a profession, and if that's your opinion, then fair dos. But whether you like it or not, that's what film criticism is, and no matter how one may care to dress it up, it all comes down to watching (rather than making) movies and then expressing – eloquently or otherwise – what you think about them. Anyone who's ever taken part in an organized test screening of an as-yet unlocked film has been, for the duration of that exercise, a film critic. The key difference is that preview-screening audiences are asked to do the job under the most egregious circumstances – immediate, unprepared, ill-considered, absolute – and with the power to change the movies, to tell the film-makers what they are doing right and wrong, and to get them to tailor their vision to the audience's perceived demands.

It's particularly ironic that while everyone is merrily blathering on about the need to break the stranglehold of professional critics and shift power towards the hallowed chalice of the audience response, it is in fact the latter which has always had the upper hand in Hollywood. Contrary to all popularly accepted notions of hierarchical power structures, professional reviewers have been several ladder rungs beneath their non-professional counterparts since the birth of cinema – or certainly before the emergence of sound, considered (wrongly) by many to be some kind of year zero for movies as we know them today. Twitter quotes on movie posters may seem like a terribly modern idea, but audience critiques are as old as cinema itself – the past rather than the future.

This brings us (as do so many things) to *Casablanca*. Now widely revered as one of the greatest movies ever made, *Casablanca* opened in 1942 to the same kind of mixed reviews which greeted *It's A Wonderful Life*, but similarly went on to become a timeless crowd-pleaser, proving once again that the opinions of critics don't amount to a hill of beans in this crazy world. Chief amongst the movie's pleasures are its bittersweet closing scenes wherein (plot spoilers ahoy) Humphrey Bogart's café owner Rick puts the love of his life Ilsa (Ingrid Bergman) on a plane with her husband Victor (Paul Henreid) and tells her to go with him because 'you're part of his work, the thing that keeps him going' and if she doesn't go with him now she'll regret it, 'maybe not today, maybe not tomorrow, but soon and for the rest of your life'. And anyhow, they'll always have Paris. 'Here's looking at you, kid' (no, don't mind me, I've just got something in my eye . . .).

Those words, along with the immortal 'beautiful friendship' sign-off, regularly top polls of audiences' favourite movie lines of all time, and deservedly so. As Woody Allen says when he quotes them to Diane Keaton at the end of *Play it Again, Sam*, 'It's from *Casablanca*, I waited my whole life to say it,' the chance finally to do so offering him a far greater sense of emotional fulfilment than winning the girl ever could. There's something so perfect and epochal about those lines that it's hard to imagine a time when they didn't exist, to imagine any of the film's variously credited writers staring at blank sheets of white paper and asking, 'OK, so how exactly are we gonna end this damned thing?'

Today the story goes that those discussions continued well into production, despite the script being based on an unproduced stage-play (*Everyone Comes to Rick's*) for which Warners had paid a handsome $20,000 after MGM balked at a mere $5,000. Worried about the censors' objections to a sympathetic married woman having what appears to be a care-free affair with a man who wears a raincoat and a trilby and looks like a goddamned gangster, the screen-writers made it clear that Ilsa's liaisons with Rick in Paris happened at a time when she believed her husband to be dead – an unwitting sin being no sin at all. As for what she gets up to in Casablanca, a neutral purgatory which appears to occupy the same amoral hinterland as latter-day Las Vegas (what happens in Casablanca stays in Casablanca), all that really matters is with whom she gets on the plane at the end – her lover, or her husband. And while Ilsa is trying to figure out who she really loves, Rick is still serving drinks to the Third Reich and insisting that: 'I stick my neck out for nobody' – a position pretty much matched on the world stage by America until the bombing of Pearl Harbor, up to which point they'd been somewhat tardy in preventing Europe from being overrun by (in the words of Eddie Izzard) a 'mass-murdering fuckhead' because they were too busy 'having breakfast . . .'

Within this global paradigm, Ilsa's romantic uncertain-ties would have struck a chord with all those ordinary Americans who had only recently been weighing up the merits of doing what they wanted to do (staying out of the war) and what they had to do (getting involved, with huge loss of life). Similarly, when Rick finally puts Ilsa on the plane with Victor, despite the fact that doing so will break his heart, it's clear that this drama has been about far more than 'the problems of three little people' all along. Yet still the writers wrestled with the issue of how properly to resolve these affairs of the heart, so powerful was the bond between Rick and Ilsa that it threatened to bulldoze everything in its path, proving that all's fair in love and war after all.

Looking back on the film several years later, Bergman would attest that she had played several key scenes with no knowledge of how the movie was going to end. When demanding that Michael Curtiz tell her which man she was supposed to love, the director would frustratingly instruct her to 'play it in between', apparently playing for time while the writers continued their quest for the perfect pay-off. Contrary to legend, such uncertainties didn't last through the entire production – the movie wasn't shot in sequence, so for at least some of the time they all knew how it was going to turn out. But the very fact that the ending was still up for grabs when the cameras first turned tells you that there's nothing 'modern' about the seemingly infinite malleability of movie narratives. (Today, the debate about 'who wrote what' on *Casablanca* remains unresolved, with Phil and Julius Epstein, Howard Koch, Murray Burnett, Joan Alison, Casey Robinson and even producer Hal Wallis forming the 'usual suspects' for any given line.)

Now ask yourself, what would have happened if *Casablanca* had been test-screened to the same audience who screamed, 'Kill the bitch!' at *Fatal Attraction* four decades later? And, just to add a personal touch, imagine yourself as part of that audience, watching the film for the very first time, being swept up in the irresistible allure of its central illicit romance which boasted an on-screen chemistry so powerful that the lead actors' respective partners would regularly accuse them of having a real-life affair, even though they barely spoke off-camera. What would you have said if the studio asked you to tell them how the movie should end? Would you have seen the bigger picture, realized the whole story had some cosmic significance greater than the plight of any of its puny characters? Would you have sat back and agreed there was only one possible ending – Rick should give up the love of his life for the greater good, and he and Ilsa should go their separate ways, never to meet again? Would you have put her on the plane and let Rick walk away?

Would you have opted for honour over heartbreak?

Would you?

Honestly?

Oh, come on; as long as you have a pulse, you would have done exactly the same thing I would – wiping away a tear and pretending to have trouble with your contact lens, you would have told the nice man from the studio that while you liked the movie very much, you would have liked it even more if, at the very last moment, Ilsa had turned to boring old Victor (whom the writers actually considered killing at one point) and said something along the lines of, 'Ah fuck it, I'm staying,' before rushing down the runway into the arms of Rick, with whom she would share a swooningly passionate embrace. Of course you would – everyone would. Everyone watching *Casablanca* wants Rick and Ilsa to be together for ever, for love to conquer all while Victor takes care of the war, leaving the lovers to live happily ever after. Of course they do – that's how the movie works. And that's exactly why no audience should be given the power to change it.

Make no mistake, wanting *Casablanca* to turn out differently is not the result of being stupid or foolish and wishing to ruin a picture you didn't understand in the first place – on the contrary, it's the result of watching the movie and getting it completely, engaging with its characters, empathizing with its situations, sharing in its joy, and (most importantly) feeling its pain. You want Rick and Ilsa to be together because that's what the movie wants you to want. Indeed, that's what the film-makers themselves wanted, having several discussions about how they could finish the picture with Rick and Ilsa boarding the plane together, leaving Victor behind – a problem they never managed to fix (thank heaven). In effect, they had written a love story so powerful that none of them wanted it to end, though they all knew it had to . . .

Of course, no one would have 'known' that more than the American audiences watching the film in 1942/3, when their country was paying the awful price of joining the war. These were audiences who needed to be buoyed up with positive messages about seeing the bigger picture, and the propagandist elements of *Casablanca* (putting aside one's own desires in the service of others) are clear, bold and powerful. Those viewers needed Rick to give up Ilsa, just as they needed Ilsa to stand by Victor. On a very basic level, Rick is America, feigning neutrality whilst hating the Nazis, eventually giving up his chance of happiness by throwing in his hat with a European man, expressing his love for Ilsa by letting her go, allowing her to carry on keeping Victor going – a crucial part of the war effort. The 'beautiful friendship' between Rick and Captain Renault is a symbolic alliance – something everyone watching the film on its first release would have understood instinctively.

But 'understanding' and 'needing' are very different to 'wanting', a central theme of *Casablanca*. Rick wants Ilsa, but Victor needs her, and Ilsa needs to go with Victor even though she wants to stay with Rick – something all three finally come to understand in that sublime airport show-down. Similarly, the audience wants Rick and Ilsa to end up together, but they understand that that can't happen, that the movie needs to end just the way it does.

And so it does.

Test screenings, for various (none too) complicated reasons, don't ask what an audience needs, only what they want, failing to understand that the two things may be diametrically opposed. If you look at the history of the process and try to tally it with critical plaudits and box office bonanzas, it soon becomes clear that (contrary to popular lore) giving an audience what they want is no guarantee of success – none at all. I once had a conversation with direc-tor Joe Dante (*Gremlins*, *The Howling*, *Matinee*) who told me that Hollywood executives placed so much faith in test screening audiences that whenever he shouted cut on a movie set he half expected to turn round and find a sofa-full of punters of whom he would have to ask, 'What did you think? Did you like the way it went? Do you like the characters? Which characters do you like the best? Who do you think should get the girl? Should we dump the other guy? Maybe we should make it a comedy, huh? Or a thriller? Whatever you want – you tell me.' Yet if you ask people whether they want to watch a movie made by someone who made a film like *Gremlins* or someone who just watched a film like *Gremlins*, the chances are they'll opt for the former. Ironically, despite the studios' 'faith in the innate wisdom of the paying public', the public appear to have zero faith in preview screenings, preferring their movies to be created *ex nihilo* by visionary film-makers.

This paradox has caused the studios to tie themselves up in knots over the years, strenuously denying the role played by preview screenings in shaping their product while simultaneously bowing at the altar of preview cards. In 2008, I travelled to the other side of the world to interview Baz Luhrmann about his career, on the eve of the Antipodean premiere of his long-awaited epic *Australia* ('what, all of it?'). A ripe, cineliterate melodrama, which I would later dub *The Wizard Queen Gone Walkab-Out of Africa With the Wind of Oz* (here all week, folks), *Australia* was a sweeping historical romance in which Hugh Jackman's manly Drover and Nicole Kidman's uptight English aristo Lady Sarah fall in love as they herd cattle across the outback, climaxing in the Japanese bombing of Darwin in 1942 during which the multifarious plot threads are all brought together in a spectacular conflagration. The interview, to be broadcast as a one-hour *Culture Show* special on BBC2, had been set up on the understanding that I would fly to Sydney and watch the film before being whisked directly to Baz's abode for our head-to-head, allowing us to discuss his entire body of work, from *Strictly Ballroom* to *Australia* and beyond.

However, when I got to the land of Oz, it became apparent that they weren't going to show me the new film after all. Instead, I had to make do with reading the script; I was left alone with a copy for precisely three hours, after which it was prised from my grasp, presumably for fear that I might upload it to the Internet, or pass it on to a reporter from AICN. The reason given for withholding the screening at the last moment was that the film still wasn't quite finished and Baz, nothing if not a perfectionist, didn't want anyone to judge it on the basis of a less-than-final cut. This is fair enough: as I have stated before, I'm all in favour of allowing film-makers to finish their work without interference from ill-judged pre-release press-scuttle. But I also happened to know that a near-complete version had been screened to (and judged by) members of the public several months earlier. The reason I knew this was because Fox co-chairman Tom Rothman had recently taken to the pages of the *LA Times* to strenuously deny claims reported in the Australian *Sunday Telegraph* that the entire ending of the movie had been reshot after a typically 'disastrous' test screening. 'Everything in that story was patently nonsensical,' insisted Rothman, who went on to say it was 'all too typical of the way the world works today that everybody picked up an unsourced, anonymous quote-filled story in a tabloid from Sydney and nobody ever bothered to check to see if it was accurate.' So just how 'inaccurate' was it? Well, Rothman's main complaint was with the allegation that Fox somehow forced Luhrmann's hand, and that he had 'bowed to studio pressure' in dropping his original 'sad ending' of the movie in favour of a 'more uplifting' rejig. 'Baz is a final-cut director,' the studio head insisted, 'and we never pressured him in any way, shape or form. He wrote the movie, shot it and cut it all himself without any interference from us at all.' What Rothman didn't deny, however, was that the test screening had happened, that changes had been made to the movie as a result, and that a key character who had originally bitten the dust was now going to live to fight another day. 'There's no reason to kill off Wolvie in this one,' one test viewer was reported to have said, urging the film-makers to change the ending so that Jackman's Drover no longer paid the ultimate price of self-sacrifice in the movie's (then) tragic finale. This view, apparently shared by many, caused Luhrmann to reassemble his key cast in August 2008 for what were inevitably described as nothing more than 'pick-up shots', but which looked suspiciously like substantial reshoots. Certainly, by the time I finally saw *Australia* on my return to the UK, both Kidman and Jackman survived the final reel. But as the director and studio head were keen to point out, there had always been several possible endings for the movie; Luhrmann had shot at least three, to give himself 'options' in the editing room. Apparently.

Unlike many critics, I rather enjoyed *Australia*, which turned out to be every bit as sprawlingly ridiculous as the title suggested, blending epic landscape photography with studio-bound artifice as it threw everything but the kitchen sink into the mix: stampeding cattle, magical wizards, moustachioed cads, handsome dinner dances, lost children, aerial bombardments and attendant firestorms – all in glorious crikey-packed hues. The result plays less like an advert for Top End Australian tourism than a celluloid jukebox of Luhrmann's cinematic passions and I had plenty of fun watching it, although even the most generous critic would have to concede it has the air of a movie redesigned by committee – at least in its final act.

That's not to say the (alleged) original ending would have been any better – who knows, I haven't seen it – or that Luhrmann changed it against his will after being told to do so by the studio. Having spent the best part of two years working on the movie, he clearly wanted it to be a hit, and if Lloyd and Keaton could listen to their audience, then why shouldn't he? What is significant is that both film-maker and studio were at such pains to underplay the importance (even the existence) of the test screening, and to assert time and time again that this was an auteur picture, the director alone having total creative power. Just as the Paramount PR department had attempted to quash any suggestion that the end of *Fatal Attraction* was being reshot to appease the audience, so those involved with *Australia* went on a charm offensive in the run-up to the film's release, the primary thrust of which was to reassert Luhrmann's role as sole visionary. In a way, I became part of that PR drive, my own interview with the director offering him an opportunity to cement his position as the man in the driving seat, on top of every aspect of the production, the general leading the troops on what was most definitely 'A Baz Luhrmann Film'.

This is the contradiction at the heart of the test-screening process. Film-makers and producers are desperate to know what audiences think, but equally eager to pretend they're not listening. They change movies on the say-so of test previews, but then deny those changes were informed by anything as vulgar as audience input. They want to know what viewers like about a movie, but are terrified to admit they took something out because the audience *didn't* like it, or put something in because they asked for it. They want the audience to tell them what to do and then forget they ever had a conversation, so they can pretend that whatever they say was exactly what they had in mind in the first place. And audiences, for all their vociferousness, don't actually like the idea that movies have been changed to please them. On the contrary, they like to believe they're made to some kind of grand design, arriving in a state of grace, perfect and complete from the very first screening. As for critics, the merest whiff that a movie has suffered post-test-screening re-cuts is enough to provoke raised noses, undercutting the auteur theory which we all know to be utter hooey anyway. All of which leads to a bonkers situation in which a film critic travels halfway round the world to interview a director about a film and they won't let him see it, but when a preview screening audience announces that it doesn't want Wolverine to get killed, they recall all the stars and shoot a new ending just to keep them happy. And then everyone has to pretend that none of it really happened.

Whether the changes made to *Australia* between August and November 2008 made it a 'better' or more popular movie we'll never know. At a cost of around $130 million, the film needed to take at least $260 worldwide to wash its face at the box-office. As it was, it took less than $50 million in America (in an age where the starting line for proper blockbuster hits is upward of $100 million) and only just scraped past $200 million worldwide, making it officially a flop – on paper at least. Would it have done worse with the original, more downbeat ending? Personally,

I'm inclined to think not; despite the post-preview changes, *Australia* had trouble finding a large enough audience to justify its budgetary overspend, a problem clearly not solved by allowing Wolverine to live. The reviews didn't help, with myself and the *Daily Mail*'s Christopher Tookey being notable exceptions to the barrage of raspberries, many making reference to the preview screening debacle which seemed only to have sealed the film's reputation as dead-on-arrival damaged goods. Even before *Australia* opened, the knives were out, with Anne Billson mocking the movie sight unseen in the *Guardian* by comparing it satirically to previous box-office hits that could have been similarly 'improved' by the addition of a happy ending. 'Let's face it,' she wrote sarcastically, '*Casablanca* would have lingered far longer in audiences' minds had Humphrey Bogart knocked Paul Henreid unconscious and hopped on that plane with Ingrid Bergman instead of sacrificing personal happiness for the greater good', reminding me of a terrific gag from Joe Dante's *Gremlins 2* in which an advert is overheard burbling in the background, merrily announcing the imminent arrival of '*Casablanca* . . . in full colour! With a happier ending!'

It's no surprise that *Casablanca* turns up time and time again in these discussions because it so perfectly encapsulates what's wrong with the tyranny of a process in which audiences are asked to act as film-makers and vice versa. Everyone loves *Casablanca* despite the fact that it breaks their hearts – or rather, they love it precisely *because* it breaks their hearts. No one in their right mind would want to change a frame of it, yet it tested badly back in 1942, and if they repeated the process today, the cards would show that the audience want Rick and Ilsa to end up together. Does this mean that Warners should change the movie to please them? No. It means that the audience should be left wanting, for that is arguably the film's strongest selling point. The genius of *Casablanca* is that, both in terms of its characters and its audience, it explores that area between what people want and what they need, understanding perfectly the sublime tension that exists between those two.

No audience will ever ask for an unhappy ending; just as you can't scare yourself by shouting 'Boo!' or tickle yourself into laughing, it's something which, by its very nature, has to be done to you, rather than by you. But having it done to you is one of the true pleasures of cinema, hence the huge and enduring popularity of weepies, a staple of movie-making since the birth of the moving image. William Friedkin once said (flippantly) that the only purpose of cinema was to make you laugh, make you cry, make you horny, or make you scared – all forms of arousal, in one way or another. Of these I would say that crying is perhaps the most fundamental response, which makes it significant that it is the one against which the preview screening process militates most monstrously. Cinema that makes us cry works precisely because it does something we don't want it to do, something requiring a level of transgression on the part of the film-maker to fulfil the masochistic desires we all understand so well, but deny so vehemently. And, in a perverse way, asking the audience what they want a film to do pretty much negates the possibility of it ever being able to do so.

My mind spirals back to a scene from *Jeremy*, an apparently incidental exchange I'd all but forgotten (contrary to my almost verbatim memory of the rest of it), but which I now recognize is probably the key to the whole movie. Jeremy is talking to his music teacher about a cello piece he's practising to play at the upcoming school concert. The teacher thinks his playing is technically fine (despite the fact that Robby Benson, bless him, has clearly never played a cello in his life), but something is still missing.

'What do you think about when you play this piece?' the teacher asks, leaning forward enquiringly as if prying into his pupil's very soul. 'What kind of thoughts go through your mind?'

Jeremy looks bewildered, his Buddy Holly glasses covering his bright blue eyes, his face hiding behind his fringe, almost unable to speak.

'Well, it's a sad piece,' he offers in a whisper, after a long and painful pause. 'It's kinda lonely . . .'

His teacher sits back, ready to deliver what I now recognize as the 'author's message'.

'Sadness is just part of it,' he explains. 'The composer wrote this piece before he was twenty. He wrote it for a beautiful peasant girl he had seen just once, in passing. Just once. So the music expresses love and parting simultaneously. The music expresses . . . life. Play it *that* way . . .'

OK, so it looks kinda dopey written down like that. But the more I think about it, the more I realize that's why I love *Jeremy* so much – because it expresses love and parting simultaneously, note-perfectly. And although I don't want it to end the way it does, I understand (and indeed understood, even as a kid) that it ends the way it must. From the moment Jeremy first masters that piece of music, there is no other possible outcome (just as there should be no other possible outcome for *Fatal Attraction* than that flagged up by Puccini's *Madama Butterfly*). He will fall in love for an instant ('in passing') and the expression of that love will also be the expression of parting – brief, transient, timeless.

Sadness is just part of it, but without it the music doesn't ring true.

The music expresses life.

Play it, Sam.

Play it *that* way . . .

EPILOGUE

HAPPY SAPPY ENDINGS

How do you want this story to end? Do you want the original, downbeat ending – the nasty, gritty, miserable one that had dramatic integrity and narrative cohesion but was hated by absolutely everyone in the preview screening? You know, like the one described so dramatically by Richard E. Grant in *The Player* when he's pitching a movie with 'no stars, no pat happy endings', where the heroine gets executed in the final reel 'because that happens – the innocent die!' I admit that when I started writing this book it had a very downbeat ending indeed: all the film critics died and nobody cared – least of all the audience. If I'd had the nerve, I probably would have thrown in an image of myself cutting my own professional throat to the strains of *Madama Butterfly*.

Blood on the floor; fingerprints on the hatchet; fade to black – The End.

'Why? Because *that happens*!'

I liked that ending, and I was determined to stick to it. No compromises! But we all know what happened in *The*

Player, right? Bruce Willis ended up saving Julia Roberts at the last moment, and Robert Altman cut away brilliantly to a shot of Grant's once-principled writer silently punching the air, having sold his soul to the devil. Bruce Willis isn't likely to run in and save me any time soon (particularly not after what I said about *A Good Day to Die Hard*, or *The Expendables 2*, or *Cop Out*, or . . . etc.), but despite my constant attempts to be a completely miserable bastard, I now find myself facing the very real possibility of a happy Hollywood ending. And, like all critics, that makes me very suspicious.

Some years ago, I wrote a book (and made a television documentary) about *The Shawshank Redemption*, Frank Darabont's adaptation of a story by Stephen King, subtitled 'Hope Springs Eternal'. A financial flop on its first cinema release, *The Shawshank Redemption* became everyone's favourite film on video, thanks not least to a finale in which the male leads (plot spoiler alert) are reunited on a sunny beach in the promised land of Zihuatanejo. I loved the movie but I hated that ending, partly because it's an opportunistic addition that makes no dramatic sense whatsoever, and partly because everyone else loves it so much, despite the fact that doing so is clearly wrong. Look at the evidence. Having taken place almost entirely within the confines of grim prison walls, King's short story ends with our narrator, Red, embarking upon 'a long journey whose conclusion is uncertain', heading off in search of his best friend and legendary escapee Andy Dufresne, whom he hopes has made it to Mexico. 'I hope I can make it across the border,' says Red, using a key word; a word repeated not once, not twice, but thrice. 'I hope to see my friend and shake his hand. I hope the Pacific is as blue as it has been in my dreams. I *hope* . . .'

Hope. Not fulfilment. Hope. As in 'Hope Springs Eternal' – which is, of course, what this parable-like tale has been about all along.

'It was the perfect ending for the story,' states Darabont, astutely, 'and therefore by extension the perfect ending for the movie.' Hence, Darabont's screenplay and first cut of the film ended the exact same way, with Red (played by Morgan Freeman, whose silver-larynx later earned him roles as the President of America, Nelson Mandela and God) on the bus reciting those same words; 'I hope . . . I *hope*'. But after Liz Glotzer at Castle Rock told Darabont that the audience would want to actually see the characters reunited (no one in Hollywood likes an open-ending, apparently), he agreed to shoot a dopey epilogue in which a sweeping helicopter-shot pans from the ocean to the shores of Zihuatanejo (actually St Croix), where a beaming, shoeless Red strolls towards the white-clad form of Andy, earnestly sanding down a boat like some extra from a Nicholas Sparks movie.

Far from hope, we end on a note of resolution, of finality, of triumph.

The audience cheered.

I died a little inside.

The rest is history.

Don't worry: you're not going to get any helicopter shots of sunny beaches, or smooth-bottomed boats, or old friends being reunited in the Miller-time glow of a feel-good finale at the end of this story. But neither are you going to get a nihilistic fade to black and the lingering

smell of death. Why not? Well because, against all my expectations (and Richard E. Grant's protestations), it turns
out that's not the reality after all. Despite the culls sweeping through the profession in the twenty-first century, film
criticism simply refuses to lie down and die. In fact, if anything, there are now more film critics around than ever
before. Yes, the staff jobs have gone and freelancing is the
future – but for those of us who never had a staff job in
the first place that really doesn't make much difference.
I've only ever been a freelancer and, significantly, so too
have my closest and most trusted friends, notably Nigel
Floyd and Alan Jones, who first taught me the ropes back
in the late eighties, and to whom I still owe a huge debt of
gratitude. In fact, looking back on the heady days of the
Dogs of Wardour Street, I don't think any of us knew what
an employment contract looked like, nor would we have
known what to do with one were it offered (eat it, probably). On the contrary, we'd huddle together in the snug of
the Nellie Dean like Soho rats, sneering at the thought of
holding down an 'office job', spurred on by the knowledge
that we were all only as good as our last review, made cocky
by the fact that we could never be fired since none of us had
ever been 'employed' in the first place. I like to think this
stood us in good stead, teaching us to be hungry and self-
sufficient, willing to work for sandwiches and the possibility
of stumbling upon an as-yet unsung masterpiece. Certainly
it prepared us for the future, where self-employment turns
out to be the only employment, and no one has a job for
life. Instead, we all live by Robert Benchley's oft repeated
maxim that 'the freelance writer is paid per piece or per
word or perhaps . . .'.

Meanwhile, despite the 'death of publishing' narrative which continues to play out around us, the regular press screenings I attend every week show little evidence of the promised collapse. Just the other week, for example, I trotted off to a Monday morning viewing at the Soho Screening Rooms on D'Arblay Street, and there were all the usual faces, present and correct, alive and kicking. There was Chris Tookey, then of the *Daily Mail*, taking up residence in the stand-alone 'throne seat' to which no one else could lay claim; there were Kate Muir and Wendy Ide of *The Times* and Larushka Ivan-Zadeh of *Metro*, occupying the middle-ground seating; in the back row, there was Derek Malcolm, now in his eighties, still out-viewing and out-writing all of us, his early years as a jockey having clearly prepared him well for decades in the cinematic saddle. Down in the front row on the left there was James King and me, with everyone refusing to sit behind me (because of my hair) except Tim Robey and Robbie Collin (because of their height); and over on the right there was Joyce Glasser of the *Mature Times* and Alan Frank of the *Daily Star*, saving a seat for Philip French, who was recently rewarded with an OBE, confirming his place as Britain's most respected film commentator (so much for no one ever building a statue to a critic).

As it turned out, Philip was on the brink of announcing his retirement. The very next Sunday, the *Observer* (the paper for whom he had first filed a column back in 1963) ran a glowing tribute announcing that the man rightly hailed as Britain's 'greatest living movie analyst' was to step down after fifty years of service, having reached his eightieth birthday in the same year that he received the

OBE. Noting that 'not all artists have a life-lease on their talent', French mused upon the changing quality of work of both directors and critics, concluding wryly that 'at least I am giving up now, while I still have my mind' – a typically self-deprecating remark from someone whose sharpness of wit will probably continue to make the rest of us look dull for decades to come.

Unsurprisingly, the *Observer* article (by Vanessa Thorpe) had a *fin de siècle* air, echoing the melancholia surrounding the publication of Roger Ebert's last review. Acknowledging his star critic's 'unrivalled international reputation', *Observer* editor John Mulholland accepted that 'many readers will find Sundays less rich without him' and conceded that 'there are readers who will feel that his writings are simply irreplaceable'. For the second time in as many months, there was a general consensus that something great was coming to an end – that the conclusion of a single critic's career held a wider sense of closure for the industry itself.

Alongside the universal praise for French's writing (even Ebert had struggled to compete with French's unparalleled depth of knowledge and unfailing even-handedness), Thorpe found space to point out that 'French believes that alongside the growing ranks of online amateur film writers, there should still be a role for an experienced critic.' This is significant not only for offering a defiant note about the future, but also for acknowledging the wide-ranging worry that French's profession was facing obsolescence thanks in part to the Internet. It signals a world in which the rise of online criticism has made it necessary for the professional print critic to justify the existence of their trade, even at the point of retirement.

The irony is that, like Roger Ebert, Philip French was already an integral part of the Internet revolution, and whilst his reviews may be anything but 'amateur' they were most definitely 'online'. Just as most modern animated features combine the skills of hand-drawn and computer-generated imagery (Japanese legend Hayao Miyazaki is no more a stranger to the digital world than *Toy Story* creator John Lasseter is to the pen-and-ink), today every print journalist has an online presence whether they like it or not. File a review for a magazine or newspaper and the chances are the physical publication will have a website to which its readers are increasingly drawn. Philip French may not have had a Twitter account (he set one up, tweeted twice, decided it wasn't for him, and cancelled it) but he had a huge following of fans accessing his 'print' reviews online. As Chris Tookey regularly pointed out, he earned a decent salary writing for a newspaper with a readership of around six million, yet the *Mail*'s web presence saw his reviews being accessed by upward of twenty million unique users, for which he was technically unpaid. Chris is an old-school print journo, yet the majority of his readers surf the web rather than read a newspaper. The same is true of all the major print titles; the question of how to monetize their online market is now more pressing than staving off the inevitable decline of their physical circulations. Even *Empire*, which has long described itself as 'The World's Best Selling Movie Magazine', seems increasingly to be shifting its attentions away from the newsagents' shelves towards the expansion of empireonline.com, investing time and energy in the development of snappy apps that give the reader an 'enhanced' online experience that may, at some point in the future, supersede the magazine itself. (In terms of films screened too late for press dates, the site already has the edge over the magazine.) Even those still wedded to the printed word are doing their bit to establish the dominance of the web.

Like it or not, we're all bloggers now – all of us trading in 'graffiti with punctuation'.

The same is doubly true of me. No matter how much anxiety its advent may have caused, I have the Internet to thank for the fact that I still have anything resembling a career. My *Observer* columns have long had an online presence; largely unrelated to the physical circulation of the paper, driven instead by alerts on Twitter and Facebook, they now have a potential international readership unimaginable a decade ago. Meanwhile, as the listeners to *Kermode and Mayo's Film Review* on Radio 5 live continue to increase (God bless them), the importance of those who download it as a digital podcast becomes ever more significant. The last time I looked, our podcast figures (2.3 million in April 2013) were pushing the programme's reach far beyond anything I had considered attainable, now made achievable thanks to the miracle of digital distribution. Stranger still, a significant proportion of the audience choose to watch the programme online, either live via the 5 live website, or later on the Kermode and Mayo YouTube channel. And whilst I remain more baffled than most as to why anyone would want to watch two bickering codgers doing their best impressions of Charles Hawtrey and an orc, it appears that what was once just a radio show now also caters for those who like their opinions to come with moving pictures.

And then there's the Kermode Uncut blog. Like the 5 live show, it relies heavily on the interaction of its on-line audience, something which has turned film criticism from a series of declarative statements into something closer to a conversation. No longer is the film critic's word final, if indeed it ever was. Now, there's an active inter-play between critics and their audience, the wit, knowledge and cineliterate smarts of whom should encourage any critic to raise their game. Far from dumbing-down, the input of online contributors has (in my experience at least) caused everyone to sharpen up, for fear of making fools of themselves in public. No longer can a critic operate from a position of ignorance without fear of correction. Despite my efforts to avoid factual errors, whenever I make them (and I do) I can be sure they will be trumpeted from the virtual rooftops within minutes of publication – and rightly so. In the same way, unsound judgements may be challenged in a trice, meaning that every critic wishing to retain their lofty position should be ready and able to defend their views in the bear-pit of the digital public gaze.

Rather than running away from this dialogue, those who wish to learn from their mistakes must embrace it. In the decade or so that I've been doing the 5 live radio show, I've learned a great deal about cinema from the listeners' emails, texts and tweets. Yes, there's a lot of unsupported blather, hostility, and sheer bitchy bloody-mindedness out there on the net, almost all of it anonymous and there-fore unworthy of attention. But there's also a genuine groundswell of honest intelligent debate to which only the comfortably numb would turn a deaf ear. If you're a visitor to the Kermode Uncut site, for example, it's entirely possible you've contributed to this book, for which I am eternally grateful (although not grateful enough to pay you, obviously). Perhaps you were one of the many who helped choose the best of those acerbic critics' quotes in the Prologue. Or perhaps you are one of the hundreds who responded so enthusiastically to a post asking for recommendations of movie websites that had captured (and held) your online interest. Those responses were (to quote the mighty Manfred Cutshaw) 'too numerous to enumerate', but included mentions for RedLetterMedia's 'Half in the Bag' (which had previously attracted the attention of Roger Ebert), and fast-talking Jeremy Jahns (whose YouTube reviews do for movies what Tobuscus does for videogames), alongside Indiewire's The Playlist and BadassDigest.com. Casting the net wider, LoveHKFilm.com was singled-out for embarking upon 'the craziest, most fool-hardy self-imposed mission, an un-paralleled attempt to document a whole genre (certainly in English, possibly also even in Chinese) and a collection of some of the best written, funny and incisive reviews on the net'. There was praise, too, for HopeLies.com, a site with which I have long been familiar, whose declared mission is to provide 'a tailored approach to online film criticism, with an emphasis on (but not limited to) Silent Film and French Cinema . . . drawing together reviews of modern theatrical releases and forgotten gems'. I had also been introduced by Twitter to the insightful Stuart Barr, who in turn led me to the online magazine Vérité, a stylish affair aiming 'to provide a platform for interesting, provocative film criticism' in the arena of independent and foreign-language film, a remit crossing healthily with that of the equally ambitious subtitledonline.com. All of these sites have a role to play in the widening field of twenty-first-century film journalism, and all demonstrate that the next generation of writers and broadcasters are not so much emerging from the Internet as making their home within it.

For the best and most industrious of these sites, there is funding to be found through advertising, which can yet sustain the kind of quality journalism that (as we have seen) 'does not come for free'. Just the other day I was in Swiss Cottage for an IMAX screening of *Star Trek Into Darkness* and I crossed paths with *Empire* news editor Chris Hewitt and Den of Geek mainstay Simon Brew, both employed as film journalists, albeit in very different media. Simon was in buoyant mood because I had recently tweeted that Den of Geek (which covers films, TV, games and comics) had been cited by two separate movie publicists as the UK online outlet they most respect, and to which they would dedicate the most time and attention. This didn't surprise me since Brew and his colleagues' combination of passion and integrity is a winning mix. I thought it was great that his site (for which I had been interviewed a few years ago) was getting some attention, and felt smugly pleased with myself for helping things along. So, after the usual exchange of pleasantries, I asked him bluntly:

'OK, tell me honestly, how many hits do you actually get?'

'What, daily? Or monthly?' he replied, unfazed.

'Either's fine,' I said. 'Monthly. How many per month?'

He paused, thinking.

'About 2.7, I think.'

'2.7 thousand? Not bad.'

'Err, million.'

'Pardon?'

'2.7 million.'

'2.7 *million*?'

'Yes, about that. 2.7 million unique visitors, yes.'

'Every month?'

'Well, most months. Last month, I think.'

'Really?'

'Yes, really.'

'Blimey, Charlie.'

'Who's Charlie?'

'Never mind.'

That Den of Geek should achieve this kind of reach is heartening, particularly since it's refreshingly free from the kind of competitive snarkiness that characterizes some other similarly themed sites. Rather than seeing them as rivals, Brew seems to view all others in the field as co-workers, toiling alongside him at the coal-face of Internet journalism, adhering to the very same principles (honour amongst film critics) I have espoused at such boring length. He's also no fan of uncredited reviews, respects the need for embargoes, understands the role of good editing, and generally thinks it's better to get things right than first – all old-fashioned values, which have helped attract nearly three million unique users a month.

As a result, Den of Geek can support (if not enrich) both editorial staff and writers, although a fair degree of unpaid good-will still goes into keeping it afloat. Brew starts work on the site every day at 5.30 a.m., 'writing the day's news

(I'm a bit picky about what we cover), proofing the features (*everything* gets edited), and getting the front of the site how I want it' – all before 9 o'clock. Then he gets on with 'other stuff'. It's a discipline that has paid dividends, and helped Brew earn a deserved name as one of the good guys of the Internet revolution.

The fact that Brew has a name worth protecting is, of course, the key to his integrity – and indeed the key to good criticism. As someone who earned his spurs in the lick-and-stick world of the Manchester print trade, I have worried a great deal over the years about the anonymity engendered by the Internet and the lack of accountability this inevitably entails. If writing this book has confirmed anything at all, it's that criticism without risk to the critic has no value whatsoever – that an opinion is only worth as much as its author has to lose: their good name; their reputation; their audience; their job. Yet after a decade of blogging in which the grounds of the publishing world have shifted beneath us, it appears this maxim has as much traction in the online domain as it does in the world of print. The landscape of publishing has changed over the last decade and the gaggle of competing Internet voices has grown exponentially, but the qualities that most reliably distinguish the wheat from the chaff in terms of criticism are still those of transparency and accountability, qualities requiring an author to make a name for themselves, and to allow that name to be open to scrutiny and investigation.

Back in the days when media studies was in its infancy, the idea that 'news' was not an absolute, but an opinion expressed by interested parties, seemed radical and inflammatory. Yet ever since the *Sun*, the biggest-selling newspaper in the UK, started overtly (rather than covertly) instructing their readers how to vote, it should have been apparent to everyone that all media outlets have an agenda. Headlines such as 'If Kinnock wins today will the last person to leave Britain please turn out the lights' splashed across the front page on election day 1992, followed by 'It's the *Sun* Wot Won It' after the subsequent Tory victory, left no room for doubt on the issue of impartiality. History has it that this was a watershed moment – the point at which journalism crossed the line from reporting the news to creating it. Yet anyone who understands the history of news journalism knows that this has always been the case. (The phrase 'You provide the prose poems, I'll provide the war', for example, appeared in *Citizen Kane* fifty years earlier, inspired by William Randolph Hearst's use of the *New York Journal* to encourage US engagements in Cuba, the Philippines and Puerto Rico). Just as every schoolchild is taught (or should be taught) that 'history is written by the victors', so the flow of information to the public has always been mediated by businesses for whom money and circulation is the bottom line. Indeed, if the much-maligned Murdoch empire was responsible for anything when printing those headlines, it was arguably making apparent what had previously been hidden.

There is a debate to be had about whether such bare-faced bias is actually more honest than the appearance of independence. Having achieved bogeyman status in the wake of the phone-hacking scandal, there can be few unaware of the political allegiances to which the so-called

Murdoch press are prey. And while I may disagree with those allegiances, at least I am aware of them, causing me to question anything I read in a Murdoch publication – or indeed *any* publication, sometimes to the point of paranoia.

I once had a conversation with the *Telegraph*'s Robbie Collin, who'd served several years in the trenches at the *News of the World*. We were talking in broad terms about the influence (or lack of it) exerted over arts correspondents by their editors – a frivolous subject, perhaps, but one that had a direct impact upon both our lives. I told Robbie I'd heard a story about a film critic filing a negative review of *The Da Vinci Code* only to discover that the review's star rating had been mysteriously increased in the published version, against his will and without his knowledge. Being an old Trot, I immediately inferred political interference, even though there was no apparent connection between the film's distributor and the paper (how's *that* for paranoia?). With hindsight, it appears more likely that the editor just panicked, worrying about the perceived 'snobbery' of the critic's review, and doubting that the film could really be that bad. Oh yes it could. Despite taking a whole bunch of money, the generally accepted opinion was that *The Da Vinci Code* was a humourless drudge of a movie, endured by most audiences rather than enjoyed. Certainly, no one was going to think a critic was 'out of touch' or 'snobby' or 'elitist' simply for pointing out some of the movie's howling faults – not least of which was the fact that the entire film appeared to have been shot in the dark. Despite Ron Howard's populist touch (his CV includes *Splash* and *Apollo 13*, both terrific crowd-pleasers), the director appeared to have been entirely overwhelmed by the thudding dreadfulness of Dan Brown's source novel, leading him to produce an uncharacteristically undramatic movie in which people ran from one darkened room to another, stopping only to point at things and explain the plot to each other. It didn't help that Tom Hanks sported a clip-on mullet that made him look like Roland Orzabal from Tears for Fears pretending to be a history teacher; or that the punchline of the narrative involved Audrey Tatou turning out to be Jesus Christ. Or something. Not even the reliably radiant Paul Bettany as a homicidal albino monk could inject anything even vaguely resembling oomph into the proceedings.

Howard was, of course, aware of the problems (most successful film-makers aren't stupid, and they generally know when they've made a stinker, even one that turns a profit) and attempted to rectify it in the crazy-go-nuts sequel by cranking the apocalyptic action up to eleventy-stupid. If you thought *Exorcist II: The Heretic* was mad, that's nothing compared to the insanity of *Angels & Demons*, which climaxes in a scene (MASSIVE plot spoilers ahoy) of papal skydiving involving a Vatican enclave, a test-tube of broiling anti-matter, an exploding helicopter, and a parachuting priest arriving Anneka Rice-style in St Peter's Square after blowing up the devil with an atom bomb. Compared to that, the sight of Richard Burton and Linda Blair stepping unscathed from the rubble of a Georgetown house which has been demolished by a plague of locusts and then sucked into the pit of hell by a vortex of evil seems positively sensible. You can say what you like about *Angels & Demons* but uneventful it ain't. Rubbish, yes; boring, no.

Anyway, back to the critic who got stiffed on his review of *The Da Vinci Code*. The story (and my immediate assumption of political interference) amused Robbie because it chimed somewhat with his own experience of working for a Murdoch paper, and the expectations which went with it. He remembered very clearly writing a negative review of *Green Lantern* (which was, it has to be said, pants) only to find a UK movie website accusing him of attacking the film precisely because it *didn't* come from the Fox stable. The allegation was patently absurd, and Robbie wrote a polite email to the blogger in question, running through a history of the Fox movies he'd savaged, proving that he had never toed any Murdoch party-line. The website never published his response, but Robbie felt that satisfaction had been achieved simply by virtue of the fact that the allegation had come from a named and verifiable source whose charges he was therefore able to answer directly.

As the Film Threat website demonstrated over a decade ago, there is as much disdain for anonymity amongst Internet journalists as there is for those in print. The idea that the Internet as a whole is some kind of unattributed bandit country only has currency in those areas where people have reason to be embarrassed about their true identities – sending abusive messages, engaging in online theft, stalking, tweeting puff reviews, or vote washing. Most online journalists worth their salt despise anonymity as much as their print counterparts, if not more so, because it undermines the very medium in which they are trying to make a name for themselves. And the fact that bloggers *en masse* seem increasingly to be rejecting such anonymity in favour of honesty and accountability offers the clearest indication yet that the 'traditional values of proper film criticism' (a phrase you probably snorted at back in Chapter One) are alive and well on the web. No matter how much has changed, some things are constant. Whatever the medium, the key questions remain the same: who is saying this; why are they saying it; and what do they have to lose by saying it? And if the answer to those questions is 'don't know'; 'don't care'; and 'nothing', then proceed with extreme caution.

Having my name in the public arena has not been without its downsides. In the course of dispensing my duties as a named and eminently traceable film critic, I've been threatened professionally, physically and legally; in person and in print; online and on the phone. I have been shot at, shouted at and sworn at. I have been stalked by post, by email, by voicemail. I have been banned, barred and blacklisted from screenings, festivals and venues. I have had arsey American lawyers yelling at me in the middle of the night and coke-addled Groucho Club habitués swearing at me in the middle of the day. I have been the target of obscene videos and outrageously defamatory remarks posted online by the unwell, the unhinged and the un-named. I have been cartooned and caricatured, imitated and insulted – in words and pictures.

All in a day's work.

And it's not just me. Every critic doing their job (or at least every critic doing their job properly) has experienced some version of this aggressively hostile fall-out. It comes with the territory, and putting up with it is the price you pay for doing what is basically a dream job – watching films all day long! Looking around me at the daily press screenings I see a mix of print stalwarts and a new generation of Internet writers, all of whom understand the cost of standing up to be counted. I see the same faces slogging through the new releases, day in, day out, enduring the highs and lows of cinema in all its myriad forms. As far as I'm concerned, that makes them 'proper' critics – just being there week after week, month after month, watching everything as a matter of professional pride, responding honestly as a matter of practice. It doesn't matter if your reviews are published online, in print, or broadcast, or whether you shout them through a megaphone at Speakers' Corner – what matters is that you wade through the good, the bad, and the ugly, all year round, producing accountable reviews that combine pithily expressed opinion, description, contextualization, analysis and (at best) entertainment, in whatever medium. Anyone who does that, and puts their name to it, is OK in my book. Whatever our personal or critical differences may have been over the years, I like and admire all those who take film criticism seriously, and I'm proud to have been able to work alongside them.

What I'm less proud of is my own critical faculty which, it seems to me, is becoming more fluid and changeable by the year. Whereas once I was stupidly certain about my opinions, age has withered that sense of single-mindedness to the point that I no longer trust myself when it comes to judging movies. As film criticism has moved into the information superhighway, I seem to have pulled over into the slow lane, with plans to drift onto the hard shoulder and stop for a picnic at the soonest possible opportunity (NB: having a picnic on the hard shoulder of a real highway is dangerous and illegal, and I use the phrase metaphorically, not literally, obviously). The more movies I watch, the more time I need to assess and weigh up their relative merits – ideally, about ten years. But as we noted before, that's not much good for a weekly film critic. The only thing you can do is get it honestly wrong in haste, and then live to regret it at leisure.

The most acute example of this in recent memory was the strange case of Steven Spielberg's *A.I. Artificial Intelligence* (which, as we know, does not have a colon). I first saw the movie in New York back in June 2001, several months before its futuristic images of the Twin Towers would spark comment in the post-9/11 fug of its UK release. Having fostered a snobby film critic's cynicism about Steven Spielberg's manipulative sentimentality, I think I went into the cinema looking for an excuse to be cross, to sneer at his populist 'dumbing-down' of what should have been an emotionally sterile Stanley Kubrick movie. And I was not disappointed – or rather, I *was* disappointed, but by the movie, rather than by my own preconceptions. It seemed to me (and several other high-profile critics) that Spielberg had taken the intelligently alienating bones of a project, adapted by Kubrick and Ian Watson from short stories by Brian Aldiss, and simply drenched them in his trademark, saccharine, string-pulling schmaltz, producing a movie that was closer to the Disney version of *Pinocchio* than to Carlo Collodi's inspirational text. In particular, *A.I.*'s oddly upbeat finale seemed a clear Spielbergian addition, a cut-and-paste from *Close Encounters* (even the 'aliens' looked the same) that attempted to put an ill-fitting smile on the face of what should have been a tragic tale.

I said all of this in my review of *A.I.* when it opened in the UK, then promptly forgot about it, mentally filing it under 'Films about which I frankly could not care less'. Even when I interviewed Spielberg for a career-overview BBC *Culture Show* special in 2006, I didn't bother to rewatch *A.I.*, merely revisiting my original review to remind myself how much I hadn't liked it. I also checked out Roger Ebert's write-up, which had been similarly (if more articulately) damning, concluding that 'Spielberg misses the real story' by asking us to 'invest our emotions in a character that is, after all, a machine' rather than focussing on the plight of the parents who project their human emotions onto a non-human subject. Arguing persuasively that Spielberg had prioritized sentimentality over intellect, Ebert stated that '*A.I.* evades its responsibilities . . . and goes for an ending that wants us to cry', something the late great Kubrick would never have done. With typical style and panache, Ebert summed up his reservations with the pithily expressed epithet that *A.I.* 'had me asking questions just when I should have been finding answers'. It all sounded pretty convincing to me.

Spielberg was, of course, well aware of the widespread negative reactions to *A.I.*, shrugging most off with good humour because, as he told me wryly, 'All the blame I get for destroying Stanley's vision are scenes that Stanley actually came up with. You know, the scenes that people can't believe that Stanley conceived and would have directed himself are the scenes that I am most credited with "spoiling". The whole ending where David and Teddy are actually rescued underwater and brought into their own future of Super-Mecha? This was Stanley and Ian's ninety-page treatment that I adapted into my screenplay.'

'So the critical version of what a Kubrick movie is like,' I ventured, innocently, 'and what a Spielberg movie is like is then interpreted in the public imagination and they get the two characters wrong?' (Note how I used the word 'they' rather than 'we' – or, more accurately, 'I'. Sneaky . . .)

'They get it completely, diametrically wrong!' Spielberg replied, laughing. 'But I think that one of the things which scared Stanley away from *A.I.* was that it was too much of a film for me, and too little of the kind of movie that he was known for as a great cineaste.'

That phrase intrigued me, because it signified an acknowledgement that whilst Kubrick was held to be a 'great cineaste', Spielberg was somehow looked down upon as merely an entertainer – particularly by critics. And the more I thought about this phrase, the more it bothered me. After all, what's wrong with being an entertainer? Heaven knows I've sat through enough movies by people who couldn't entertain if their lives depended on it. How come I had fallen in line with critics who worshipped Kubrick's lack of sentimentality, when I am nothing if not a rank sentimentalist? All of which made me start to wonder whether I had got it wrong about *A.I.* – although not enough to make me go back and re-watch the movie.

What finally did it was a quiet word from my better half, Linda, who had been writing a book about Spielberg and children, and who said in passing one day:

'You know you're completely wrong.'

This was nothing new.

'Wrong about what?' I asked, trying to narrow it down.

'About *A.I.*,' replied Linda.

I decided to stand my ground.

'No I'm not,' I replied.

'Yes you are.'

'But . . .'

'Completely wrong.'

The dog looked at me as if to say, 'Told you so,' and then went to lie on the sofa, daring me to tell her to get off.

'Oh right. OK. Sorry.'

'You need to watch it again,' said Linda, going to sit next to the dog, who was clearly loving this.

'I see.'

'This evening, in fact. You're going to sit down, and we're going to watch *A.I.*'

'But I don't like *A.I.*,' I pleaded pathetically.

Linda gave me a stern look.

'You're completely wrong about it.'

The dog rolled on her back and stuck her legs in the air, apparently overcome with joy. Linda tickled the dog. The dog yawned and spread herself out even further on the sofa, as if to demonstrate that there was no more room and I would have to sit on the floor.

I went to tidy my office.

That evening I sat down and watched *A.I.*

And it turned out I had, indeed, been completely wrong about it.

Bugger.

During the opening movement I got a flash of what Joe Morgenstern must have felt like re-watching *Bonnie and Clyde* back in 1967 – that strange skin-crawling sensation of looking at a movie you've seen before, but never actually watched. Far from being fluffy, ponderous and a bit boring, which is what I'd thought first time round, *A.I.* now seemed to cut straight to the chase, establishing a complex dramatic situation (grieving parents, surrogate robot child, man/machine divide), raising touching and intelligent philosophical questions about the human condition (the nature of love, the 'reality' of artificial emotion), turning from tragedy to adventure to existential fairy tale in an instant. I think I first shed a tear about fifteen minutes into the film – by the time it finished, I'd pretty much cried my own bodyweight in salt-water. The performances were great, the design ambitious, the score stirring, and the script heartbreaking. As for the finale, about which I had previously griped, it now seemed so utterly essential to the narrative that I simply couldn't imagine the movie ending without it. It was as if the Blue Fairy had flown from the pages of her storybook, waved a magic wand over my head and turned me from a robot critic, unable to feel any emotion, into something approaching a 'real boy'.

I was overwhelmed.

'You were right,' I said to Linda.

'I know,' she replied.

'I was wrong.'

'Yes you were.'

'I think I should apologize . . .'

Linda smiled. 'Whenever you're ready . . .'

'. . . to Steven Spielberg.'

'Oh, right. Off you go, then.'

And so I did.

Not immediately, of course. Like everyone else in movie land, I have to wait for the chance to tell film-makers how wrong I've been about their work. I still haven't got round to apologizing to John Boorman (it's definitely on my 'to do' list), although I did say sorry to David Lynch about *Blue Velvet* some years ago, so at least I've made a start. But in the case of Spielberg, I had to wait until he was in Paris doing press for *Lincoln* to confront him with the error of my ways. And so it was that in December of 2012, more than a decade after I'd first publicly misjudged *A.I.*, I finally got to say sorry.

I started uncertainly.

'Look, I'm a film critic,' I said somewhat redundantly, 'and I'm sure that in the position you're in, what film critics say doesn't make the slightest bit of difference.'

OK, nice touch, start on the back-foot, bland generalities, all friends here, blah blah blah. Now, get to the point.

'When I first saw *A.I.*,' (here we go) 'I was not a fan of it.'

Big deal. No one was a fan of *A.I.* What makes you so special?

'It was not a movie which engaged with me.'

Right. And?

'I thought it was a misfire.'

OK, you've told him you didn't like it (more than you did during that *Culture Show* interview, you cowardly swine). Now move on to the important part; the bit about you being wrong; the apology.

'In the last few years, my wife Linda, who's a professor of film' (oh that's right, drop that in about her to make you sound smarter), 'became really obsessed with *A.I.*, and she said to me, "You've got this film wrong, you need to watch it again." So I started watching it again and found myself reduced to floods of tears, and it is now my favourite Steven Spielberg movie.'

OK, pretty good, if a little too much personal information. So now on to the 'apology' part, right?

Wrong.

'And I wondered whether your own relationship with your back catalogue fluctuates in the same way . . .'

You're kidding? You're trying to make this about him in order to wriggle out of you saying sorry.

'. . . or has it always been that you know the ones that you love and you know the ones that you're not so proud of?'

What a rubbish question.

'Um . . .' said Spielberg, as well he might. 'Well,' he continued, clearly unsure what the hell I was getting at, 'I don't give myself the opportunity, except through the eyes of my own children, to see my films, to watch my movies. So I haven't seen *A.I.* in a long, long time. And the reason I haven't is that I haven't shown it to my kids yet. So I really don't look at my movies, although I keep promising myself that someday I will. I want to see *Hook* again because I still don't like that movie and I keep hoping that someday I'll see it again and perhaps like *some* of it!'

Blimey, this is making me look really bad; Steven Spielberg is now criticizing his own movies, being self-effacing and funny and wise, and I'm just sitting here like an arrogant arse, laughing along with him about the fact that even he hated *Hook*, while failing to do what I had promised to do. I felt like Fonzie (not for the first time) in that episode of *Happy Days* when he finds himself physically unable to say that he was wrong ('I was wrrrsshhh, I was wrreeeerrr, I was wrrrooagh . . . I was not quite right').

Spielberg, meanwhile, was on a roll.

'*A.I.* of course is a sentimental favourite of mine,' he declared, 'because it's really the first time ever I think anybody's worked with a ghost. [Damn, that's a good line. Why didn't I think of that? Oh, yes, it's because I'm not Steven Spielberg. Doh!] And I did – I had Stanley Kubrick with me every single day shooting that picture. It was his story from beginning to end. It was my screenplay, but it was his ninety-page treatment, which he wrote with Ian Watson, which was very detailed, on which I was able to base my screenplay. And so that movie has a very special place in my heart because Stanley is one of my most important godfathers.'

Follow that, Kermode.

'Well, I'd just like to say officially . . .' I began, falteringly, 'on behalf of film critics . . .'

No, don't blame *them*, this was *your* mistake; man up and admit it.

'I got it wrong when that film came out.'

Finally! And . . . ?

'And I apologize to you.'

About bloody time.

'Because it's a masterpiece.'

Which indeed it is.

There was a peculiar silence. I felt a weight lifting from my shoulders. It was a novel feeling, not one with which I was familiar, and I kind of liked it. It felt like . . . chocolate. Or candy floss. Or something sticky and saccharine that had previously seemed unhealthy, but suddenly and bizarrely didn't seem sickly any more.

Just sweet.

Does that make any sense?

This was a big moment for me, and apparently something of a novelty for Spielberg too.

'Well, let me tell you,' he said, clearly attuned to the enormity of the proceedings, 'this has only happened to me once before; when Vincent Canby panned *Close Encounters*, and then three years later changed his mind and wrote a glowing review.'

Hey, look, everyone, Steven Spielberg just compared me to Vincent Canby! Sort of. A bit.

'So this is only the second time this has ever happened to me so . . . thank you!'

Jeez, this was strange. Lovely, but strange.

'And thank you, Linda, for seeing *A.I.* again, and watching it with your husband.'

We were moving into unchartered waters – my head giddily spinning, a whole new world of good-naturedness opening up before me.

'That meant a lot to me,' continued Spielberg, apparently holding an imaginary conversation with my wife in which I was merely an onlooker.

'It meant a lot. What he just said.'

Thank you, Mr Spielberg.

Thank you, Linda.
Thank you.
Thank you.

Some time later, I was in Bradford, preparing to perform a live musical accompaniment to the 1929 Russian silent movie *The Ghost That Never Returns* with Neil Brand and the Dodge Brothers. It's a really strange movie – dark, tough, revolutionary, packed with panopticon prison riots and delirious dream sequences for which I had been honing my limited skills on the theremin. I'd become oddly obsessed with the strange sci-fi noises of that instrument, patented in 1928 by Russian inventor Leon Theremin, hence the connection to *Ghost*. Played by simply waving one's hand around in front of a large electronic aerial, the theremin is a bafflingly futuristic device which perfectly encapsulates a bizarre dichotomy. Since it features no frets or keyboards, the theremin was in theory an immediately accessible instrument which could be played instantly by anyone, without need of musical training. It was, in effect, a piece of democratizing technology which would enable even the most rank amateur to produce beautiful music from the mere wafting of their arms. The irony, of course, is that without frets or keys, the theremin is actually all but impossible to play – or at least impossible to play well (and if you've seen the Dodge Brothers playing *The Ghost That Never Returns*, you'll know what a theremin being played badly sounds like). Despite being created to prove that anyone could be a musician, the theremin actually proved the opposite – that while anyone can make screaming, babbling electronic woops and bleeps, it takes effort and talent to make anything approaching music.

I think there is a lesson in this.

A few weeks had passed since my Spielbergian epiphany, since I had resolved to start being nicer to everyone in general and movies in particular, to stop looking for the bad in everything and instead seek out the good. As I approached my fiftieth birthday, I vowed to spend more time praising cinema and a little less time burying it. After all, a little more positivity in the world couldn't hurt, could it?

I flipped open my laptop to check the IMDb, the Internet site of choice for even the most old-fashioned inky. A link led me to the *Variety* site, where respected *Village Voice* and *LA Weekly* alumni Scott Foundas had recently been installed as the paper's new Chief Film Critic, a significant signing. As I browsed, I noticed a tweet alerting me to a story in the *Independent* gleefully announcing that 'Mark Kermode had better watch out'. Apparently, some affronted luvvie was threatening, for the umpteenth time, to smash my face in – something the paper did not see fit to challenge. The piece was sloppily written by someone who (by their own admission) had seen very few of the terrible movies made by their subject. That the 'professional geezer' was making threats was not news; that a respectable broadsheet now considered calls for violence against critics to be jovially acceptable was simply a sign of the times . . .

I snapped the laptop closed and felt something stir in my stomach.

What would Horatio Alger have done?

I checked my diary for the next day's screenings, which started with *G.I. Joe: Retaliation* in 3D, before moving on to a retrofitted 3D re-release of *Finding Nemo*.

I flipped on my phone to find a text telling me that the 3D fantasy *Jack the Giant Slayer* had dominated the weekend box office.

I glanced at the trade press, which hollered that production was now afoot on Michael Bay's next movie, the as yet officially untitled *Transformers 4* – in 3D.

I grabbed my double-bass, my harmonicas and my beloved theremin, tied up my red Docs, and bounced out onto the Bradford streets, the fire in my belly rekindled.

I was a man on a mission, a man on the move, and just sick enough to be totally confident.

Now, where the hell did I leave that hatchet . . . ?

Index

INDEX

INDEX

INDEX

INDEX

INDEX

INDEX

INDEX

picador.com

blog
videos
interviews
extracts